blem... What Is Excessive?... How To Prevent A
?... Prevention Advice For Puppies And Newly
g Why Dogs Play-Bite Us... Play-Biting Is Painfu
n Advice... Four Paws On The Ground... Initial Triggers That Teach Dog
wanted Greetings... Water And Sound De... And Tast
ith Aggression – Aggression Toward Pe... And Fea
Circumstances: The Crucial Factor... Types Of... rd Peopl
ific Triggers... Dominance Aggression In Public Places... Fear Aggressio
ive Dogs... How To Remedy The Situation... Redefining Who's Leader.
ning... Controlling The Dog In Your Home... The Food Toy Reward... O
ine Attitudes. **Aggression Toward Other Dogs** Fear Aggression... Th
ence... Cyclical Aggression... The Rehabilitation Plan... Getting To Know
ur Dog Is Attacked In Public... Practical Attack Avoidance Techniques
d Dog In The Same Pack Hidden Currents... A New Dog In The House
n... What To Do If A Fight Takes Place... Canine Divorce. **Possessiv**
And Don'ts. **Aggression Over Food** Retraining Program... Obedienc
on When Grooming Why Dogs Show Aggression... Breed Problems
ging Taste Buds... In The Home... Following Their Noses... Obedienc
Up Your Dog... Using Muzzles. **Sexual Problems** Marking Territory
nergy... Scent And Taste Deterrents... Obedience Training... Don't Pa
minant Aggression... Hypersexuality. **House Toilet Training** The Nev
ges... The Cage Solution... If Separation Anxiety Is The Cause... Territor
age Of Command... Collar And Leash... Puppies And Less Determine
termined Pullers... How To Fit A Face Collar Onto A Dog... Using A Bod
ntain Pack Position... Do's And Don'ts With A New Puppy... Introducin
ts Of The Same Sex... In Conclusion. **Phobias And Fears** What Cause
oud Noises... Overcoming The Fear... Household
evention Advice... Week 1... Week 2... Week 3... Further
g Discs... Scent Deterrents. **Eating Animal Feces**
es Of Other Animals... Line Training... Redirect You

BREAKING BAD HABITS IN DOGS

BREAKING BAD HABITS IN DOGS

Learn to gain the obedience and trust of your dog
by understanding the way that it thinks and behaves

Colin Tennant

Second Edition

BARRON'S

Contents

▶ Notes On Using This Book

This book sets out to explain what goes on inside a dog's mind and to make sense of why dogs behave as they do, particularly why they appear to behave badly (to our way of thinking). It also gives advice on training exercises and other measures that can be used to remedy bad behavior. Used sensibly, the programs described in this book are quite safe, but readers must be aware that some dogs are powerful animals that may, on occasion, behave unpredictably. Dogs that display characteristics such as aggression should always be approached with caution; if in doubt, seek the advice of a qualified dog trainer or behavior practitioner first.

The information and recommendations in this book are given without any guarantees on behalf of the author and publisher, who disclaim any liability with the use of this material.

 Readers will see that in this book I sometimes recommend that a problem dog should be referred to a dog trainer or a canine behaviorist. Both professionals should have a clear understanding of canine psychology and the reasons why some dogs behave badly. However, do be aware that few behaviorists — especially academically qualified ones — can train dogs to a high standard. This is something that you should know before you seek help.

When following the advice given in each chapter, readers should decide which training measures to use, bearing in mind their circumstances and the age and breed of the dog in question. In some cases it would not be practical to use all the methods described at the same time.

Revised second edition for the United States and Canada published in 2010 by Barron's Educational Series, Inc.
© Copyright 2010 by Barron's Educational Series, Inc.
Originally published by Interpet Publishing in 2010
© Copyright 2010 by Interpet Publishing
Vincent Lane, Dorking, Surrey RH4 3YX, England

All inquiries should be addressed to:
Barron's Educational Series, Inc.
250 Wireless Boulevard
Hauppauge, NY 11788
www.barronseduc.com

Library of Congress Control Number: 2009940538
ISBN-13: 978-0-7641-4548-3
ISBN-10: 0-7641-4548-7
Printed in China   9 8 7 6 5 4 3 2 1

▶ The Author

Colin Tennant is Britain's leading expert in dog behavior and obedience training. He operates a canine behavior center, providing advice and assistance for owners of dogs of all breeds. In 1975 he served in the Cheshire Police Dog Section and is Home Office-qualified as a police dog handler. Colin began his career in canine behavior and obedience training at the Asoka Training School in Manchester. In the early 1980s he founded the London Dog Training Group specializing in one-on-one training for problem dogs.

Colin has trained animals for more than 100 television shows and has made several instructional DVDs dealing with training problems, as well as the care of cats and other pets. He lectures around the world, and is a frequent contributor to national newspapers and magazines. He is employed as a consultant by the media and has provided expert advice on dog behavior and training to the BBC and other national TV networks, as well as to radio programs and filmmakers. He is Chairman of the Canine and Feline Behaviour Association based in Great Britain, Principal of The Cambridge Institute of Dog Behaviour and Training, and senior behavior practitioner at his Canine and Feline Behaviour Centre in Hertfordshire.

Contents

CHAPTER 11 **Dealing with Aggression**

Contents

► Introduction

► Origins of the Dog

The dog curled up by your feet has been man's faithful companion for thousands of years. Originally domesticated from its wild cousins, the dog is now one of the world's most popular pets, with millions sharing our homes. We find many of their characteristics familiar and loveable, but we often fail to appreciate the natural inheritance that they carry with them (the characteristics that make them dogs). We tend to demand that all pets we domesticate should fit in with our lifestyle. To understand dogs' behavior, it helps to know something about their history and innate nature. In essence, nothing that we teach dogs is natural to them. By contrast, every behavior that they exhibit (including the ones that conflict with us) is natural, but often these behaviors are inappropriate in our environment, which causes distress to dogs and owners alike. Therefore, we should understand that training is a journey of learning for the dog. It requires the owner to be patient and understanding of the dog's inherited drives that evolved to equip them to live in a natural setting, not in our world. Fortunately for us, they are the most adaptable pet animal that we keep domestically.

► The Early History of Dogs

Archaeological excavations have revealed that dogs have lived around man for thousands of years. The ancient Egyptians kept dogs for many purposes; they worshipped the jackal-headed god Anubis, and dogs were often buried next to their masters, which indicates how greatly the Egyptians respected their dogs. The Ancient Greeks, Chinese, and Romans also kept and trained dogs and afforded them great status in their respective societies. One famous Japanese emperor owned 100,000 dogs that all enjoyed royal protection.

Over time man has bred dogs selectively to enhance those canine abilities of which he has need, and to harness the instincts he finds most useful. For example, Collies have far better herding instincts than any wolf, and German Shepherds have more confidence and guarding/shepherding ability combined. The sight hounds are swifter than a wolf. Mastiffs were bred for their strength and fighting qualities, both against men and other animals.

Left: *Toy dogs are particularly affectionate and faithful companion animals. Despite their small size, they can be very effective guard dogs.*

Above: *For people who live alone, dogs can be a lifeline, providing affection and friendship in an otherwise empty house. Their company can even have beneficial health effects, helping to counter depression and speeding up the time it takes to recover from an illness.*

Over four hundred breeds exist worldwide, and each year more are added to the list. Looking at them you may wonder what our ancestors were trying to achieve with their selective breeding. A Chihuahua, for instance, isn't suited for herding or guarding, for it weighs no more than 3 or 4 pounds (2 kg). The Chihuahua, the smallest breed in the world, was bred purely for human fancy – often to provide personal companionship for aristocratic ladies. The Pekingese is a similar example.

Above: *Big dogs...small dogs...whatever their size, dogs have provided us with companionship for thousands of years.*

Working Breeds

The shepherding breeds are, without a doubt, the most malleable dogs that respond to human training, and are thus the ones most commonly found working alongside man. I use this term to describe the breeds that actually work alongside man in the modern world. This includes police dogs, guide dogs, sheepdogs, assistance dogs, and others. The essential role that dogs now play in society is demonstrated admirably by the sniffer dog.

Right: *Mastiffs are big and powerful dogs which have for centuries been bred by man as fighting dogs, both for use in battle and when hunting wild animals. Despite their fierce appearance, they have quite placid temperaments.*

Many a drug runner's face drops at the sight of the approaching sniffer dog in an airport lounge.

Companionship

Most dogs are acquired as family pets. Evidence from the Society for Companion Animal Studies at Glasgow and Cambridge universities clearly shows that people live longer and lead happier lives when they own a dog. The elderly and single people benefit greatly from owning a dog: it helps them meet other people on walks, keeps them fit, and provides a rewarding source of companionship. As society becomes more stressful, dogs and other pets will no doubt continue to satisfy important social and psychological needs for many people. However, is this necessarily good for the pets? We shall see.

This dog needs a firm hand.

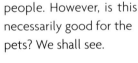

If not properly trained, a Mastiff may prove difficult to handle when taken for a walk.

TRAINING DIGEST

Below: *The German Shepherd is an extremely versatile working dog, as well as one of our most popular pets.*

We should understand that training is a journey of learning for the dog. It requires the owner to be patient and understanding of the dog's inherited drives.

Over time man has bred dogs selectively to enhance those canine abilities of which he has need, and to harness the instincts he finds most useful.

Evidence clearly shows that people live longer and lead happier lives when they own a dog.

Introduction

Above: *Appearances can be deceptive – the Labrador looks like a picture of domestication, but deep down inside there beats the heart of a wild animal.*

and desire. When we read about someone being bitten by a dog, we recoil in disbelief and assume that this is an unusual occurrence. The fact is that if we expect dogs to be what they are not (as we often do), we will be disappointed when they behave badly or unsociably. Or – if you wish – like a dog enmeshed in the human world.

Dogs are bound to feel fed up when we leave them at home alone while we enjoy an evening out. They are pack animals, not solitary creatures. The dog may not understand our reasons, but they do learn to adapt to our strange, non-doggy behavior and peculiar environment. Getting along together is a two-way process.

If you truly understand your dog and respect him, you will be fascinated

▶ Domestic Problems

Despite their value in the home, too many people choose dogs that are unsuitable for their homes and lifestyles. It must be remembered that a pet dog is in essence a wolf in Labrador's (or any other breed's) clothing. Man has done a good job of disguising the real wolf through breeding, so that we can no longer see the wild animal lurking inside our dogs. We don't see it until the dog begins to behave badly or (as I would say) like its cousin, the wolf.

This self-deception is the crux of many of the behavioral problems that I encounter and that will be featured in this book. Dogs know what they are; most owners don't. It can take some time

and many consultations before they realize that they have willingly been breeding, loving, and caring for a moderated wolf in their home.

▶ Man's Best Friend

Most people take dogs for granted. They expect that they will be loyal, obedient, friendly, sociable, and dependable friends who attend to our every word

Below: *Dogs instinctively always have an eye for food. Therefore, they must be trained to distinguish between your table and their own food bowl.*

Above: *When dogs meet, they often circle one another, sniffing the anal and genital areas. They use scent as a way of gathering information about the world.*

▶ TRAINING DIGEST

▶ It must be remembered that a pet dog is in essence a wolf in Labrador's (or any other breed's) clothing. Man has done a good job of disguising the real wolf through breeding, so that we can no longer see the wild animal lurking inside our dogs.

rather than let down when your dog behaves like a dog. So let's now examine some examples of dog/wolf behavior that we can all recognize.

▶ Sniffing and Rolling

Dogs sniff each other, humans, and urine and feces deposited by other dogs and animals. Why? Because that's their messaging system, the equivalent in many ways of your eyes checking a sign or an advertisement in a newspaper. It advertises their presence. Scent is also important in the hunt for food.

Food equals survival, so most animals have powerful instincts in this crucial department. Until taught differently, they will gladly take any food they sniff out or see from a dog bowl or the street, or even from your coffee table. Dogs are predators and scavengers, and finding

Above: *By nature, dogs are pack animals like their wolf ancestors. It is not surprising that they look out of sorts when forced to spend long periods of time on their own in the house.*

free food is a slice of luck not to be ignored.

Because of their great scenting ability, dogs like rolling in animal manure to mask their own smell – much to the disgust of most owners. They also mark dead prey by rolling and impregnating their own scent on the carcass, thereby laying claim to it. They do it instinctively, but we see it as a dirty habit.

▶ The fact is that if we expect dogs to be what they are not (as we often do), we will be disappointed when they behave badly or unsociably. Or – if you wish – like a dog enmeshed in the human world.

Food equals survival, so most animals have powerful instincts in this crucial department. Until taught differently, they will gladly take any food they sniff out.

► Introduction

► Pack Rules

Most dogs will strive to establish their ranking status vis-à-vis other dogs or any humans with whom they come into contact by body language. In cases where dogs are very dominant-aggressive, they exhibit it through growling, biting, or

Above: *Domestic dogs have inherited the wolf's innate awareness of the dynamics of pack behavior. Pack animals have to learn to fit into a pack hierarchy, and this explains why many pet dogs seek to dominate other dogs with which they come into contact through aggressive displays.*

aggressive physical intimidation. If you understand this wolflike behavior, you will be better able to train, control, and respect your dog. Remember, these instincts have helped the wolf to become one of the most successful species in the world.

Above: *This juxtaposition of pictures is revealing – the domestic dog crouching ready to play behind its toy and the wolf waiting alertly in the snow look remarkably similar. Much of the behavior of a dog is influenced by its wolflike instincts.*

Dogs are hunters so it's normal for them to chase a moving object, whether it's a jogger, a cat, or a squirrel. Larger dogs may knock over valuable household items or even jump up and knock us over in their enthusiasm to greet us upon our return, just as they would greet fellow pack members returning from the hunt. However, in the wolf pack, other dogs stand conveniently on four legs and at muzzle level, where they can be licked for food rewards without jumping up. With humans, it's a different story.

► Pack Behavior

Dogs love digging in soft soil or sand and they enjoy burying bones or toys; this is their way of saving food for a rainy day. They do not intentionally mean to damage our beautiful lawns. They simply cannot see any harm in this instinctive action. Dogs, particularly

males, also mark territory through urination and scent gland secretions; this is the dog's way of marking out his hunting areas to secure his food supply and of letting other dogs know of his presence in the locality.

When you return home from shopping, watch your dog's reactions. Your dog will sniff you all over with excitement because we have many scents on our clothes and shopping items. They act like puppy wolves excitedly welcoming the adult wolves back from a hunting trip. In fact, domesticated dogs retain juvenile characteristics all their adult lives as a consequence of their domestication, which we believe is what makes them so malleable and responsive to training.

Dogs often lick us with great enthusiasm. They particularly like our faces, though the feeling is not always mutual! This is the dog's method of reinforcing body contact with the pack and showing deference to higher-ranking pack members – and of requesting a mouthful of regurgitated meat.

Dogs will wander, if not restrained, over great distances. They like meeting and investigating other dogs; sniffing the genitals and the anuses of other dogs is a great source of information and a display of politeness that often diffuses tensions. Dogs also like using their voices and may bark, howl, or yap as an expression of their mood or excitement.

Wolves do all these things too, except barking, which is a rarely used part of their vocabulary.

It must be appreciated that these behaviors are normal, though they may not always be appropriate for our circumstances. In fact, behavioral problems are very much specific to circumstances. For example, a dog that chases squirrels in the country is probably not a problem dog for its owner, but a dog doing the same thing in a busy city park may be considered a danger by its owner because of the distress it causes to other park users, and the likelihood of its running into the road while in pursuit of its prey.

▶ TRAINING DIGEST

▶ **Most dogs will strive to establish their ranking status vis-à-vis other dogs or any humans with whom they come into contact by body language.**

Behavioral problems are very much specific to circumstances.

Right: *During the formative stages of puppyhood, the dog is becoming part of the family pack.*

Left: *Dogs – and wolves – are vocal creatures. Dogs use their voices to communicate with other canines. Wolves use vocal signals to warn of danger and to summon other pack members.*

Above: *It's natural for dogs to bark as a warning or a call for help, but persistent barking is a nuisance that can ruin the enjoyment of owning a dog.*

► Introduction

► Inherited Dominance

I do not adopt a rigid view of dominant dogs. Dogs vary so immensely in character, temperament, and behavior that hard and fast rules do not apply. My experience of dealing with many thousands of badly behaved dogs has taught me that trying to prejudge their behavior is unsuccessful in terms of rehabilitation or training.

I follow the safe route in all dog training and when acting to modify unacceptable dog behavior. If you follow my rules, ideally the dog will be prevented from displaying excessive dominance; at the very least the behavior should be altered to a manageable level. Wolves naturally and constantly suppress one another, and we humans also need to suppress our dogs' natural inclination to try to dominate us if this is a problem. However, in most dogs it is not.

► Dog Training and Behavior

Most bad behavior in dogs can be altered or prevented by obedience training to establish new rules by using the methods described in this book. This is why it's so important to set the ground rules when a new puppy or

► DOG TRAINING – NINE TIPS

1 Before you begin training your dog, be sure you fully understand the exercise and commands you are about to teach. Do not attempt any exercise if you are in doubt.

2 The motivation for your dog to learn is praise delivered in a pleasant tone of voice, pack behavior, food, and games. Remember this throughout the training program.

3 Dogs do not understand our language, even though many owners assume they do. You can be sure that if the dog seems to be continually making errors, the fault lies with the trainer who is not communicating the message clearly enough to the animal.

4 When training, the dog may begin to lose interest. If this is the case, get him to do an exercise he likes and can achieve, praise him for it, and finish training. Play a short game and try again later in the day.

5 Never leave a long recall line on your dog when the animal is left unattended. If the connection ring gets snagged and caught on an object, the dog could be strangled. Fixed (non-slip) collars are best when training.

6 Be aware that different breeds make progress in training at different rates. It is not important whether your dog learns quickly or slowly, as long as it does learn and changes for the better.

7 The training lessons should be short. Start with perhaps ten minutes at first, and then gradually – if the dog is not losing interest – extend the lessons. Many short lessons are more beneficial than one long one.

8 Train when your dog is alert. Tired dogs or dogs that have just eaten don't do well.

9 Avoid making repetitive commands. Dogs are not deaf or stupid. Repeating "Down" ten times does not help. Keeping silent between commands helps the dog to differentiate between the sounds that you are making and understand what you want.

Below 1: *Children can benefit greatly from the pleasure of playing with a well-behaved pet. But they, like dogs, need to learn the rules.*

Below 2: *The dog must be taught to defer to human pack members.*

Below 3: *Dogs do not generally view young children as high ranking. Obedience training helps to modify that perspective.*

1

2

3

adult dog arrives. Whether you train using books, DVDs, a training club, or a private instructor, obedience is a necessity and a continuing process throughout the dog's life. Dog training is not dissimilar to human learning – it should continue from birth to death and be constantly reinforced. And remember that dog training is intrinsically linked to solving many dog behavior problems.

The bottom line with dogs is that you lead or are led. Dogs work on a black-and-white system of leadership – if you teach your dog what it can and cannot do and accompany clear, concise commands with the relevant reward, the chances are that your leadership and authority will be respected. Certainly dogs that are trained well and understand how to follow a series of commands properly are happy dogs. They rarely get into trouble, because they have learned the do's and don'ts of living with people. So the general behavior of dogs is much

improved by one critical factor... modifying their natural instincts through obedience training.

Dogs work, train, and become good companions when the rules are clear. They cannot live beside us in harmony if they try to lead the human pack. So read this book and learn how to lead. By all means, give your dog all the fun, leisure, and outdoor activities you can. Let your children enjoy the companionship and learning curve of dog ownership, but most of all respect your dog for what it is – a versatile and intelligent animal that has left the wild to share the lives of humans like us.

TRAINING DIGEST

▶ Most bad behavior in dogs can be altered or prevented by obedience training to establish new rules by using the methods described in this book.

The bottom line with dogs is that you lead or are led. Dogs work on a black-and white system of leadership – if you teach your dog what it can and cannot do and accompany clear, concise commands with the relevant reward, the chances are that your leadership and authority will be respected.

Left: *A dog that is taught to be obedient to commands will generally be a happy dog in the home.*

1: How Dogs Learn

Just like people, dogs learn through association. The dog will want to repeat an action that is "rewarded" with a pleasant consequence, such as a gift of food or a pat on the head, but it will be disinclined to repeat actions that meet with unpleasant consequences, such as discipline or a verbal expression of disapproval. This is called learned behavior. However, unlike us, dogs do not reason; they cannot imagine the consequences of a specific action in the same way that we can — and that's the crux of most problems that dog owners experience. We tend to think that if we show a dog a slipper that it has previously chewed and shout "No," it will make the connection between the chewed slipper and our disapproval — because that is how we would construe the matter.

Well, it's unlikely to make that connection. We may treat a dog like a human but, remember, it can only react like a dog.

▶ The Critical Period for Learning

The time when dogs are most sensitive to learning is between five and twelve weeks of age. This is a fast- and short-track learning period. I find it important that puppies should be imprinted with obedience training commands and reward techniques during this time. It conditions them to respond to all future advanced training aimed at encouraging positive manners and acceptable behavior. If they are to develop normally, pup-

Below: *You need to reprimand a dog or puppy for bad behavior within two seconds of the event, so the dog can link your displeasure to its actions.*

Use a firm tone to command.

pies should be socialized with people and animals and exposed to as many experiences around the home and in the outside world as possible.

Dogs continue to learn throughout their lives, but it is harder to modify the behavior of older dogs with embedded habits. These early weeks are the best time to teach good social manners and obedience, and to introduce the dog to what behavior is acceptable and what is not. However, don't give up with older dogs; they can unlearn the bad behaviors they've acquired; they just take a little longer and will test you now and again to check whether you've relented and will let them get their own way. The one trait dogs do have in abundance is persistence.

▶ Inherited Behavior

Dogs naturally inherit certain drives and behaviors. The degree to which this is

true is influenced to an extent by the dog's breed; for example, a Border Collie has strong herding instincts and an acute eye for movement. When a dog like this does not enjoy the usual stimuli or get enough exercise to satisfy its energetic instincts, it may relieve its frustration in

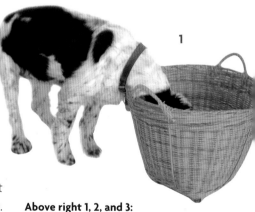

1

Above right 1, 2, and 3:
Beneath a dog's domesticated exterior is an animal whose instincts derive from life in the wild. It is only natural that they should be inquisitive.

Right: *Dogs are most responsive to corrective training in the early weeks of their lives.*

another way – perhaps by chasing cyclists or joggers. A ball is often used to redirect such behavior. An anxious or calm temperament can also be inherited, but more often than not this characteristic is exacerbated by the behavior of unwitting owners. Dogs are brimming with moderated wolflike natural drives

Children can help with basic obedience training.

that have evolved to enable them to survive in the wild, not in your home. Redirecting these innate drives is very important.

The search for food is a basic instinct.

2

3

▶ TRAINING DIGEST

▶ A dog's behavior is conditioned to a degree by its breed. Dogs with a herding instinct have tons of energy and need lots of exercise.

We may treat a dog like a human but, remember, it can only react like a dog.

The time when dogs are most sensitive to learning is between five and twelve weeks of age. This is a fast- and short-track learning period.

Dogs continue to learn throughout their lives, but it is harder to modify the behavior of older dogs with embedded habits.

How Dogs Learn

Inherited behaviors cannot be removed, but they can be altered and lessened or redirected toward less aggravating behavior. However, you will have to accept that terriers will always be highly triggered and prone to bark, and hounds will be liable to follow scents and appear deaf to commands at times. *But do not despair!* In most cases, evidence of a poor temperament, for example a dog that exhibits fears and phobias, is generally due to lack of socialization as a puppy. This sort of behavior can be improved. Some breeds have more robust temperaments than others. Toy breeds can be more hyperactive and timid, which is probably due to the fact that they are unnaturally small in a world full of people with big clumsy feet.

▶ Voice Tone

Words in themselves are meaningless to a dog. If you watch a good dog trainer in action, you will notice that they use tone of voice with great flexibility. A word (sound) should be delivered clearly and crisply in short, sharp, one- or two-syllable units. In terms of communication, praise and confidence-building words mean a lot to a dog. Don't use long, wordy phrases when trying to teach a dog a new lesson; it will simply take longer for the dog to decipher your message.

▶ Reward

To recap, dogs learn by association. Praise – whether in the form of words of encouragement, stroking, or food – is a potent bonus for a dog, and when used in training it produces excellent results. If we command our dog to "Sit" and praise him warmly at the same time, the dog will quickly learn that this action is a rewarding one. Repetition will reinforce this message and produce the desired result. Food, toys, and even exercise or time spent with you can all act as powerful reinforcements when teaching a dog new behavior. Rewards, when combined with good timing (see below), produce a well-trained dog. A dog that sees you as leader is also more likely to listen and watch out for your commands, and reward by tone of voice can be very important to a dog.

You can use rewards to reinforce good behavior or after a training session.

Above: *Time spent playing with your dog helps build up the bond of friendship between you.*

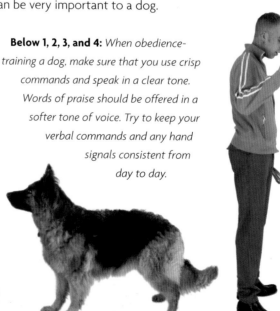

Below 1, 2, 3, and 4: *When obedience-training a dog, make sure that you use crisp commands and speak in a clear tone. Words of praise should be offered in a softer tone of voice. Try to keep your verbal commands and any hand signals consistent from day to day.*

The dog is sitting attentively and is responsive to command.

1

2

Discipline

Just as a reward is effective in teaching a dog to do something that we approve of, discipline is effective in discouraging a particular behavior. There are many ways of showing a dog that he is doing something undesirable, such as saying "No" firmly, and holding him by the loose skin of the neck or by the collar and looking into his eyes. For example, if a dog playfully nips your hand, take the dog by the collar, simultaneously command "No," and stare into the dog's eyes for a few seconds. Dogs dislike this type of admonishment and soon find that the Alpha (pack leader) stare resulting from nipping is an unpleasant consequence that they would rather avoid.

Unfortunately, it is human nature to be impatient; as a result, people use punishment much more often than is necessary to modify canine behavior. It is possible to train a dog while only rarely having recourse to punishment. Rather than hitting a dog when he jumps up, it is much better to teach him to sit and stay, preventing him from being tempted to jump up in the first place. Try to anticipate when the dog is about to jump up and command "Sit." This positive approach is a much better option than falling victim to the negative urge to punish the animal when the action is done. It's worth remembering that dogs did not evolve to fit into a human lifestyle. In fact, it's amazing that they do manage to get along with people so well, considering how little we each know about dog communication.

► TIP

► Try looking at the world from the dog's point of view – puppies (below) have to cope in a world populated by giants.

► TRAINING DIGEST

► In most cases, evidence of a poor temperament, for example a dog that exhibits fears and phobias, is generally due to lack of socialization as a puppy. This sort of behavior can be improved.

Praise – whether in the form of words of encouragement, stroking, or food – is a potent bonus for a dog, and when used in training it produces excellent results.

Try to anticipate when the dog is about to jump up and command "Sit." This positive approach is a much better option than falling victim to the negative urge to punish the animal when the action is done.

The command "Down" is accompanied by a clear movement of the hand and an inclination of the upper body.

3

The dog has responded correctly.

4

How Dogs Learn

Getting Your Timing Right

Timing is critical to all training commands and actions. If you want a dog to learn in a particular situation, the praise or punishment must be given within two seconds of the action taking place. Whether you are offering words

Below 1 and 2: All the family can take part in obedience training a dog, but it's important that parents should teach children the commands and actions to employ, and that all members of the family are consistent when using them.

of encouragement or discouragement, if you wait too long you may as well not bother. For instance, there is no point in calling your dog in the park, getting irritated when it does not respond immediately, and when it does eventually come back, giving it a smack for not returning sooner. The dog will not associate the punishment with something that happened a minute ago; it will simply associate the punishment with coming to you – not the desired result at all. So praise a dog immediately when it obeys your command – it will quickly get the message.

Aim for Consistency

It is important that everyone who is involved with correcting your dog's bad behavior acts consistently so that the dog does not get confused. If someone is inconsistent in reacting to a problem behavior, especially when the problem is embedded in the dog's mind, you will make little progress. You will end up with a dog that sometimes obeys and sometimes doesn't. The psychology is similar to child-rearing. Make sure you know exactly what training program you are following, and explain it thoroughly to all family members and any other

The command is clear and the hand action is unambiguous.

The dog stays as commanded and is alert to its owner.

1

2

Above 1: *Dogs are not ageist — they are quite prepared to defer to and obey other members of the family pack, even relatively young children. Note how this Dalmatian is standing, looking alertly at the girl as she gives a hand signal to sit, much in the same way as he focuses on the mother in the picture on the opposite page.*

Above 2: *The girl's signal is distinct and her voice commands are short and crisp, as her mother has taught her. The result is that the dog is sitting obediently and waiting for further commands. Consistency reaps benefits.*

TRAINING DIGEST

▶ **Timing is critical to all training commands and actions. If you want a dog to learn in a particular situation, the praise or punishment must be given within two seconds of the action taking place.**

Make sure you know exactly what training program you are following, and explain it thoroughly to all family members and any other people involved. Remember, for positive results, be consistent.

people involved. Remember, **for positive results, be consistent.**

Another one of our human failings is our reluctance to be critical of ourselves. Nearly all owners who consult me about their dogs' behavioral problems repeat the same mantra: "He won't listen, I've told him ten times, he just won't learn." I often film them trying to instruct their dog and then play the tape back to them. This is what they hear: "Oscar, sit, sit down, sit here, stop it, just sit Oscar, Oscar, **sit down,** you bad dog," and on it goes. Now what use is that? The command is "Sit." How the dog is supposed to realize that one word in all that ramble should lead it to a sitting position defeats me — and the dog. People usually get the message after watching the tape. It can be quite

amusing and we can laugh about our human foibles. Remember that we are conditioned to teaching other humans who can solve problems with their big brains and complex reasoning abilities. Dogs just do not work that way.

Left: *It's all about timing. If you praise a dog for its good behavior or admonish it for poor behavior, do so within two seconds of the event. If you delay longer than this, the dog will not associate your reaction with its action.*

▶ **Praise a dog immediately when it obeys your command — it will quickly get the message.**

27

How Dogs Learn

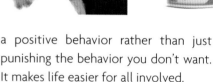

Guilty or Not?

Many people describe their dog as looking guilty when it has urinated on the carpet or chewed the leg of a chair. They infer from this that their dog knows that it has done wrong. In most cases, the dog looks guilty on your arrival not because it feels any remorse, but because it has learned to read your body language or tone of voice and it associates these with your anger and subsequent behavior toward it. Dogs do not feel guilt as we do. Only when you accept this fact can retraining begin. Showing signs of being frightened is not evidence of a guilty conscience; it's straightforward fear.

Above 1, 2, and 3: *If you spot your dog doing this, you will almost inevitably interpret its expression in picture 3 as a guilty look. But the dog is not feeling guilty – it is more likely apprehensive because it knows your body language and expects a punishment.*

Don't expect your dog to value material possessions. It can't tell the difference between designer clothes and a pair of old, worn-out jeans. To a dog there's no such thing as your food and his food, it's all just food – until it is taught otherwise. Dogs need to be taught step-by-step if they are to end up as good, sociable companions. And when you are trying to correct a dog that has done something wrong, if possible do try to praise

Left: *It is difficult to harden your heart and not respond to the pleading looks, but the Ignore response is a very powerful way of discouraging behavior that you want to deter.*

a positive behavior rather than just punishing the behavior you don't want. It makes life easier for all involved.

IGNORE – A Powerful Leader Statement

If your dog tries to dominate your life by excessive attention-seeking using learned techniques like barking, jumping up, nudging, pawing, whining, etc., introduce the **Ignore** response to your dog. In my view this is one of the most effective training methods that we can use. Put simply, you ignore the behavior that you wish to stop or reduce, and conversely give attention to behavior you wish to encourage. That's the easy part; the hard part is ignoring very calculating, clever dogs that display inordinate persistence in order to get their own way. These dogs are often skilled in manipulation. If you persevere and are consistent, you will find that few dogs go on repeating a behavior that is found to be unrewarding. Puppies or less practiced adult dogs are, of course, much more responsive to the Ignore method of training.

Freely available food is a powerful temptation to a dog.

2

3

To give an example – suppose your dog keeps pestering you. You say, "Get off – stop it," or perhaps you push the dog down physically, or give the dog eye contact. Many dogs see these actions as rewarding, even if they are accompanied by an aggressive tone of voice. The art of Ignore psychology is to remain aloof; imagine your dog isn't there, even though he's driving you crazy. After a week or so of being unable to gain your attention, the annoying behaviors naturally begin to fade. I have yet to find a dog that did not alter significantly when the owner employed the Ignore training correctly and consistently.

Above: *When dealing with dominant dogs, it is often helpful to restrict their movements by using a wall-mounted hook to which their leashes can be secured.*

IGNORE – RECAP

When your dog is pestering you or attempting to get your attention, remember the following:

• **Don't give him eye contact.**

• **Try not to shove or push the dog away physically – he may interpret this as play.**

• **Don't shout at the dog.**

• **Use the hook restriction program for a persistent dog when necessary (see pages 48–51).**

• **Implement the Intelligent Leadership program (see pages 44–47), which will markedly improve behavior.**

HOW DOGS LEARN – RECAP

• **Tone of voice and the ability to use your voice effectively in training are vital.**

• **Rewards should be given simultaneously with, or within two seconds of, a command being given.**

• **Reprimands should be given simultaneously with, or within two seconds of, a command being given.**

• **Timing and consistency are vital so that a link between the trainer's commands and the desired action is consistently forged.**

• **Ignore is a powerful learning tool that dogs understand.**

2: Training Equipment

Intelligent Dog Training

When dogs need training, the first essential is a collar and leash. Most dogs respond well to this and the results are generally good. A dog, like a child, needs an education to prepare it for life in our world. If it does not learn what it

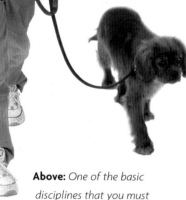

The leash is looped to shorten it so that the dog stays close to the walker.

Above: *One of the basic disciplines that you must teach a dog is to walk to heel on a leash. Once the dog has learned to obey, even children can safely walk the animal.*

can – and cannot – do, it will eventually do just what it wants and act purely on instinct. Conflict with its owner is almost inevitable unless you take the leash.

For example, it is instinctive for a dog to eat any food available, not only in the dog bowl but even off the dining room

table. To a dog it is simply natural behavior, until taught otherwise. In fact, a human baby will do exactly the same until it is taught not to, and yet while most people view the baby's action as innocent, the dog is labeled a thief and bad. That perception or expectation of the animal is unfair to the dog and it highlights how human perceptions and expectations of dog behavior really need to adjust.

Breaking Bad Habits

Many companies produce excellent and innovative equipment to help assist the dog owner in reeducating the dog and correcting its behavior. This section explains what is readily available and how it should be used. Unfortunately, equipment is all too often employed as a quick fix, but without some instruction in training methods, quick-fix solutions are usually doomed to failure. However, when the equipment is used by people with experience and knowledge of canine behavior or with the assistance and guidance of a qualified dog trainer or canine behavioral practitioner, it can help speed up retraining and help to ameliorate even very severe cases of bad behavior.

Most equipment is suitable for use both with sensitive dogs and puppies (SDP) and with determined and dominant dogs (DD), but some is only to be used on DD dogs. When reading the descriptions in this chapter, assume that

the equipment described can be safely used on both SPD and DD dogs unless otherwise stated.

Flexible Leashes

Leashes that extend and rewind have many uses in helping to reform a dog's behavior. I use one when introducing a family dog to a new pet, whether it be a cat or dog. It allows flexible distance on

Below: *A well-fitting and sturdy collar is a must for any dog that is going to share your home. It enables you to take a firm hold of the dog should the need arise, and by attaching a leash to the collar you can keep the animal securely under your control.*

Left: *A flexible leash is very useful when you want to introduce a dog to another pet in the household. The fact that the line unreels from the holder allows the dog some freedom to move forward and make the acquaintance of the other animal, but you can pull back the leash if it shows signs of aggression.*

GUIDANCE ON LEASHES AND COLLARS

▶ **Dog leashes:** Leather leashes are the best. Ideally they should measure about 4 to 6 feet (1.2–2 m) in length.

Dog collars: Again, leather is preferred, but nylon collars are also useful.

Half-check collars: These are safe to use as a half-check collar does not fully tighten on a dog's neck.

Check chains and slip collars: These tighten on a dog's neck as it pulls but do not choke it. They should only be used in specific circumstances and with a qualified trainer – they are *not for general use* and should never be used on puppies or small breeds.

the leash, which enables the dog to move as close to the new pet as you wish without your immediate presence imposing on the dog. Dog-to-dog aggression is another area where the flexible leash is useful. Many dogs react aggressively to other dogs when attached to a leash. However, when the handler uses the flexible leash, the absence of the expected restriction takes the edge off the antagonist. The handler is not nearby to "support" the aggressor, so the dog has to stand alone. This flexibility often reduces tension and thereby aggression.

▷ **Long Lines**

Use nylon line (between 20 and 50 feet/6–15 m long), which can be purchased from a boating shop. Place a dog hook at one end to attach to a collar, and form a loop for handle at the other (always wear gloves when using the line). This is very effective when used in recall training with a young dog.

Above and right: *The flexible leash unwinds from a spool in the container against the pressure of a spring. By pressing a button near the handle, the line can be locked in any chosen position.*

The girl is keeping the dog on a flexible leash for control.

Training Equipment

Dog-walking Harnesses

Such harnesses are fitted to the dog's body and a leash is attached to the top of the harness. They work by making it uncomfortable for the dog to pull the owner when on a walk, and conversely they are comfortable to wear when the dog stops pulling.

Car Harnesses

These allow you to secure your dog in the back of the car by attaching the harness to a seat belt. They are useful when a dog's movements in the car need to be controlled and can be helpful when dealing with dogs that suffer from car sickness (see Chapter 18).

Face Collars

(for determined difficult dogs only)
Like the harness, this is used to stop dogs from pulling, but in this case it fits over the dog's muzzle. It allows the dog's mouth to open as usual so that it can breathe normally. When the dog pulls ahead of its owner, the face collar checks the dog's head back toward the owner, making it uncomfortable or awkward for the dog to pull. They teach the dog that walking alongside you on a loose leash is comfortable for both parties. They are particularly good for large dogs or when the

Right: A dog-walking harness discourages a dog from pulling by exerting pressure under its "armpits."

Right: This Labrador is perfectly comfortable while walking calmly by its owner. But if it were to surge ahead, the face collar would cause its head to be pulled up. As the inset picture shows, dogs can still open their mouths to pant in a face collar.

owner is not particularly mobile or able to control powerful dogs that pull. They also have a calming effect on some aggressive dogs.

The Muzzle

(for determined and dominant or aggressive dogs only)
This is useful for all problems of aggression or for dogs that scavenge food. When first using a muzzle, it is most important to introduce it slowly so that the dog does not associate it with a bad experience. Dogs get stressed and often panic when first wearing a muzzle

or face collar, which is a fact that manufacturers generally play down. However, the stress that you experience when a dog pulls is worse, while a dog that tries to bite someone may land you in legal trouble. If introduced properly, within a few weeks the dog will accept these devices without any further stress. Most people rush the introduction and then get worried by the dog's stressed reaction to it. Here's how you should do it. The method also applies to face collars. First get the dog to sit while wearing a leash and collar. Have several juicy treats in hand. Put the muzzle on the dog (it

must be able to open its mouth with a muzzle fitted) and then reward the dog with a treat fed through the muzzle. Leave it on the dog for a few minutes, remove it, then give another food reward. The dog should now associate wearing the muzzle with a reward.

This needs to be repeated three times daily for about ten minutes each time **for three days**. On day four, attach the leash and fit the muzzle to the dog as usual, then walk the dog a short way in the house or yard and reward the dog at frequent intervals. If the dog panics or attempts to rub its head on the floor (which is normal), distract it with the food and use your leash to make it sit.

It's also useful to leave the muzzle on the dog in the house twice daily for about ten to fifteen minutes. When the dog begins to accept the muzzle without fuss, you are beginning to reach normalization. Most dogs resent the muzzle or face collar at first, but quickly adapt and associate it with food rewards and walks. Once you can walk the dog around the house or yard without adverse reaction, you are ready for normal outdoor use.

Healthy Food Diet and Food Rewards

Food is an aid often used in my obedience training – it can be a very powerful influence in behavioral training. Food is vital for body maintenance and significantly affects behavior in dogs. I believe that dogs, like people, should be given a healthy diet that is free of

chemicals or additives. This removes the possibility of colorants or other chemicals in the diet affecting behavior. I call this a "clean diet." Clean food does not require taste enhancement, added vitamins, and the like. Good food has all necessary dietary requirements.

Food is used in many of the programs outlined in this book, especially to deal with aggression and anxiety-related

behavior. I have found that dogs' behavior can change considerably when they are fed a clean diet, such as fresh meat cooked with vegetables and rice. There certainly appears to be an advantage in feeding your dog food that you have prepared yourself or obtained from a high-quality manufacturer.

The Food Toy

Rubber toys in which food can be concealed are used to help cope with separation anxiety problems, destructive behavior, aggression, and teaching dogs to be alone for short periods in the yard or other rooms in the house. Dogs are kept occupied as they work at the toy to get at the food contained in it. It is also useful for puppy training and for stimulating all dogs mentally.

▶ ## MUZZLE RECAP

▶ **If you accustom a dog to wearing a muzzle by using treats to reward calm acceptance, it should get used to it reasonably quickly. Traveling to the park by car (left) also rewards the dog for wearing a muzzle with the prospect of a walk together.**

A cage-type muzzle (far left) has a mesh of slats through which you can give a dog treats and food rewards while it is still wearing the muzzle.

▶ ## FOOD TOY RECAP

▶ **The food toy is very useful in diverting a dog from a bad behavior by giving it a pleasurable distraction on which to concentrate instead.**

It is amazing how long a dog will play with a food toy in order to take out every scrap.

Training Equipment

Deterrent Sprays

These products are harmless, unpleasant-smelling liquid sprays that are very useful in the early stages of teaching puppies not to chew valuable household furnishings and items. They come to learn by their own experience and by exercising individual choices.

I have recently used one to stop Saphie, a puppy Cairn, from chewing. Puppies are naturally inquisitive and Saphie, like all puppies, explores her world with her teeth and nose. Under my desk there is a jungle of computer wires and cables. I can't see what she is doing all the time so I spray the electrical cables with the bitter spray every day. First experiences are critical in dog training, and once she has experienced a taste of that spray, the electric cables are very much off the menu.

Remote Training Collar

(for determined and dominant dogs only) This is a scent collar that works by remote control at short distances and emits a jet of pungent-smelling, but harmless, citronella spray. I have used this to help teach recall to dogs that ignore other training methods in order to get them back on command.

Stopping dogs from scavenging food or eating animal and bird feces, which could ultimately make them very ill, can also be helped with the collar. To use the collar effectively, you do need to understand how dogs learn. Timing is essential and it is vital that you get help from a dog trainer to learn how to

Above: *The remote training scent collar can be activated at long range by the use of a small handheld control device.*

correctly operate the device. It is not intended as a way for you to relieve your frustration and punish the animal – it should never be used in that manner. Though the spray is innocuous, like all training devices, it can still spook a few dogs when inappropriately used; this is why you should not operate it without expert help.

Training Discs

These devices have two distinct applications when used effectively. When they are thrown near a misbehaving dog, the discs interrupt the action the dog is pursuing and they also produce a negative association related to the surprise sound. Preconditioning the dog to react to the sound of the discs is the second way of using the

discs. You can use a bunch of keys to obtain a similar effect, but the discs are far more practical in application and will work on most, though not all, dogs. Be careful when using them with puppies, however. Without a doubt, dogs are suspicious or fearful of the sound they make.

The discs work in the following way:
- The dog learns a sound (the clatter of the discs) and associates it with whatever it is doing wrong. Dogs don't like the noise and have an innate fear/suspicion of the unknown.
- It associates the sound with a command, "No."
- Eventually the dog responds instantly to the command "No" without the discs being used.

Most dogs learn to stop an undesirable behavior when the discs are used.

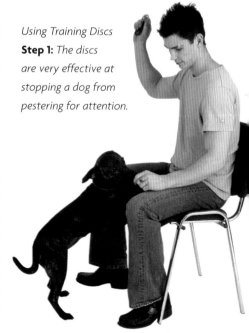

Using Training Discs
Step 1: *The discs are very effective at stopping a dog from pestering for attention.*

Eventually you can wean most dogs off the sound of the discs, but occasionally very persistent dogs will need a reminder of the discs being thrown.

How to Use the Discs

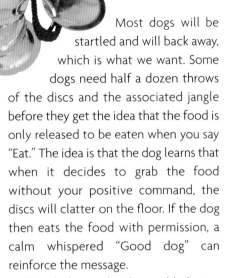

Most dogs like food, so using a collar and leash for control, take a tasty treat between two fingers, and with the dog nearby pretend to place the food on the floor. When the dog goes to grab the food, shut your hand tight, preventing the food from being taken, and **simultaneously** throw the discs down near your hand while commanding "No." If you are dealing with a really greedy dog that catches your fingers with its teeth, get somebody else to control the dog by attaching a collar and leash for added safety.

Most dogs will be startled and will back away, which is what we want. Some dogs need half a dozen throws of the discs and the associated jangle before they get the idea that the food is only released to be eaten when you say "Eat." The idea is that the dog learns that when it decides to grab the food without your positive command, the discs will clatter on the floor. If the dog then eats the food with permission, a calm whispered "Good dog" can reinforce the message.

Now let's use that learned behavior to cope with other problems like jumping up, barking, or stealing food. Once the dog gets the message that "No" means "No" in association with the sound of the discs being thrown or rattled in your hand, you can transpose the training technique. For example, if your dog is pestering you for attention, command "No" and simultaneously throw the discs down near the dog's feet. This should stop the unwanted action. When order is restored, a calm "Good dog" can be said.

Step 2: By commanding "No" while throwing the discs on the ground, the dog comes to associate the sound of the discs with the order "No."

Step 3: After a while the dog should respond to just the command "No" without the need for the discs to be thrown as a reinforcement.

TRAINING DIGEST

Deterrent sprays (above) use bitter-smelling, but otherwise harmless, sprays to discourage a dog from unwanted behaviors. This application should stop the dog from play-biting the young girl's arm.

By using training discs (below), you can teach a dog that it can only take a treat when you command "Eat." If the dog lunges at the food unprompted, the discs are thrown noisily on the floor near the dog's food.

Training Equipment

Dog-Stop Alarms

(for determined and dominant dogs only)
These aerosol-type alarms work by emitting a sharp, high-pitched noise when activated by the owner. They startle the dog long enough for you to interrupt what it is doing and issue a counter-command or offer a reward for another action. For example, if the dog begins to show aggression toward another dog, you activate the alarm – the behavior is interrupted – you then heel off with the dog either using voice commands or some toy or treat as a distraction.

Above: *It pays to condition and train a dog to spend time on its own in its bed. The dog will feel secure there, and you can use the command "Bed" when you want to be left alone.*

Above: *Dogs love playing with tug-of-war-type toys like this. Be careful with dominant dogs, however; they may view the game as a contest they must win.*

Water Pistols

Water pistols (or even clean plastic bottles) can be used to squirt water at a misbehaving dog. They work rather like the dog-stop alarm by giving the dog a shock, and are especially useful when puppies begin to nibble electrical wires, plants, etc.

Dog Beds

When a puppy is first brought into the home, it feels very insecure and a little lost. Adaptable as dogs are, one can help the process of acclimatization by teaching the dog that it has a place where it can lie without being in the way of pedestrian traffic around the home. I usually put a small bed in a cage or puppy pen when a puppy first arrives. The puppy finds the texture and warmth reassuring and, as it is kept in the pen for short periods and at night, it is naturally conditioned to sleep in the soft, warm bed. As the weeks pass and the puppy's feelings of security and well-being increase, I begin to move the bed around the kitchen area. As the puppy is now conditioned to sleep or rest in the bed, it will seek it out for sleep and relaxation.

As time goes by, I add another link to the training routine by giving the command "Bed" and pointing to it. I train the dog to go to the bed and lie down, and I reward it with a treat. This command is useful when visitors arrive who do not necessarily want dogs near them, or when you are occupied around the house and don't want the dog to interfere. You can put the bed in any part of the house, or even in the car, and the dog will still relax in it.

Dog Flaps

These are like large cat flaps and are generally used when house-training dogs or to allow dogs access to the yard when you are out.

Indoor Cages and Pens

These are useful for toilet-training a puppy, and in controlling a dog that exhibits destructive behavior.

Car Ramps

Teaching dogs how to get in and out of cars is a major task if the dog is large and the owner isn't very strong. Ramps *(left)* help to teach dogs what you require and allow them to get into a car until they are old enough to jump in and out of their own accord.

Carrier Cages and Crates

Carrier cages/crates and dog guards are useful in a car from a safety point of view and can help prevent unwanted behavior like jumping around on the car seats.

Dog harnesses are also useful, especially if you drive a sedan rather than a station wagon. They are made in a variety of sizes and clip on to the rear seat belts. They are comfortable for the dog to wear and prevent them from jumping around. They also help stop dogs from becoming over-excitable because they are restrained.

Above: *Nowadays toys for dogs come in a wonderful array of shapes, sizes, and colors. Playing with your pet helps form a strong family bond.*

Toys and Balls

These are essential for all sorts of mind-stimulating games to assist the dog's mental development, and are also used in the programs that deal with separation anxiety and recall training.

Whistle

The whistle is an essential adjunct to recall training; the use of a whistle for this purpose is described fully in Chapter 4.

TRAINING DIGEST

Dog-stop alarms and quick squirts of water from a water pistol startle a dog long enough for you to interrupt what it is doing and issue a counter-command or offer a reward for another action.

Put a small bed in a cage or puppy pen when a puppy first arrives in your home. The puppy finds the texture and warmth reassuring and, as it is kept in the pen for short periods and at night, it is naturally conditioned to sleep in the soft, warm bed.

Carrier cages/crates and dog guards are useful in a car from a safety point of view and can help prevent unwanted behavior like jumping around on the car seats.

Toys are essential for all sorts of mind-stimulating games to assist the dog's mental development.

Left: *An indoor cage or pen is invaluable when you are trying to toilet-train a young puppy. It is also sensible to teach a puppy from an early age that it is normal to spend time on its own away from you.*

3: The Dominant Dog

Left: *A textbook case of a dominant dog pulling on the leash, quite oblivious to its owner's commands.*

Dominant, boisterous, pushy, in the way, always tripping you, in your face – these are words that people use to describe the dominant dog. You can describe the dog any way you wish, but in general we are talking about a dog that dominates parts of your life in a way that is detrimental to what should be an enjoyable and happy relationship. In fact, these dogs are like children who have not been taught consistent discipline from a young age. Neither of them understands our values of right and wrong. However, there the similarity ends because you can explain to a child what you want, but dogs live only for the moment, and explanations are just a waste of breath. In a way, dominant dogs live in a vague world where all the normal good and positive signals of communication between owner and dog have become blurred. This would not be the case in the wild – wolves are exact in their behavior, and for the pack to function and operate smoothly there must be few misunderstandings between pack members.

▶ Problem Signs

Dogs that dominate often exhibit some or all of the behaviors mentioned above. In addition, these dogs will often dive through doorways before you, or be the first to get into or out of the car without waiting for a cue from their owner. They are often more inclined to pull on the leash and to drag their owner in the park from one dog to the next or from one sniff to another. Significantly, when doing this, the dog never turns its head to view its "pack leader's" reactions because it does not feel the need to do so, even though the owner is tugging on the leash and shouting all sorts of commands at it. Such ineffectual owners are nothing more than background noise to a dominant dog. Some people may describe such a dog as simply untrained, but it is more than that – this type of behavior teaches the dog that it leads on issues that matter to it.

1   2   3

Above 1, 2, and 3: *How often is this little scene played out? Your dog runs to fetch a toy, comes hurtling back, and drops it at your feet, expecting you to play. Dominant dogs try to set the domestic agenda; instead, you must assert your control.*

Owners describe how they use various ploys to divert the dog or fool its skills of anticipation so they aren't dragged here and there. Do any of these complaints sound familiar: "I never pick my car keys up first," "I can't get the dog's leash on the collar because he gets so excited," "I have to put the dog in the car before my children because otherwise he will knock them over", "I can't leave him outside a store because he barks," "I can't get the cat's food ready without locking him in another room." What is constant here is the "I can't" refrain. The dominant dog rules supreme – aren't dogs clever!

Causes of Dominance

Dominant dogs have a strong innate drive to be the leader. Although the strength of this varies from dog to dog and breed to breed, dominance is very much compounded by how they have learned, through endless practice, to get your attention and their own way.

There is no equality in dog society; you either lead or you are led. This does not mean that we humans cannot develop a trusting and enjoyable relationship with our pet dogs. On the contrary, a dog that knows its position in the hierarchy of the family pack is undoubtedly a happy and contented dog. More-over, it is a less anxious dog.

The following programs are quick ways of psychologically teaching your dog how to behave

Above: Pawing, nudging, and butting in when you are busy are other ways in which a dog tries to assert its dominance.

in the way that you want. You must show by your example and your behavior, as well as by lack of response to their demanding overtures, that you are the leader. Remember, you are trying to accustom a dog that did not evolve to live in a human household to coexist with humans who don't speak "wolf language."

Right: Top dog! You could not ask for a more graphic illustration of how a dog can sometimes seek to dominate its owner.

Left: Airedales are strong and energetic dogs. On occasion their assertiveness can make them hard to handle.

TACTICS USED TO GAIN CONTROL OF THE SITUATION

- Adopting a doleful, sad look
- Fetching a toy
- Grabbing something that attracts your attention
- Nudging your hand for strokes
- Pressing their body against you or leaning on you
- Non-acknowledgment of owner
- Ignoring your commands
- Sitting on your foot
- Whining
- Pawing
- Barking

The Dominant Dog

Altering Behavior

To change the way a dog behaves, you have to keep rewards very clearly defined and offer them only for the behavior that you wish to teach or encourage. Unpleasant behavior, like jumping up on you or pestering endlessly for attention, **can** be stopped without confrontation. The dog is obviously not aware that you have normal, everyday chores to fulfill. Like a young child, it has no concept of time or responsibility – only what it wants to happen at that moment.

You will need some additional equipment and training procedures to bring the seriously embedded, unpleasant behavior under control when dealing with very strong-willed dogs or dogs that have been badly behaved for a long time. Though no fault of their own, this is often the case with rescue dogs. Though dog-training equipment – such as training discs – will help achieve a quick result in the short term, for the long term the same dog will have to learn how to behave well. You can only do this by treating it like a dog and not as a little human. This means altering its behavior by patient, long-term, non-confrontational training methods. Obstinate, bad behavior has to be remolded. However, dogs are malleable creatures and, when given clear directions backed up with suitable rewards, are able to change.

If you carefully read the section on how dogs learn (pages 22–29) and understand that the dog's learning association time is about two seconds, you will know that you must link an action to a reward or unpleasant experience (discipline) within that time frame. I deliberately avoid the word "punishment" here because, in my view,

Below 1, 2, and 3: *Defining dominance is very difficult at times. What one owner considers bad behavior, such as jumping up and demanding attention like this, may not be a problem at all for another owner.*

Getting your attention means that the dog is getting its own way, just what the dominant dog wants.

1

2

The noise of the discs startles the dog and causes it to get down.

1

2

Above 1, 2, and 3: *As the section on training discs in Chapter 2 explained, any action either to reward or discourage a dog from a particular type of behavior must take place within two seconds of the event to be effective.*

3

3

it is the wrong word to describe what you are trying to achieve. However, the word does seem to fit into the human concept of retribution and I occasionally use it for fluidity in the narrative, but do try to remember that a dog does not view punishment, nor understand the meaning of the word, as we do. The human concept of punishment means nothing to a dog. It simply learns that an action is followed by an enjoyable experience or it is not. If an action ceases to be enjoyable or if it goes unrewarded, the dog will eventually cease to act in this way.

TRAINING DIGEST

▶ To change the way a dog behaves, you have to keep rewards very clearly defined and offer them only for the behavior that you wish to teach or encourage.

Obstinate bad behavior has to be remolded. However, dogs are malleable creatures and, when given clear directions backed up with suitable rewards, are able to change.

The human concept of punishment means nothing to a dog. It simply learns that an action is followed by an enjoyable experience or it is not. If an action ceases to be enjoyable or if it goes unrewarded, the dog will eventually cease to act in this way.

Below: *It's obvious that he thinks that he's the top dog in the household, but that attitude can be changed.*

The Dominant Dog

Jumping Up for Attention

A common example of unacceptable behavior is exhibited by the dominant dog that is big and pushy and jumps up on you. This can hurt, and the behavior has to be stopped. Dogs instinctively want to be near your mouth, just like their wild counterparts, where jumping up can lead to food rewards in the shape of regurgitated morsels of food from a senior pack member. Another reason most dogs jump up is because as puppies they were offered touch, voice, and/or food rewards when they cutely placed their little puppy paws on your lap when you were seated. In time the behavior

Right: It's hard to resist a puppy when it puts its little paws against your leg looking to be pet. But by continually indulging the puppy, we may imprint a behavior pattern that seems less acceptable later in the dog's life when it still climbs up for attention. Praise should only be given when the puppy or adult dog is on four, not two, legs.

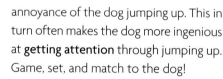

becomes more prolific due to more rewards (unwittingly offered) and, as the dog gets bigger, so does the problem.

As an adult dog the game is now fixed in its psyche. Humans will often employ a strategy of avoidance to minimize the

Below: Dogs are smart and quick to size up a family group in order to figure out who is most likely to give in to their demands for attention.

annoyance of the dog jumping up. This in turn often makes the dog more ingenious at **getting attention** through jumping up. Game, set, and match to the dog!

As the dog gets bigger, more agile, and faster, the action becomes more unpleasant and people begin to push the dog off after an initial gentle pat (reward) or a stroke, thinking, "That's enough, he'll be satisfied with that." The dog that leads reads this as a powerful reinforcement reward – the pat does not signify "Now go away," but is interpreted as a pat for being persistent. By resolutely forcing its attention onto visitors to the home or family members, it demonstrates its right to be noticed and rewarded.

Some people are more strict or less disposed to indulge the dog, and often you will see a dog make choices about whom to pester in order to get the most attention. This beautifully demonstrates their ability to learn how to get a reward and to anticipate from whom the best rewards will come. They learn quickly, but if you know how to teach a dog what you want it to learn, you can turn this aptitude to your advantage to retrain dominant dogs.

The Human Factor

Certain types of dog owners are more likely to be dominated by their dogs than others and they are occasionally on the receiving end of aggressive displays (not necessarily biting). It is not unusual for people who are not particularly assertive, or who have vague personalities, to spoil their dogs endlessly, treating them like children. They avoid facing up to an annoying behavior, preferring to live in hope that it will mend itself. Of course, these people are most at risk of ending up with a dog that does not behave as they would wish.

Certain dog breeds seem to have an innate propensity to dominance, and some of these are the so-called "guard breeds" like Rottweilers, Dobermans, and Mastiffs. But other breeds, too, like Cocker Spaniels and English and Welsh Springers, plus many of the terriers, can display this temperament. Small breeds like the Shih Tzu may look like loveable

On its hind legs, the Dalmatian stands nearly as tall as the woman.

Above: *This picture illustrates the problem when large dogs try to assert dominance through jumping up. The lady owner is leaning back, showing amusement mixed with some anxiety at being on the receiving end of this display.*

bundles of fluff, but despite their small size they are frequently dominant and aggressive by nature. The giant breeds like Maremma Sheepdogs, Pyrenean Mountain Dogs, and Bernese Mountain Dogs can also exhibit their fair share of aggression. However, essentially all breeds can start to exhibit dominant behavior if they are not offered leadership or intelligent behavior and temperament development by their owners during early training.

TRAINING DIGEST

Humans will often employ a strategy of avoidance to minimize the annoyance of the dog jumping up. This in turn often makes the dog more ingenious at getting attention through jumping up.

Certain dog breeds seem to have an innate propensity to dominance, and some of these are the so-called "guard breeds."

However, all breeds can start to exhibit dominant behavior if they are not offered leadership or intelligent behavior and temperament development during early training.

Above: *The bigger the dog, the bigger the problem can be when it insists on getting on your lap.*

The Dominant Dog

Intelligent Leadership Program – A Structured Psychological Demotion Plan

The following suggestions are not to be viewed as punishments or means of retribution. They are ways of starting a new regimen in which you are established as the leader and your dog accepts you as such. It will learn how to behave and become well-mannered and good-tempered. I find that even fear-driven dogs tend to become more obedient and less fearful when this behavioral program is implemented.

It is recommended that the following program be introduced over a period of one or two weeks.

• If your dog sleeps in your bedroom, ban it from there immediately. This includes the stairway. Use a baby gate(s) to restrict access if necessary.

• When walking around the house, make your dog get out of your way. Do not walk around it. Use your foot to nudge the dog gently out of the way. If your dog is aggressive or may bite, do not use this method. Instead, push a broom ahead of you to clear a pathway.

• Give no treats (except for reward or training purposes).

Right: *Don't allow the dog to barge ahead and push through a door before you. Shut the door firmly in his face to deny him the privilege of going first. Continue to do this until he lets you take precedence.*

Left: *He'll get his food only when you have finished eating.*

• Remove all toys, balls, chews, and similar items. Only use them when you choose to do so, especially when they are linked to new training.

• Stop petting your dog for no reason, and I mean totally. All petting is now **earned**.

• If there are certain rooms, seats, or areas that the dog habitually occupies, make sure that he knows that you must have access to those places without

1

2

- Ban the dog from bedroom.

- Make the dog get out of your way around the house.

- Treats are restricted to training sessions.

- Pack away toys and only get them out for training.

- Petting must be earned.

- Ensure that you have unrestricted access to all areas of the house.

- You go through doors first.

- The times of your dog's meals are your decision.

1: *Dominant dogs like to take possession of, or occupy, significant parts of the house, such as the living room sofa or your nice, comfortable bed. You must take charge, command the dog to get off the bed, and ban the dog from the room totally.*

2: *Keep the door shut and, if necessary, use a baby gate to keep upstairs totally off limits.*

Below: *Pack up the toys and put them somewhere out of the dog's reach.*

Playing with toys will now be something that you, not the dog, initiates.

any confrontation or expression of resentment. Use an adjustable baby gate to prevent access to stairways or rooms if necessary.

• Don't let your dog go through a doorway before you. If he tries to push ahead of you, slam the door in his face (make sure that the door does not hit him). You may have to slam the door many times each day to get the dog to learn to wait. He must defer to you. The dog learns that when you call him through a doorway, it is safe. When he pushes ahead of you, the door slams shut.

• When preparing your dog's food and/or your own meals, make sure that your dog is aware that he will be given his food only when you are ready. You must be seen to be in charge of all food resources.

• When watching television or reading a book, don't unwittingly pet your dog when nudged and nosed as you almost certainly will be. **Ignore him**. Alpha wolves ignore the solicitations of lower-ranking pack members unless it suits them – that is what keeps them as leaders. They decide whom to acknowledge and when.

The Dominant Dog

• If you live in a house of standard size, only allow your dog into the living room by invitation between three and six times daily for periods of between half an hour and one hour. Then tell it to leave, and use a leash and collar if necessary to make sure the dog obeys your command "Out."

• If you are using the hook restriction program (see below), try having several hooks positioned in different rooms to help you when first teaching the dog to stay out of your room.

You may wonder what the point is of having a dog if you cannot touch or praise him. Well, you have to make a choice: either you put up with the problem and watch it become progressively worse and worse, or you become tough and decide to do something about it so that you can both enjoy a happier and more harmonious relationship later on.

How long should the above methods be pursued? Well, that depends on many factors, including how badly behaved or dominating your dog is and how long the problem has been in evidence. I find that after about three months, one can ease up on some of the ignoring and the absence of petting procedures, but many dogs have to be kept on the new regimen for life, otherwise they return to their old ways. There are no hard and fast rules. You have to judge your own circumstances and gauge the results. Remember that this plan is not designed for well-behaved dogs.

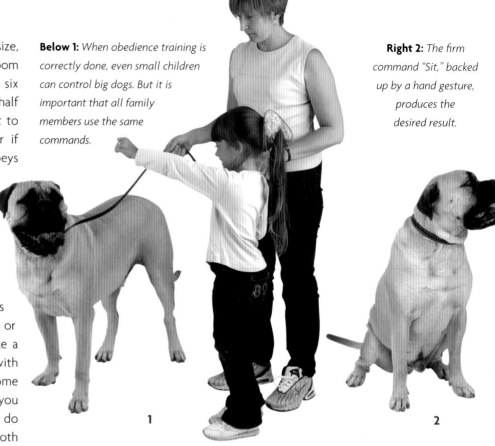

Below 1: When obedience training is correctly done, even small children can control big dogs. But it is important that all family members use the same commands.

1

Right 2: The firm command "Sit," backed up by a hand gesture, produces the desired result.

2

▶ How to Take Charge – Intelligent Dog Training

Obedience training to dogs is what schooling is to children, a way of educating the child or, in this case, the dog, to fit into our complex society. Dogs that understand the basic commands of "Sit," "Stand," "Down," "Stay," plus the recall "No" and "Good boy/girl" have a communication language that benefits both parties. Like children, they need time to learn, and repetition is a great teacher. The more consistent you are with your commands, the easier it is for a dog to learn. Dogs can be confused when they are expected to act in response to an alternative word for the same command if they have not learned it.

Having trained your dog to obey certain commands, you can then use this control to influence its behavior. For example, if it will not move off the couch we can command "Come," then "Down" and then "Stay." Your dog will understand the new ideas and, with the prompting of tone-of-voice rewards and maybe a treat, it will learn to obey and accept you as leader. This will take time. However, **it does work if you are consistent** and patient and make the necessary long-term effort. Now many

Below 3: *Here, the dog is responding to the command "Down" and again, the child motions to show the dog what to do. The mother keeps hold of the collar and leash during the exercise to ensure that the dog is under control at all times.*

3

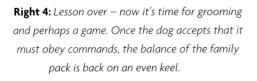

Right 4: *Lesson over – now it's time for grooming and perhaps a game. Once the dog accepts that it must obey commands, the balance of the family pack is back on an even keel.*

experienced readers may say, "I've tried all that but he's still difficult." Read on because I have some new methods to help you to control your dog.

4

▶ TRAINING DIGEST

▶ **Below:** *This is the situation that you are trying to rectify. The dog has become habituated to getting its own way – the unfortunate owner is on the floor.*

After about three months, one can normally ease up on some of the ignoring and the absence of petting procedures if the intelligent demotion program is working, but many dogs have to be kept on the new regimen for life, otherwise they return to their old ways.

Dogs that understand the basic commands of "Sit," "Stand," "Down," "Stay," plus the recall, "No" and "Good boy/girl" have a communication language that benefits both parties.

The Dominant Dog

Phase Two – The Hook Restriction Program

The next step is to implement structured training routines that will prevent your dog from performing ingrained bad habits. You will now make the decisions about what happens around you and when and how your dog will behave. I call this reforming the dog's familiarity of its home geography – i.e., your house and yard.

People Arriving at Your Home

This section describes how to change and calm your dog's behavior in the home. I concentrate on the house because that is where most people seem least able to control a dominant dog. It is the center of your joint worlds – a busy meeting place particularly if children are around. After the following training regimen has been put into practice, clients normally tell me how quiet and well-behaved their dog has become. "He's a different dog." It's really quite simple to accomplish – here's how to do it.

The Kong is a rubber toy that is used for play. We use it in many dog behavior programs. However, you can safely adapt several toys that are strong, non-edible, and have a central cavity that makes extracting sticky meat foods a slow affair

Below 1, 2, and 3: *By using a food-filled toy in association with the hook restriction method, a dog comes to associate being tethered with a pleasant reward.*

Above: *Owners frequently touch their dogs to stop them from pestering visitors – the dog interprets this as a reward and keeps on doing it.*

for your dog, keeping its mind occupied as it tries to remove the food.

Dogs that are over the top and leap boisterously all over visitors can be made to learn that the arrival of visitors will be rewarded with a pleasant experience that has nothing to do with

Right: *If a visitor takes notice of a dog that is demanding attention, the dog has won a small victory and may repeat the action.*

jumping up. We are aiming to redirect their energy onto this new toy and the associated links of a hook and leash, as explained below. The toy is attractive because it is stuffed with your dog's daily diet, and that means all of the diet, not just treats. Hide the dog's food dish away for a few months. Of course, a bowl of water should still be available.

How the Dog Sees the Situation

To retrain a dog that dominates your lifestyle, it is important to understand who is leading and who is led. Most of these dogs have learned a set of "triggers" to which they respond. The owner then reacts to the dog and is, in consequence, led. For example, a guest arrives at the door. That is the dog's trigger and he starts to become very excited. Usually he will have learned how to avoid being caught and controlled, so when the guest enters your home, it's a free-for-all. As you and your guest walk to the living room, the dog will demand to be pet, jumping up, barking,

and performing other disruptive behavior.

You may try your best to control the dog's actions, but experience has taught it how to persist and wear down most people's resistance. When a dog forces itself on people, they generally stop to pet it, believing that by making this concession the dog will be satisfied. Once acknowledged, they think it will stop. Most owners also "pet touch" their own dog when trying to calm it down or stop it from misbehaving. The dog learns that his actions produce this flurry of touch, eye contact, and voice acknowledgment. Success is the dog's reward, and so the disruptive behavior is embedded. There is no motivation to stop, so it does not stop and the dog is prepared to put up with the occasional display of anger from its owner.

The dog has learned the following scenario:

The door bell/knocker sounds. I (the dog) must act quickly and become excited because there are two powerful rewards.

1 The visitor is forced to stroke/pet/ stop and pay attention to me as a dominant dog.
2 My owner pets me (just holding the dog qualifies as a reward), shouts at me, and generally gets equally excited by the arrival.

The chaos that ensues is often inadvertently made worse by the actions of the owner until the dog becomes a complete nuisance.

TRAINING DIGEST

▶ You can safely adapt several toys that are strong, non-edible, and have a central cavity that makes extracting sticky meat foods a slow affair for your dog, keeping its mind occupied as it tries to remove the food.

We are aiming to redirect their disruptive energy onto this new toy and the associated links of a hook and leash.

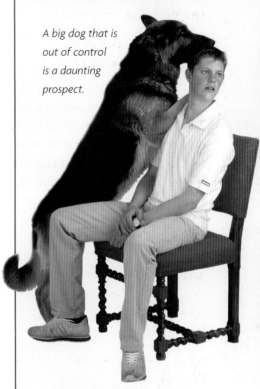

A big dog that is out of control is a daunting prospect.

Above: *A dog that persistently does this to a visitor will quickly start to lose you friends, unless you do something about it.*

The Dominant Dog

How to Take Full Control

The first remedial action is to halt your dog's well-tried disruptive routine in its tracks. **You** must decide what will happen in the house and when. Patience for the first five days is critical. No anger, no shouting, no manhandling of the dog. Dogs are basically opportunists and will seek every opportunity to practice their tricks. This new routine is also manipulative, making use of the fact that dogs love their leashes and associate them with being walked, so getting the dog on a leash should not be too difficult.

Equipment Required

In the short-term, use of the training discs or a water pistol (see pages 34–37) will probably stop, or at least interrupt, your dog's shenanigans. The dog will now associate jumping up with the unpleasant sound of the discs clattering on the floor, only if they are used consistently when the dog jumps up.

You will also need a leash — 4 to 6 feet (1.2–2 m) long — and two or more hooks attached to a baseboard, wall, or other solid fixing point around your home. A food-toy filled with natural wet food (no dry food) is also required. If one hook is set into a baseboard about 4 in (10 cm) from the floor, you can easily drop the end loop of the leash over it. Don't fix the hooks in a walk-through area. Remember to ensure that any baseboard used is firmly fixed, as a large dog could pull a loose one away from the wall.

While you are at home, place your dog on the hook, using a leash and collar, for about twenty minutes at a time, three times a day. Condition the dog so that you only release him when he is quiet and relaxed. If he becomes over-excited when you approach him, walk away immediately. Say nothing. If repeated several times over a week or so, the dog will come to learn that

1 and 2: Getting your dog accustomed to spending time on its own attached to the hook helps to break the pattern of disruptive behavior.

3 and 4: The dog starts to learn that you call the shots. The use of the food toy also helps to reinforce the quiet behavior that you want to encourage.

1   2   3

you only release him when he is quiet. The dog is now partly conditioned to a new set of rules, which will help with visitors and family arrivals. Now we are ready for the test run.

1 Before your guest arrives or upon hearing the doorbell ring, place the leash and collar on your dog.
2 Secure the leash and collar over the hook. Don't forget to give the dog the toy stuffed with food.
3 If the dog barks incessantly, transfer him to another hook situated in another room. Ensure that you ignore the dog's protests.
4 Answer the door, invite your guest in, and tell him or her not to acknowledge your dog at all.
5 Once the dog has settled down or after about fifteen minutes let him loose, but keep him on his leash for control.
6 You and the guest must not acknowledge the dog at all.
7 If the dog brings toys or uses other actions to obtain attention, ignore these, too.
8 With some very badly behaved dogs, use the training discs as instructed if

4

the dog barks when attached to his hook, or when he is released from the hook.
9 Another powerful reward for behaving well is the release, but only do this when your dog is quiet.
10 If you approach your dog to release him and he begins to become over-excited, walk away as you did in the early conditioning program.

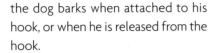

11 After a few weeks of training, calmness should be the norm. Your dog will have learned that praise, touch, and rewards are only given at your command and when you want.

I tend to use this method until the dog willingly runs to the hook and leash upon hearing the doorbell. After a few months when I have stopped the dog from imposing on visitors, I will only use the hook and leash on occasions where I have the doors open to the street or when it's difficult to keep an eye on the dog. The hook, in some ways, is similar to a child's playpen from a safety point of view. If the psychological Intelligent Leadership program has been used at the same time, you should by now have a much calmer and happier dog.

Praise and touch rewards only happen when you say so.

Above: *If your dog remains quiet on the hook while visitors are present, you can eventually reward it with a quiet word of praise and release it from the tether.*

TRAINING DIGEST

While you are at home, place your dog on the hook, using a leash and collar, for about twenty minutes at a time, three times a day. Condition the dog so that you only release him when he is quiet and relaxed.

After a few weeks of training, calmness should be the norm. Your dog will have learned that praise, touch, and rewards are only given at your command and at a time when you want.

The Dominant Dog

A Good Time When Tethered

Some dogs are seriously difficult or are very vocal on the first few occasions when you restrict their movements. But

Below 1, 2, and 3: When your visitor arrives and rings the door bell, restrain your dog's excitement, and attach the leash to its collar before you open the door.

they can also be helped. This is where the rubber food toy comes in. I simply fill it with a portion of their meat-based food. Always use healthy dog food for this program. Avoid foods that contain chemical additives, as they may be influencing your dog's behavior. **Do not use heavily processed foods** – the meat has to be sticky and of meaty texture to lodge inside the toy and be sufficiently

well-packed that it is difficult for your dog to extract food from it.

If you know that guests are coming, only feed your dog that day through the food toy. Stuff it with food and place it in a plastic container or bag in the fridge. Your dog should have had no food prior to your visitor's arrival. Planning these training exercises in advance is critical if you are to change

1

2

3

4: Drop the loop of the leash over the hook and give your dog the food-stuffed rubber toy to occupy its attention.

5: Now you can enjoy your guest's company while also appreciating a placid dog – at last.

4

5

A placid, well-controlled dog is a wonderful companion.

your dog's temperament and help him to view the hook restriction as a fun exercise.

When the guest arrives, attach the dog to his collar and leash and place the leash loop over the hook before you invite your guest into the house. Give the food toy, stuffed with food, to your dog and answer the door, ushering your guest into the room.

With repetition, your dog will associate getting his food with the arrival of guests. Moreover, it will take time for him to extract the food; his mind will be concentrated on the food reward rather than trying to pester the guest. Over time the repetition will imprint the desired behavior and your dog will become less dominant or overbearing with visitors.

Once you have reached a stage where your dog behaves calmly, accepts the food toy and food, and happily runs to his hook and leash, probably after a few

months' training, it is time to dispose of the hook and use only the leash and collar and the food toy placed anywhere in your room. Bring your guest in and sit down while the dog tucks into his treat. The final stages are just to place the toy on the floor while the dog is no longer tethered or on a leash. By using this approach in combination with the psychological demotion program and other methods outlined in this book, you should now have a well-behaved dog that can receive some petting when you choose to give it, and which will interact with people in a calmer and more controlled way. Another benefit is that the peaceful atmosphere enables dog and owner to develop a mutual language that is clear, and the dog is now able to learn new positive behaviors more willingly.

Always be attentive, however, and be aware that some dominant dogs can revert back to their old disruptive ways.

RECAP – BEHAVIOR DENIED

- Dashing to the front door is no longer allowed – reward removed.

- Pushing in on family or visitors is impossible to achieve – reward removed.

- Diving on people who are sitting down or demanding petting constantly is now barred – reward removed.

- Running from room to room has stopped – reward removed.

RECAP – NEW REWARDS

- Being on the hook tether is now rewarded with a toy full of food.

- Being released only happens when the dog is not over-excited – the reward is being released.

- Approaching people calmly and not jumping up is rewarded with a stroke.

- Shouting and threats from annoyed people has stopped.

- Responding to obedience commands and actions produces more rewards.

4: Recall – Dogs That Don't Come On Command

One of the questions I am most frequently asked is how to persuade or command a dog to come when called – the exercise trainers term the recall. Why is it that so many people have trouble with this exercise? One answer, taking a dog's point of view, is that most owners of difficult dogs simply bore or have bored their dogs to death during walks. There is much truth in that – we ourselves would pay little attention to a family member who ignored us most of the time – but it is not the whole answer. More often than not the problem arises because we fail to understand basic canine psychology.

Let's look at it from the dog's point of view. As a dog develops from a puppy, through adolescence, and into an adult dog, it explores all the wonderful varied smells in its environment, plays with all the dogs it can, and generally investigates everything that is happening in the vicinity. These pleasures are constantly reinforced by enjoyable repetition. Of course, while all of this is going on, you are the last thing on your dog's mind – or rather you become just that if the dog has not been trained to come when you call.

When you call your dog, it's simply a matter of whether the motivation to obey you outweighs the attractions and distractions of where the dog is at that moment – and that's the crux of the problem. Most people love letting their dogs run free in the park to play with other dogs. This is important for your dog, so that it can socialize and learn how to interact with other dogs – a vital part of building up a sound temperament. But it is just as important to ensure that exploration and socialization take second place to your commands, so you have to provide the motivation for the dog to find you more interesting than whatever else it may be doing at the moment. This is not an easy task – at least for people who want to put the minimum effort into walking the dog.

Another source of difficulty arises if your dog is a dominant or alpha type who wishes to make sure that all other dogs within sight are aware of his presence. This means marking territory with urine and subsequently tearing around the park, pestering other dogs to assert his importance. There are other reasons for poor recall, but the methods to improve recall are the same.

▶ Prevention Advice

From the day you get your puppy (or, indeed, adult dog), spend time in play to capture and keep its interest. One of the simplest and most useful games to play is the retrieve, using a ball or some other favorite toy. My young dogs soon learn that I am the pack leader and the center of their world. I teach this by constantly developing games with balls, soft toys, and other chase actions. The time I put in during the first six months of owner-

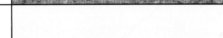

▶ When you call your dog, it's simply a matter of whether the motivation to obey you outweighs the attractions and distractions of where the dog is at that moment.

Below: Dogs love making friends with other dogs when out on a walk, and sometimes ignore their owner's cries to come back.

Left: Is this what happens when you call your dog back to your side during a walk? It is extremely frustrating when your cries are met with complete indifference by the dog, who is much more interested in exploring the sights and smells of a new environment.

Below: This is what we want – the dog returns obediently when the owner demands it. It is important to condition your dog early in its life to accept you as pack leader. Use toys and balls to make walks fun so that the dog has an incentive to come when called.

ship enables me later on to perfect the recall. The dog still enjoys play with other dogs, but learns that when you command, it obeys – and willingly because you are the leader and are fun to return to.

Owners who fail to implant this basic idea find that in certain situations their dogs ignore their frantic calling, and that belated attempts at teaching the recall fall on deaf ears. Their dogs return to them when they are ready, not when called.

▶ You have to provide the motivation for the dog to find you more interesting than whatever else it may be doing at the moment.

From the day you get your puppy (or, indeed, adult dog), spend time in play to capture and keep its interest. One of the simplest and most useful games to play is the retrieve, using a ball or some other favorite toy.

Recall – Dogs That Don't Come On Command

Correcting the Habit

Let's now look at some training methods to reverse this habit. It is important to remember that punishing a dog for not coming (all too often the natural human reaction) simply makes matters worse. Dogs are not inclined to come when punished, and trying to punish a dog after the event (or when you have caught it) does not allow it to make the connection between the punishment and its own actions. See the section on how dogs learn (pages 26–27).

Call the dog's name to gain its attention.

Extended arms and a welcoming body posture reinforce the verbal command to "Come."

Add some extra words of praise as the dog approaches you.

1

2

3

4

Above 1 and 2:
When teaching the recall using a collar and leash, use about a 6 ft (2 m) length of leash so that the dog can move a little distance away from you initially.

The dog recognizes its name and turns its head.

Above 3 and 4:
When the dog is paying attention to you, give the command "Come" and encourage the dog through your body language to approach you.

Before deciding which training method to adopt, you need to take your own dog's character into account. For training purposes, dogs can be classified in two basic groups: the dominant

Use the command "Sit" to complete the exercise.

5

Praise your dog.

Above 5: *Give the dog lots of verbal praise – "good dog" – and a rewarding pat when it comes back to you as commanded.*

and/or determined dog (DD) and the sensitive dog or puppy (SDP). Unless otherwise described, each of the training approaches considered below is suitable for both canine types. If you are unsure of how to classify your dog's personality, select an SDP approach first and see how you progress.

Leash and Collar Recall

Leash and collar recall is the basic system of training a dog to come. Even if you have tried and failed teaching the recall off-leash, it is still best to go back to the beginning and start again with the basics of leash control and the commands "Sit," "Stay," and "Come."

Put your dog's collar on, and attach a 6 ft (2 m) leash or a flexible leash to the collar. Tell the dog to sit and stay, then walk away about 5 feet (1.5 m). Stop, turn, and after a few seconds:

- Clearly call the dog's name (to gain its attention).
- Give the command "Come."
- Bend down invitingly and, when he moves toward you, offer praise as the dog nears you.

After many practices you can add the "Sit" command so that we have the recall exercise in its entirety: name, come, sit, good dog.

Now many of you will already have achieved this, but the recall off-leash poses greater problems. At least if your dog can achieve the above, we know that it understands what we want from a recall before the next training techniques are used.

Right: *Dogs respond warmly to praise from their owners. Use verbal praise, petting, and stroking as rewards for good behavior.*

REASONS WHY A DOG WILL NOT OBEY YOU

- Owners have allowed the dog to find its own pleasures from puppyhood.

- Owners do not take on the alpha (leader) role immediately.

- Owners do not train the puppy to come when otherwise distracted.

- Owners delay the start of formal training until the puppy is too old.

- Owners do not teach the recall in all situations, including the home, from eight weeks.

- Owners select a breed that is too difficult to train in relation to their level of experience.

Recall – Dogs That Don't Come On Command

▶ Sound and Food Recall

Dogs have good hearing and most dogs enjoy eating. This method takes advantage of both of these facts. If your dog isn't so keen on food, it will be more difficult, and you may need to use special treats rather than regular food rations.

You'll need a dog whistle and some food. Change your dog's food to a healthy, meat-based type. Before you start this method, introduce some time for play while you're out walking your dog – this helps to teach your dog that doing things with you can be fun. The recall training should be practiced every day for fifteen minutes, twice a day (perhaps while you're out walking your dog) in a quiet area with as few distractions as possible. When you feel confident and your dog begins to enjoy the training, you

1: When practicing the sound and food recall, use the command "Come" and reinforce it by blowing on a dog whistle.

1

The promise of a food reward ought to get the dog moving.

2

can progress to using an area where there are distractions present.

Do not feed the dog for one whole day. You can begin training the following day in the quiet area you have chosen – preferably your own yard. Divide half his normal daily food allowance into about ten portions and keep it in a container – this is less messy.

Left: *Most dogs love a treat, so the use of food rewards is a powerful way of imprinting good behavior and letting the dog know when it is doing the right thing.*

Now show your dog a portion of food in your hand and run backwards. As you run, give the command "Rover, come!" in an excited voice and blow the whistle once. Reward your dog with the food as soon as he comes to you. You do not need to make the dog sit at this stage. Repeat this ten times, then end the lesson. Any food you haven't used can be given to your dog on the final recall after you have attached his leash.

Now your dog has a real incentive to come when called, for a dog's stomach usually rules his mind. You can use the second half of his food ration for lesson two later on in the day, or give

2 and 3: *The dog has seen that you are holding a food reward and should approach you eagerly in the expectation of getting a tasty morsel of food.*

3

He's done it! Repeat this exercise up to ten times per session.

4

Above 4: *Give the dog the food as soon as it comes to you. The "Sit" command can also be given at this stage.*

RECAP

• Dog learns that food arrives during walks, not at home.

• Dog learns that the new whistle sound corresponds to food rewards.

• Dog learns that the second command, "Sit," causes the delivery of instant food reward.

TRAINING TIPS

• Don't only call your dog to put his leash on when you are ready to go home.

• Call your dog at least ten times per walk to embed the recall (always make him sit).

• Play a game of some sort during each walk.

• If your dog is still reluctant to come when called, miss out another day of its food rations, and then try food recall again.

him the remaining half of his meal when you return home. Continue the training for another three days, until your dog comes when you command and whistle each time. Keep the dog on the hungry side during the first two weeks' training.

For weeks two, three, and four, give your dog half his dinner (in portions) on his daily walk. Once you have him responding quickly, drop the verbal commands and use the whistle only, though you may praise him verbally as he runs toward you. Now introduce the sit. At the end of the month you need to wean him slowly off the food.

Continue feeding your dog the remaining food (if any) in the evenings, but take two or three small portions of food with you on his walks, and use this intermittently to reinforce his recall.

Eventually you'll only need to give food rewards occasionally – no more than once or twice a week – so your dog doesn't know when a food reward will come. However, you should continue to praise your dog whenever he comes – whether it is with or without food. It requires perseverance, but it is worthwhile in the end.

Recall – Dogs That Don't Come On Command

The Long Line Recall

(for determined and dominant dogs only)
This program, I feel, is one of the most successful when the handler is skilled and consistent – timing is critical. Start by obtaining a length of line, similar to curtain cord – i.e., strong and thin (many yachting shops sell suitable line). You will need the line to be about 30 feet (9 m) in length. You may also find it useful to wear a gardening glove to prevent burn marks on your hand if the line should unexpectedly be pulled through your fingers. Next, tie a loop handle about 6 inches (15 cm) long at one end and connect a dog clip (like the one you usually have on the end of a leash) to the other end. Attach the clip to your dog's collar and you're ready to get started.

Begin your training in a garden, yard, a quiet part of the house, or any other peaceful place with no distractions. When using the line in the garden, a shorter length, maybe 10 to 15 feet (3–4.5 m), is adequate and much easier to handle. Make sure there are no obstacles that might entangle the cord. When out in the park avoid trees, posts, or any other objects that the line may snag on. Open, grassy spaces are best.

Release your dog in your chosen area and let out the line. If your dog runs off, simply drop the line and follow on foot (never hold the line except when checking the dog). Eventually your dog will stop at a distraction – whether it's a tree to sniff or another dog. Now you should take hold of the trailing line at any point along its length; gather any slack and then command your dog, using his name, to "Come." If he doesn't respond, tug the line sharply to distract him. Immediately walk backwards, still holding the line. If he responds and comes toward you, praise him enthusiastically. If he ignores you, repeat the command "Come," simultaneously checking him on the line until he does respond. When he arrives, tell him to sit and praise him lavishly. A small treat may also be offered.

Above 1 and 2: *The long line recall technique can be practiced in open spaces where there is no danger of the line snagging an obstacle. A shorter line can even be used in the yard.*

Practice Makes Perfect

Continue to practice in the quiet place you have chosen for the first few weeks, until you have reached a standard whereby the dog responds to your commands without the physical reinforcement of a tug down the line.

The next stage is to practice all of the exercises in different locations, including a variety of public places.

At first he will be distracted. This is normal, but now you have to work harder. Allow the dog to run free, with the line trailing on the ground. Command "Rover, come" only, and if you get no reaction give a check down the line to interrupt and stop the dog from ignoring you. As the dog's collar is checked and he looks at you, bend low and praise him, "Clever dog," making your voice as excited as possible. Most dogs will then run toward you, at which point you

Below 1: *Make sure that you take up any slack in the leash before calling your dog and commanding him to "Come."*

1

Crouching down helps to gain the dog's attention.

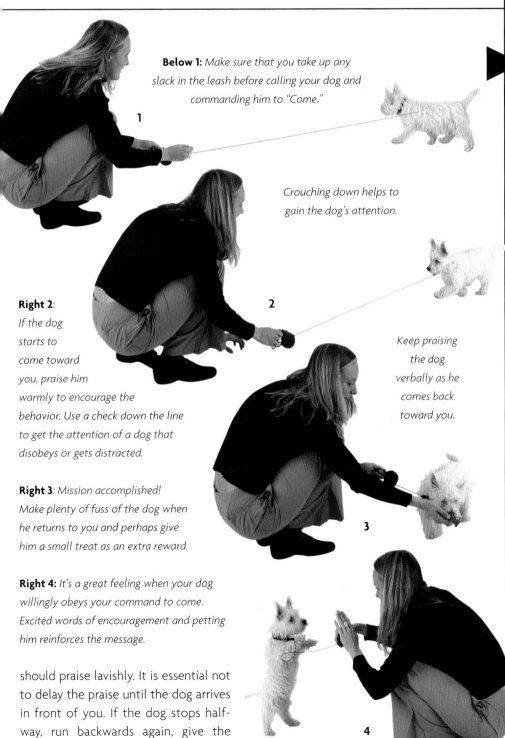

Right 2: *If the dog starts to come toward you, praise him warmly to encourage the behavior. Use a check down the line to get the attention of a dog that disobeys or gets distracted.*

2

Keep praising the dog verbally as he comes back toward you.

Right 3: *Mission accomplished! Make plenty of fuss of the dog when he returns to you and perhaps give him a small treat as an extra reward.*

3

Right 4: *It's a great feeling when your dog willingly obeys your command to come. Excited words of encouragement and petting him reinforces the message.*

4

should praise lavishly. It is essential not to delay the praise until the dog arrives in front of you. If the dog stops half-way, run backwards again, give the "Come" command again, and reward any response with excited praise.

TRAINING DIGEST

► When using the long line method of training the recall, make sure that there are no obstacles that might entangle the cord. When out in the park avoid trees, posts, or any other objects that the line may snag on. Open, grassy spaces are best.

Right: *By giving a check down the line if the dog does not respond to the command "Come," you are able to attract the dog's attention at a distance.*

► Take hold of the trailing line at any point along its length. Gather any slack and then command your dog, using his name, to "Come." If he doesn't respond, tug the line sharply to distract him. Immediately walk backwards, still holding the line. If he responds and comes toward you, praise him enthusiastically.

As the dog's collar is checked and he looks at you, bend low and praise him, "Clever dog," making your voice as excited as possible. Most dogs will then run toward you, at which point you should praise lavishly.

Recall – Dogs That Don't Come On Command

Practice on Walks

Once the dog is at arm's length, gently take the line about 3 feet (1 m) from the collar and tell the dog to sit. (The line is now used like a leash.) Praise the dog for sitting and then, after about thirty seconds, release him with the command "Free," letting the line out again. Repeat the exercise as many times as you wish. You should call your dog several times on each walk for practice. In this way your dog won't expect to be called only once, at the end of your walk, and then attached to the leash and taken home. Also try altering your walking routine and the routes that you like to take occasionally. These actions will prevent your dog from anticipating when he thinks the walk will end and the usual "I don't want to come" syndrome.

The psychology of the training is this: dogs do not measure distance, so in its mind the line could be anything from 50 to 100 yards (45 to 90 m) long. Providing you pick the line up at different lengths on different occasions, he will generally not realize that you never call him from more than the line's length away.

If the dog reaches the end of the line (and no other distractions are nearby), drop the line just before it tightens – the dog then trails it behind, oblivious to the fact that you have dropped the end of it. If the dog subsequently runs off about 100 yards (90 m), quickly catch up to the end of the line, pick it up calmly, and call him. If he comes immediately, praise him and run backwards. If he ignores you, give a sharp check down the line.

Dealing with Distractions

The dog may find various distractions more interesting than you, or what you are trying to teach it. This is a time when a number of owners give up because their dog may appear to be regressing. This is not the case! The dog is simply making choices based on past experiences that were generally in its favor.

The dog does not forget what you have taught it, but instantly associates your command with either your positive enforcement of obedience, or your lack of it, in the past. You want your dog to be obedient in all circumstances. **Do not give up – continue!** Within a few days of consistent reinforcement, the dog will respond to your commands.

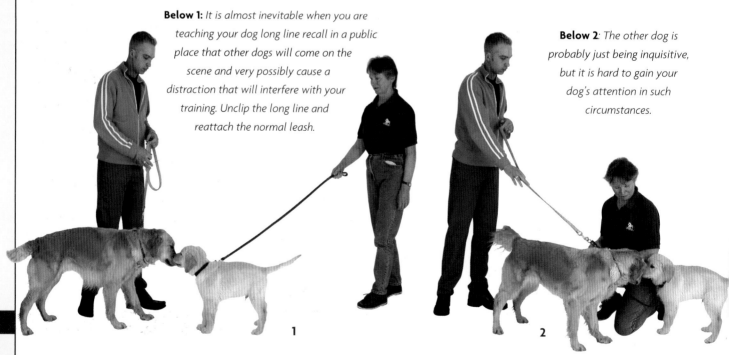

Below 1: *It is almost inevitable when you are teaching your dog long line recall in a public place that other dogs will come on the scene and very possibly cause a distraction that will interfere with your training. Unclip the long line and reattach the normal leash.*

Below 2: *The other dog is probably just being inquisitive, but it is hard to gain your dog's attention in such circumstances.*

1

2

Above 1: *Always praise your dog as it comes obediently toward you on command.*

Above 2 and 3: *A stroke and a "good dog" show that you are pleased. Then command your dog to "Sit" and again praise it when it obeys you.*

When you are training in a public place, other dogs may run up to you and your dog. Their intentions may be friendly, or their owners may have little or no control over them. Under these circumstances, especially in the first few weeks of training, it is best to heel your dog off briskly to another area. In difficult circumstances I simply connect the leash to the dog's collar and disconnect the line, leaving it on the ground to pick up a few minutes later. This avoids entanglements – especially if you have someone else's uncontrollable and boisterous dog around you. Your dog cannot be expected to learn while other dogs are jumping all over him. There is also a danger of the line getting caught around both of the dogs, and this situation should be avoided.

Line training works well on most dogs. The only exception is very large dogs that aren't sensitive to being checked unless you use excessive force, which is not recommended.

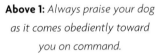

Below 3: *The best course of action is to call your dog to heel and head off to a quieter part of the park.*

▶ RECALL – RECAP

• **Your dog learns that when it ignores you a check comes down the line.**

• **Running backward as you call it encourages a dog to come to you.**

• **As the dog runs to you and when it reaches you, praise it, then give the command "Sit" and more praise. A treat may also be a pleasant reward for coming when called.**

• **When the dog runs to you, act pleased – and interested.**

Above: *It is important for puppies to socialize with other older dogs, but they do get in the way of training exercises and are liable to cause distraction in the early stages of training.*

Recall – Dogs That Don't Come On Command

▶ Sound and Toy Recall

Dogs have good hearing and most dogs enjoy playing with a favorite toy; this method utilizes both of these facts. However, if your dog isn't so keen on toys, you will first have to teach the Long Line Recall (see above) before following these instructions further.

You'll need a dog whistle, as in the long line training and a toy (ball, squeaky toy, etc.). Start by removing all toys from the house and placing them in a secure cabinet. Select a favorite toy and take it with you on your walk to begin training the same day in a quiet area you have chosen.

Now show your dog the toy in your hand and run backwards, simultaneously and excitedly commanding, "Rover, come!" and waving the toy in the air in an excited manner. Reward your dog by throwing the toy once and allowing him to retrieve and give it back to you (use a long line or leash trailing if your dog refuses to give the toy up). Repeat this ten times, then end the lesson. Throw the toy for your dog on the final recall, then attach his leash and head home.

Now your dog has a real incentive to come when called, for a dog's motivation to retrieve and participate in interaction with the owner normally overrules its desire to follow other distractions. When you return home, make sure no toys are available to the dog, with **no exceptions**.

Lock away all toys at home so that the dog will get extra enjoyment out of playtime in the park.

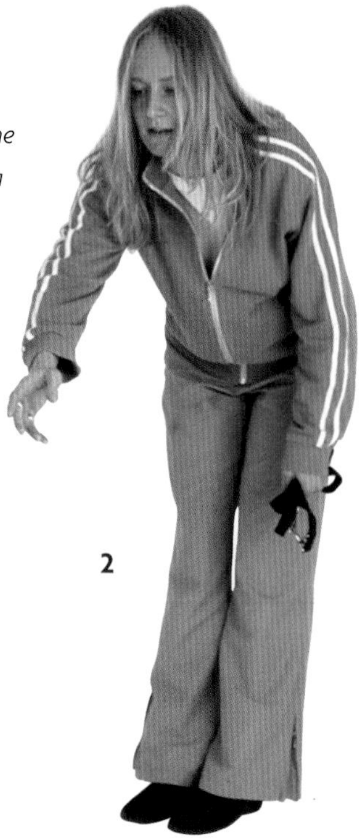

1

2

***Above 1–4:** You can use the fact that most dogs love retrieval games to your advantage when teaching recall. When the dog obeys your command to "Come" and the associated whistle signal, it is rewarded with a fun game of fetch the toy.*

Continue the training for another three days until your dog comes on command each time that you call him, using the toy method.

For another month continue this routine on his daily walk. Once the dog responds instantly, try keeping the toy out of sight until the dog comes right up

3

This lesson can be repeated up to ten times on a walk. Then allow the dog one final fetch before heading home.

4

▶ SOUND AND TOY RECALL – RECAP

▶ • Dog learns that toys are only available during walks, not at home.

• Dog learns that coming when called is rewarded by an exciting game.

• Toy reward is gradually phased out but reward of praise continues.

• Any item that encourages a dog to come to you can be used.

1

to you. Drop the verbal commands and use the whistle only – although you may praise him as he runs toward you. At the end of the month you need to wean him slowly off the toy, so use it to reinforce his recall intermittently.

Eventually you'll only need to throw the toy reward occasionally, so your dog doesn't know when the rewarding game will come. When I say occasionally I mean no more than once or twice a walk. However, you should continue to praise your dog at all times when he comes, whether it's with or without the toy. It does require perseverance.

1, 2, and 3: Once the dog has learned the lesson that coming when called is rewarded with a game, you should gradually phase out the use of the toy but keep praising it for being obedient.

2

Praise your dog every time it comes back to you when called.

3

Recall – Dogs That Don't Come On Command

Hide-and-Seek Recall

Dogs are pack animals and, though your dog may not come back on command, he will still generally keep you in view – even at great distances. This method manipulates your dog's natural instinct to stay with the pack.

Take your dog out to a large open space with plenty of hiding places. Release your dog in an area where there are few dogs, and quickly run off and hide. Let your dog see you. Many dogs quickly run back to where you are, both out of curiosity and pack instinct. Over a period of weeks keep hiding, but gradually make it more difficult for the dog to find you. When you are discovered, offer a small treat like ham pieces or a favorite toy so the dog has a reward for coming, and give him plenty of dramatic and excited praise.

Without the recall command being issued, I have found that most dogs actually become acutely attentive to your location and by default listen and begin to come on command.

Citronella Collar Recall

(for determined dogs only)
The citronella spray collar is another innovative electronic device that is remote-controlled. When used with knowledge – an important factor – it is excellent in teaching DD dogs the recall. It works on the same training psychology as the long line except that the line is replaced by the remote-controlled collar. The battery-powered collar is

Below 1: *The citronella collar can be remotely activated by pressing a button on the small hand controller, which transmits a signal to the collar.*

1

filled with a citronella liquid, which is harmless to dogs. When the hand device is depressed, a jet of citronella spray is released from the collar beneath the

dog's chin, forming a cloud of vapor in front of the dog's nose. This has two possible results:

- The sudden, strong-smelling spray alarms the dog, who escapes back to an owner who is happily calling the dog to them.
- The dog's play or investigation is abruptly interrupted, giving it the opportunity to hear and respond to the "Come" command once more.

For the dog, it's an unpleasant experience to be startled by a sudden burst of citronella if it ignores its owner's commands. Most dogs decide that the best reaction is to run to their owners for attention, support, or whatever. You can then complete the recall exercise. The dog does not associate the unpleasant experience it had over there with you standing over here. However, it quickly

*Remember to
praise your dog
when it comes
on your call.*

2

3

Above 2: *The collar emits a
cloud of bitter-smelling spray,
which startles the dog.*

Above 3: *The dog will normally stop what it is doing
and either return to you for reassurance or be
attentive to your command to "Come."*

associates coming to you with praise and a treat. It is essential that you fully understand timing in dog training before using the citronella collar. See the section on timing in Chapter 1, How Dogs Learn, before employing this method.

Try to avoid calling the dog if you are unable to reinforce the command, even if that means that the dog goes where you may not want it to. In this way the dog does not have the opportunity to disobey your command — so it does not learn that disobedience is an option.

▶ REINFORCERS

▶ **Favorite treats – I recommend chicken or ham pieces.**

Favorite toys, balls, etc. Don't give the toys to the dog at any other time except during training. Gather up all the toys at home and lock them away.

The pleasure of playing a game with you.

The dog's daily dinner given in portions as a reward.

Lower left 1: *There are various reinforcers that you can use to encourage good behavior. Treats and retrieve games played with toys or balls are all rewarding for the puppy or dog.*

Lower left 2: *If you plan to use toys as part of the recall training program, lock them away at home so that the dog can only enjoy playing with them on your terms.*

1

2

5: Separation Anxiety – Home Alone

Dogs and people love each other's company, and that is the reason most of us own dogs. Indeed, dogs often become more inextricably linked with our lives than we realize. Like their cousins (wolves), dogs are gregarious by nature and unsuited to leading solitary lives. That's almost certainly why we get along with them so well. From a dog's point of view, we are the family pack, and so, whether he lives with one person or a large family, he instinctively enjoys, and needs, our company. Leaving a dog alone regularly for long periods is not kind and does not equate with responsible dog ownership. However, like wolves and even humans, dogs can adapt to spending reasonable stretches of time in their own company without suffering severe and long-term psychological problems.

For most well-adjusted dogs, anxieties rarely develop to the point of causing problem behavior. However,

some dog owners find that leaving their beloved pet for even a short time can result in the most extraordinary behavior, and this is what I will explore in this chapter. Reactions to being left alone can take many forms including barking, howling, self-mutilation, excessively boisterous behavior on the owner's return, destructiveness, and

even biting the owner as he or she leaves the house. All are caused by a sense of stress and can be grouped under the heading of separation anxiety.

This can be a severe problem, as was the case with a Golden Retriever bitch I dealt with that nipped several family members as they were about to leave the house in the morning (combining separation anxiety with a touch of dominance aggression). A Labrador owner recalled how her dog just wandered off to her son's bedroom when left alone and chewed through two pairs of handmade leather shoes. Leather is an attractive chewing material to many anxious dogs. It can be a comforter – in the same

Below 1 and 2: *Dogs and humans get along well together – that's why we value their company and let them share our homes.*

1

2

The dog has realized that he is about to be left on his own.

way that some people binge on chocolate when they are feeling down. The fact is that dogs do chew when they are puppies – that's normal canine behavior. We become understandably upset when our treasured goods are

4

3

Below: "Please... I don't want to be alone."

Left and above 3 and 4: *Displays of destructiveness while left alone such as this are typical of dogs that suffer from separation anxiety. Generally, such dogs have not learned a degree of self-sufficiency and have become dependent on their owners' company.*

Dogs are remarkably sensitive to the warning signs that you are about to leave, such as picking up house keys or putting on a coat.

damaged by the dog – that's just normal human behavior. However, if we, as owners, try to understand our dog's needs and general behavior, most of the unpleasant circumstances that I have described are avoidable.

Separation Anxiety – Home Alone

▶ General Causes

This problem nearly always arises when a puppy is spoiled or not conditioned to accept an appropriate routine. As a youngster, it may have been allowed to sleep in its owner's bedroom and received constant attention, or its cute and cuddly appearance may have attracted excessive fussing from visitors and family alike. The unwitting result can be a dog that thinks it has a right to demand attention whenever it wishes, and that this is normal behavior. If you respond to a dog every time it blinks its doleful eyes at you, you could have a separation anxiety problem in the making. Often I describe these dogs as helpless when alone. The bottom line is that we actually cause the problem ourselves by misguided acts of kindness when the dog is demanding.

Dogs that literally go everywhere with their owner, day and night, can also turn out to be owner-dependent. Understandably, therefore, separation anxiety is more common in single-person households, especially when elderly people live alone with a dog as their sole companion. If only you and the dog occupy a house, then naturally you will be together most of the time. But there are measures you can take to teach your dog to be self-sufficient, without forfeiting a close and rewarding relationship.

Another possible contributing factor, though it is often overlooked, is the breed of dog involved. Dogs that are nervous or great natural attention-seekers may receive or solicit extra care and attention from sensitive owners in their early years, causing an excessively close bond and over-dependency to develop. Toy breeds and endearing varieties with humanlike facial features can also trap people into responding to them more like little humans than actual dogs.

Right: *Children love showering attention on their cuddly pets. But if circumstances change – the children disappear to school all day, for instance – the dog can become unsettled, missing all the fuss that he craves.*

Left: Excessive pampering can create a situation where the dog becomes totally reliant on its owner's company.

- Dogs have not learned from puppyhood to spend time alone, but are given free run of the home with human company in all rooms.

- Some owners give their dogs too much attention, often to satisfy their own emotional needs, thereby teaching the dogs to be helpless.

- Some dogs learn to be wholly human-orientated, ignoring their own kind, which causes imbalance and insecurity.

- Small, cuddly breeds tend to attract excessive human attention, so separation anxiety can be more common among toy breeds.

Below: Barking is a common symptom of separation anxiety – not good for you, the dog, or your neighbors.

A sudden reduction in the amount of time and attention you give your dog may well upset him. For example, a dog that has been tenderly nursed through an illness may become distressed when it recovers and the extra fuss suddenly stops. Of course, dogs' personalities vary, so another dog may take this situation in stride, with little or no change in its behavior. Again, a sudden change in the owner's lifestyle – for example, if an owner who has previously been at home all day takes up a job outside the home – will affect the dog. A highly dependent dog will find it most difficult to be alone without the normal company of a family member.

Are You the Problem?

I would argue that dogs are blameless and that we are always the problem. I have been dealing with dogs and their owners for very many years, and this has taught me a great deal about canine-human relationships and the complex ways that we condition our dogs for our own psychological comfort and needs. We are usually not aware of this, but in some cases this interdependence can develop to an unhealthy level. If circumstances change suddenly – for example, if we acquire a new partner or a different job – and the dog is no longer needed as much, it may react badly and develop separation anxiety.

Dogs that have inherited an insecure nature often want attention and company on demand, which compounds the separation anxiety problem. When you comply with your dog's demands, it comes to expect attention every time it asks, until the habit becomes firmly embedded. When there isn't enough attention, i.e., when you are not around, separation anxiety may occur. Barking and destructive behavior are usually the most common signs of separation anxiety, probably because these behaviors produce some emotional relief.

Separation Anxiety – Home Alone

Prevention Advice

The ideal solution is prevention, so I'll cover that first. If you have a puppy or a new dog, teach it that it is normal to be left alone for periods of half an hour to an hour several times a day – and for longer at night. This should be done gradually, starting with five minutes per session. It is, of course, much easier with a puppy than with an adult dog. Teach your puppy that it has its own area (or pen or cage) where you will visit it. Never give the dog access to your whole house. If the puppy starts to cry when it's alone in its pen, wait until silence occurs, then go in and make a mild fuss, but not too much, otherwise you may encourage separation anxiety. Don't let the dog think that every time you come to its area it will be let out; sometimes leave the dog in and sometimes let it out. In other words, be unpredictable in order to avoid reinforcing expectations of attention.

With an attention-seeking dog, many people fall into the trap of petting it whenever it solicits affection. When they think they've shown it enough attention, they stop and expect their dog to understand that they've been fair. What they

don't realize is that the dog has no concept of fairness. All it knows is that if it persists, it can obtain the attention it wants. This only serves to reinforce the dog's dependency on and control over the owner's time and attention.

Reducing Dependence

If possible, start this program during a long holiday weekend. Begin by reducing the amount of attention your dog receives during a twenty-four-hour period to twenty-five percent of what it was. Ignore all the dog's attempts to solicit attention, whether by nudging you, bringing toys, or looking pleadingly to be pet. You'll find this hard at first, but

you and all your family and friends must be consistent.

Next, start leaving your dog on its own in a room of the house for periods of five minutes while you are still in the house. If the dog begins to cry, bark, or sound excited, don't go into the room. When a gap in the barking comes, wait two minutes then go in casually, saying nothing and keeping the contact low-key. On no account should bursts of excitement from the dog be reciprocated. Then wander around for a few minutes and let the dog go free in the house. Ensure that no one pets the dog, no matter how much it solicits praise. The dog's initial puzzlement or even worse behavior will

"I wonder if he'll pet me?"

Right 1, 2, and 3: *When you are working with your dog to reduce its sense of dependence on you, avoid the temptation to pet it whenever it pesters you. Use the Ignore response instead.*

1

2

Above: *Try to accustom a dog from puppyhood that it's normal to spend periods of time on its own. The use of an indoor cage is helpful when doing this.*

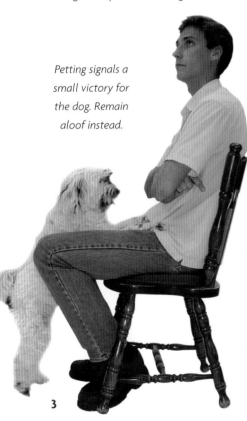

Petting signals a small victory for the dog. Remain aloof instead.

soon give way to acceptance of the new arrangements after a few days.

If this regimen is adhered to, it slowly teaches the dog that it's no big deal to be with you or without you. You should aim to leave your dog alone for five-minute periods, working up to four to six times a day. When this is achieved without any commotion, slowly begin increasing the period your dog spends alone up to the desired time to fit in with your social patterns. If you introduce this program gradually over several weeks, you'll have a greater chance of success. But it is important that the regimen continues.

You can combine this method with the next one by giving the dog a part of its dinner via a specially designed food-stuffed rubber toy (explained below) when it is on its own in the kitchen. This means that the dog is actually rewarded for being out of your company. Your dog should also receive its toys and food when not in your company.

TRAINING DIGEST

▶ If you have a puppy or a new dog, teach it that it is normal to be left alone for periods of half an hour to an hour several times a day – and for longer at night.

Ignore all the dog's attempts to solicit attention, whether by nudging you, bringing toys, or looking pleadingly to be pet. You'll find this hard at first, but you and all your family and friends must be consistent.

You should aim to leave your dog alone for five-minute periods, working up to four to six times a day.

Above: *The toy-fetching routine is another tactic to gain your attention. It may seem hard-hearted, but you must ignore the bait that the dog is desperate that you take.*

Separation Anxiety – Home Alone

The Use of Food

Using food rewards to modify your dog's behavior produces positive associations with your absence. The most useful aid is a tough rubber toy designed to be stuffed with food, which the dog has to remove bit by bit. Instead of gulping his dinner down in a flash, he has a time-consuming but rewarding new hobby.

- Keep your dog in the kitchen area when you are out.
- Change his diet to a healthy food.
- Feed your dog his daily dinner only through the toy.
- If you are out three times in one day, split the day's ration into three portions.
- Use the toy and stuff it with food when you are about to leave your dog.
- Place the toy on the kitchen floor and let the dog work on extracting the meat each time it is placed on the floor.
- You can still use this method even if you are not going out. Leave the dog in the kitchen three times daily for about fifteen minutes, and each time leave him the toy with a portion of his dinner inside. This will accustom the dog to positive rewards when you are out of the room, even though you may still be present in the house.
- Do not feed your dog or give him treats at any other time. All food must be fed through the toy.
- If your dog does not consume the food in the toy, place the whole thing in a plastic container in the fridge until the next lesson. Very few dogs will ignore the food in the toy by the second day.

The combination of the two methods described had a ninety-five percent success rate last year at my center with dogs from a wide range of breeds suffering from separation anxiety.

Two's Canine Company

Another way to occupy your dog during your absence is to see if you can "borrow" on a temporary basis a friend's or neighbor's dog that can keep him company. You need to make sure it is a dog that gets along well with yours, and

Above: *Dogs that get along well together will often pass the time happily, playing and keeping one another out of mischief.*

Left: *When it is time to go out and leave your dog alone at home, consider using food as a diversionary tactic to keep its mind off being on its own.*

Below right 1, 2, 3, and 4: *The beauty of the toy stuffed with food is that the dog really has to work at it to extract the food. While he is concentrating on it, nosing it around on the floor, and trapping it with his paws, the fact that you are out of the room is forgotten.*

1

Below: *Introduce your dog to the food toy by giving him his daily food ration through a toy placed on the kitchen floor in place of a conventional food bowl.*

The food that you use in the toy should be meaty and moist – dry food does not work as well. By cramming it into the toy and compressing it, you create a diversion that occupies the dog's attention and rewards its persistence with food.

that they are left somewhere they can play without wrecking anything or causing any damage around the house. The best combination is usually a dog and a bitch. However, this method will not work if your dog is specifically over-attached to you personally and does not like playing with other dogs.

2   3   4

▶ Using food rewards to modify your dog's behavior produces positive associations with your absence.

Feed your dog his daily dinner only through the toy. If you are out three times in one day, split the day's ration into three portions.

Another way to occupy your dog during your absence is to see if you can "borrow" on a temporary basis a friend's or neighbor's dog that can keep him company.

The best combination is usually a dog and a bitch.

Above: *Another simple ploy to deal with separation anxiety is to arrange for your dog to enjoy the company of another while you are out.*

Separation Anxiety – Home Alone

▶ Exercise the Energy

Try lengthening your dog's exercise periods prior to leaving him alone, and make more effort to tire him out. Throw a ball and run around or let your dog play with other friendly dogs. Don't just go for a lethargic stroll. Then when you arrive home leave your dog on its own for a while. If he's tired, he's much more likely to settle down and go to sleep. As in the previous method, gradually build up the time that you leave your dog alone.

During walks and exercise, you can praise and touch your dog as much as you'd like, especially when obedience training him. While you are working on dealing with separation anxiety, you will usually find as a bonus that your dog becomes far more obedient around the house and in the park.

▶ Important Tips

1 Do not allow your dog to decide when attention should be forthcoming. Let any attention be on your terms. You decide when enough is enough. So for the next few months always ignore your dog if it requests attention.
2 If the anxiety is triggered by your leaving the house, pretend to leave several times a day. Go through all the motions, including putting on your coat and going to your car. With so many false starts to contend with, your dog won't be able to predict when you are leaving, and this should disrupt the ingrained anxiety behavior.

3 Whenever you return home or when your dog has been in another room on its own for a while, don't greet it effusively or over-excite it. Instead, adopt a low-key approach – calm verbal praise is sufficient. In this way your dog will not look upon your return as a big deal. Better still, ignore the dog completely for the first five minutes.
4 Remember that many dogs that crave attention consider being pushed off or reprimanded as a form of reward. Simply stand upright with your hands at your side if your dog jumps on you. Pause, then sit down again. Repeat until the dog loses interest. Don't give the dog any eye contact.

1

Below 1, 2, 3, and 4: *Dogs may start to show signs of anxiety when they anticipate that you are about to leave the house. By making a number of "false starts" throughout the day, you can confuse the dog's expectations and reduce its anxiety.*

Are you going out, or not? The dog is no longer sure what this routine is leading up to.

1   **2**

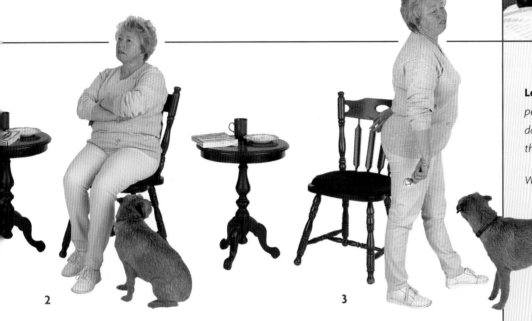

2

3

▶ In Conclusion

I have found that most dogs respond well to the above methods, and that eventually you can reinstate a moderate amount of affectionate response – in other words a relationship that both of you still enjoy. However, a few dogs are so conditioned to effusive displays of affection from their owners, that praise and fuss always have to be kept to a minimum to prevent the dog's anxiety from becoming unbearable again.

▶ RECAP

- **Teach your dog to be alone, initially for short periods.**

- **Use food rewards (the daily ration given via the food-stuffed toy) so the dog develops pleasant associations with the fact of being separated from you.**

- **Treats given at other times are not helpful in solving this problem.**

- **Some dogs like a chew when alone.**

- **Don't allow your dog treats (including toys) when in your company, except when you are out on walks.**

For all the dog knows, you may turn around and come straight back. What's there to worry about?

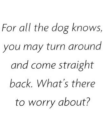

3

4

6: Excessive Barking

For dogs barking is a natural form of communication, and they do it for innumerable reasons. A dog would hardly be a dog if it didn't bark sometimes. However, when barking becomes prolonged or excessive it can be a problem. Strangely enough, the dog's ancestor, the wolf, rarely barks. Howling is its forte – it is a way of transmitting messages to others of its kind.

There are several reasons for excessive barking or howling. Some owners encourage a puppy to bark to develop its guarding ability. In other cases, the owners have unintentionally encouraged it to bark from puppyhood. Whenever the dog barked, its owners appeared and gave it attention. Finding this behavior rewarding, the dog quite naturally continued to bark more and more. This is especially true of puppies.

Some dogs bark from stress when separated from their owners. Others bark from boredom when they don't have enough stimulation. A dog whose routine is changed so that its owner can't spend as much time with it as usual may become frustrated and anxious – this is another cause of excessive barking or related problem behavior, such as

destructiveness (see also the advice provided in Chapter 5 on separation anxiety).

▶ Prevention Advice for Puppies

The ideal solution is prevention. If you have a puppy or a new dog, teach it that it's normal to be left alone for periods of half an hour to an hour several times a day, and for longer at night. This should be done gradually, starting with five- to ten-minute periods.

Also teach your puppy that it has its own cage, pen, or area where you will visit it. Don't, as a norm, give it access to your whole house or apartment. If, while the puppy is alone in its pen, it starts to cry, wait until silence occurs before going in and making a mild fuss of it. Verbal praise is sufficient, but not too much. If every time a dog barks you appear on cue – either to reprimand it or to comfort it in some way – the

Above: *We expect dogs to bark when the doorbell rings – in fact it is useful to be alerted to people approaching the house. But when the barking goes on and on, the behavior becomes unacceptable.*

barking behavior will be maintained or may get even worse.

It is natural for dogs to bark when visitors knock or ring the doorbell. Most owners don't mind this – territorial guarding is natural dog behavior. But don't let the dog overdo it, otherwise you could end up with an excessive barker. Most dogs that drive their owners crazy by barking at the door excessively were taught when to bark but not when to stop.

Above: *This dog is mooching around aimlessly and generally giving the impression of being thoroughly bored. In situations where they lack stimulation, some dogs take to prolonged sessions of barking as a way of relieving their boredom.*

A dog must learn to spend time on its own without resorting to barking the house down.

1

Get the dog used to spending time in the cage.

2

3

Above and right 1, 2, and 3: *Dogs that have become accustomed to spending lots of time with their owners during puppyhood may resort to barking later in their lives when they are left on their own. A good way of preventing this problem from developing is to teach the dog during its formative months that it is normal to spend time alone in a cage, pen, or kennel away from the rest of the family.*

TRAINING DIGEST

Some owners encourage a puppy to bark to develop its guarding ability. In other cases, the owners have unintentionally encouraged it to bark from puppyhood. Whenever the dog barked, its owners appeared and gave it attention. Finding this behavior rewarding, the dog quite naturally continued to bark more and more.

Some dogs bark from stress when separated from their owners. Others bark from boredom when they don't have enough stimulation.

If every time a dog barks you appear on cue – either to reprimand it or to comfort it in some way – the barking will be maintained or get even worse.

Some dogs don't like being left alone in the yard or in an adjacent room, and as a result will bark until the owner attends to their needs, which normally means giving the dog access to human company again. What a powerful reward!

Barking While the Owner Is Home

Some dogs don't like being left alone in the yard or in an adjacent room, and as a result will bark until the owner attends to their needs, which normally means giving the dog access to human company again. What a powerful reward! No wonder dogs learn to bark. If your dog is this type of barker, then follow the Intelligent Leadership and Ignore programs (see pages 28–29, 44–45), and read the section on separation anxiety-related barking (see pages 72–73) for more advice.

Excessive Barking

How to Stop or Reduce Barking

If possible, start this program during a holiday or long weekend. Begin by reducing the amount of attention the dog receives during a twenty-four-hour period. Ignore all the dog's attempts to solicit attention, whether by

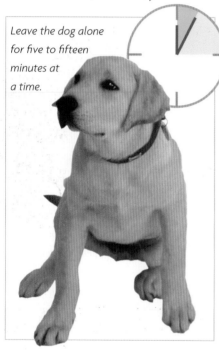

Leave the dog alone for five to fifteen minutes at a time.

Above: *The key to stopping a dog that persistently barks when it is left on its own is to accustom it gradually to spending short periods of time alone several times a day.*

nudging you, begging you to bring toys, or just looking to be pet. You'll find this hard at first, but you and all your family and friends must be consistent.

Start leaving the dog on its own in a room of the house for periods of five minutes while you're still in the house. If

Right: *This training program relies on you significantly reducing the amount of attention that you give your dog.*

the dog begins to bark, do not go into the room. When a gap in the barking comes, wait thirty seconds, then nonchalantly wander in and say hello, but keep the praise low-key. On no account should bursts of excitement from the dog be reciprocated. Then wander around for a few minutes and let the dog go free in the house. Ensure that no one pets the dog, no matter how much it solicits praise. The dog must not associate being with you as a reward for its barking.

Anxiety-Related Barking

Many dogs are over-attached to their owners and appear to be incapable of spending time on their own. Use the following methods on such dogs to change their view of spending time alone. It is normal in human society for people to spend time alone even though we are a gregarious species. Wolf society is also pack-oriented, but wolves can and do spend time alone, and domestic dogs are equally equipped to adapt to being on their own. There are several approaches we can use to help them do so.

Food Inducement

Food is on a dog's mind most of the time, and if it's not, we can easily induce them to think food, or at least make

DEALING WITH FUSSY EATERS

▶ Most dogs learn to be fussy eaters through their owner's actions, when food refusal is rewarded by the substitution of tastier food. Dogs that are known fussy eaters should go a full day without food before you begin training to increase their natural hunger pangs. Dogs are not designed to eat daily; this is a custom imposed by humans. Toy dogs can be trickier to deal with since their small size means lower food requirements, but the principle remains the same. Do not restrict eating practices if the dog is old or unwell.

Above: *Don't respond or go to your dog while it is barking – reward its silence, not its demands for attention.*

dinnertime more exciting. Always use healthy dog food for this program. Avoid any foods containing additives, which might influence your dog's behavior.

You will need a tough rubber toy designed to be stuffed with food (see Training Aids). For the next five weeks your dog will receive his daily food intake only through the toy and in your absence. Divide his day's ration into five portions to stuff into the toy. If he

ignores the food in the toy, simply place the whole thing in a plastic container back in the fridge until the next lesson.

If the dog eats the food willingly, he will have learned to do so in your absence and will associate your absence with a powerful food reward that takes time to extract. He is being rewarded for being separated from you. If your dog barks or scratches to attract your attention, ignore him. Only enter the dog's room when he is silent. He must not associate his barking activities with your arrival. Remember – **no treats or food at any other time!**

Warning
Except in exceptional circumstances, dogs should not be left on their own for an entire day.

TRAINING DIGEST

▶ For the next five weeks your dog will receive his daily food intake only through the toy and in your absence. Divide his day's ration into five portions to stuff into the toy.

Above: *The food-filled rubber toy described in Chapter 2 is a powerful training aid. Instead of barking when alone, dogs learn to anticipate the reward of a food treat.*

▶ If the dog eats the food willingly, he will have learned to do so in your absence and will associate your absence with a powerful food reward that takes time to extract. He is being rewarded for being separated from you.

Excessive Barking

▶ Helpful Distractions

Some trainers recommend leaving a radio on while you're out to keep the dog company. This works in a few cases. Even more effective is the use of a tape recorder to play back the sound of your own voice to the dog while you are away.

Some dogs that bark when left alone can be distracted by leaving them food treats or a favorite toy to keep them busy until your return. You will need to prevent access to toys and chews when you're at home so that they become a special treat associated with your absence.

▶ Excitable Barking for Attention

This type of barking can be a social nuisance when it gets excessive. The way to deal with it is by using counter-conditioning. For example, if the dog barks when it sees you eating, stop

Above: *His Master's Voice? The sound of a radio playing quietly in the background, or even a tape recording of your voice can help some dogs become used to spending periods of time on their own without resorting to fits of barking.*

feeding the dog by hand and only give it food in its bowl. Don't allow the dog any food reward if it stares or barks at you. Employ the Ignore program (see pages 28–29). Better still, don't allow the dog in your presence when eating.

If your dog reacts with boisterous barking when you take the car keys or pick up its leash and collar or your coat,

simply confuse the dog's ability to anticipate your actions. This is done by altering walk times whenever possible, picking up the aforementioned articles five or ten times a day, or even putting on your coat and walking to the front door only to return to your sofa. This saturates the dog with so many false starts not leading to the expected result that (unless he's really stupid) the message will get through.

Never shout or scream at the barking dog to shut up, as this often increases the atmosphere of excitement as far as the dog's concerned: "My owner grabs my leash, I bark wildly, my owner shouts with me, I jump up and down, my owner waves his arms at me; oh, isn't it fun!"

Training discs, when properly introduced, are a very effective means of stopping this type of behavior in attention-seeking, dominant, boisterous dogs. While the dog is barking, throw the discs (or a large bunch of keys) near the

Below: *Food chews can keep dogs happy for hours while their owners are out of the house.*

Play is a great way of stopping a dog from getting bored when it is left on its own.

Above left: *Toys help a dog enjoy time spent alone, although not many dogs know how to skateboard!*

Left: *Try to keep calm and not shout at a dog that barks persistently. A raised voice may just make an excitable dog even more excited.*

dog's feet so that the sound startles him into silence. When your dog stops barking, don't make a fuss of him and stir up the excitement again. Wait impassively for a minute of silence, then limit your praise to a softly spoken "Good dog."

Above: *Some dogs start barking when they see their owners eating in anticipation of the reward of a treat from their hands. In such cases, only feed the dog through its own bowl and don't give any treats or rewards while you are eating.*

Left: *If your dog barks when you put on your coat for a walk, confuse its expectations by making repeated false starts. Walk to the door, stop, and return to the front room again.*

RECAP

• **Don't reward barking behavior.**

• **Put an end to the cues that elicit barking.**

• **Keep calm – shouting only adds to the excitement.**

• **Remember: dogs bark naturally, but they learn to bark excessively only when owners unwittingly reinforce this behavior.**

• **Interrupt the barking by throwing training discs near the dog at the time of barking only.**

Excessive Barking

Barking in the Car

Most dogs love cars and all the accompanying excitement of going for a drive. They associate cars with fun – being with you, going on a hunt, a walk in the park. Riding in the car has all the visual stimulus of a hunt, with other dogs and animals flashing by. Dogs that express this excitement by barking non-stop in the car are a big problem for many people. Prolonged or excessive barking is aggravating, and when it occurs right in your ear while you are driving, it can be dangerous. Many a driver has had an accident while trying to quiet a dog in a car, normally in anger.

Above and above right: *A food-filled toy (left) is a useful distraction – it occupies the mind of a persistent barker who might otherwise be creating mayhem in the car. If your dog shows destructive tendencies when left alone in the car, try confining him in a travel cage or behind a dog guard (above right).*

Using Deterrents

More sensitive dogs, and dogs that are caught in the developing stages of the barking habit, may respond well to spray deterrents. When traveling, take a water pistol along on the journey. When your dog starts to bark, squirt the water in its face, simultaneously giving the command "No" in a firm voice. Don't raise your voice, or the dog will think you are joining in and take this as encouragement to bark!

Alternatively, you can use a commercially produced deterrent spray, which squirts a fine mist of harmless but very bitter liquid into the air. It's difficult for

a dog to bark while tasting such a pungent smell. By the way, you won't like the taste either! You can also buy a special remote-controlled collar that squirts citronella spray when the dog barks, but this should only be used with the expert help of a trainer or canine behavior practitioner, as some dogs are very sensitive to the jet spray or accompanying sound. Alternatively, you could use the training discs as outlined in Chapter 2. For safety

reasons, if you are driving it is best to have a friend sitting next to you on car journeys to apply the deterrent for the first four or five sessions, and occasionally thereafter.

If you are consistent, most dogs will find the experience distracting and unpleasant. As soon as you have thirty seconds of silence, quietly praise your dog verbally in a low-key voice. Don't pet him or make a fuss of him, as this will simply re-excite him. Your dog should learn that silence brings pleasant praise as a reward, and that barking means trouble. I also find that placing a food-stuffed toy in the car serves as a pleasant distraction for the less serious cases.

Redesigning the Car Space

Some dogs suffer from separation anxiety when left in the car. They may take out their frustration on the car interior, or simply attempt to escape, chewing and scratching and causing damage that may be quite extensive. Owners of such dogs will find that the use of a traveling cage fitted in the car not only keeps the dog safe en route but enables you to keep your car interior in good condition. Also consult Chapter 5 on Separation Anxiety for more advice relevant to this problem.

Restraints

Alternatively, it is worth trying a head-collar, which has a calming and controlling effect on most dogs. Head-

Above 1 and 2: *As the pictures show, this is not a training method to use if you are driving a vehicle on your own. Instead, ask a friend to accompany you on a car journey while your dog is restrained by a travel harness in the back. If it starts to bark, your friend can throw the discs while commanding "No." When the dog falls silent, quietly say a few words of praise.*

collars are made in various styles and sizes to fit most breeds. Initially, many dogs dislike wearing them (as with all muzzles and collars). Accustom your dog to the head-collar gradually by fitting it for a few minutes each day in the home (see also pages 32–33 for detailed advice on how to introduce a dog to a head-collar).

Finally, place the dog, fitted with head-collar and leash, in the car. The leash should be about 4 feet (1.2 m) long and made of nylon or leather. Connect it to a fixture in the car, leaving the dog

room to sit and lie down only. Unable to jump around wildly because of the restraint, the dog will become calmer and less prone to bark.

Car harnesses especially made for dogs are also helpful for restraining wild movements, and stop dogs from jumping to and fro as they work themselves up into a barking frenzy.

Below: *It's natural for dogs to bark, but don't let the habit get out of hand.*

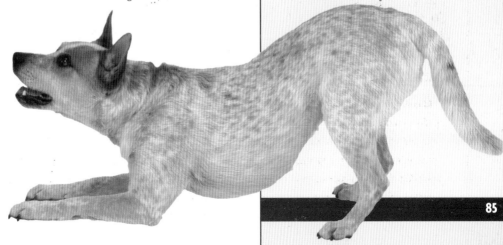

TRAINING EQUIPMENT TO TACKLE BARKING

- Training discs – thrown near dog.
- Water pistol – squirted at dog.
- Deterrent spray – squirted in the air near dog's head.
- Remotely activated spray collar (under expert supervision only).

SUMMARY

- Nip the barking habit in the bud – don't let it build up into a big problem.
- Reward silence, not barking.
- Have a helper in the car initially.
- A squirt in time teaches silence.
- Consider the use of a dog guard or traveling cage in the car.
- Accustom your dog to a harness or head-collar.
- Don't shout.

7: Excessive Attention Seeking

Attention seeking — what does this actually mean? After all, most dogs are "show-offs" who love attention. Dogs wouldn't be dogs unless they did. In fact, dogs that seek our attention are the most trainable, and trainers develop a host of methods to attract a dog's attention in order to teach it obedience and general sociable manners. However, when the attention-seeking dog interferes with your lifestyle or stops you from getting on with your normal daily chores to the point of actively causing you annoyance, this behavior becomes unacceptable.

This problem is often caused by over-indulging the dog in puppyhood. It is easy for a cute puppy to attract a lot of attention, and all too easy to produce a dog that thinks it has a right to demand attention whenever it wishes. Dogs that go everywhere with their owner, day and night, can also turn out to be excessive attention seekers, though more often than not they develop separation anxiety, another common behavioral problem.

Above: *It is easy to fall under the spell of puppies and small dogs and to indulge their whims whenever they want attention. But it is not always a good idea, as the dog may start to view such attention as its right.*

Below: *Dominant dogs like to grab their owner's attention. Petting and stroking are indicators that the dog is viewed as a high-ranking member of the pack, and it may behave aggressively to other dogs in the house to reinforce its status.*

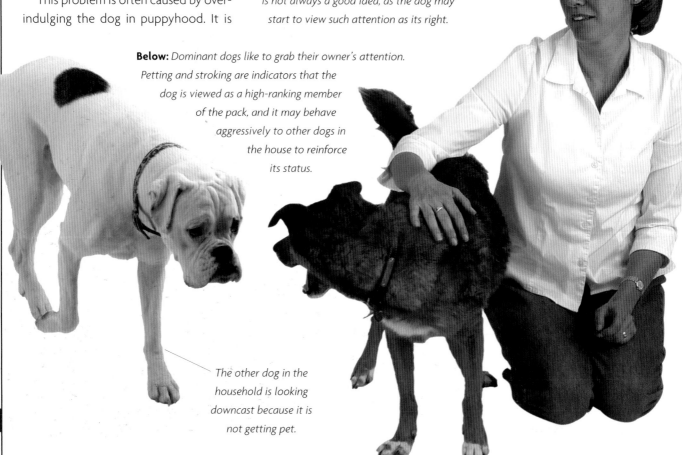

The other dog in the household is looking downcast because it is not getting pet.

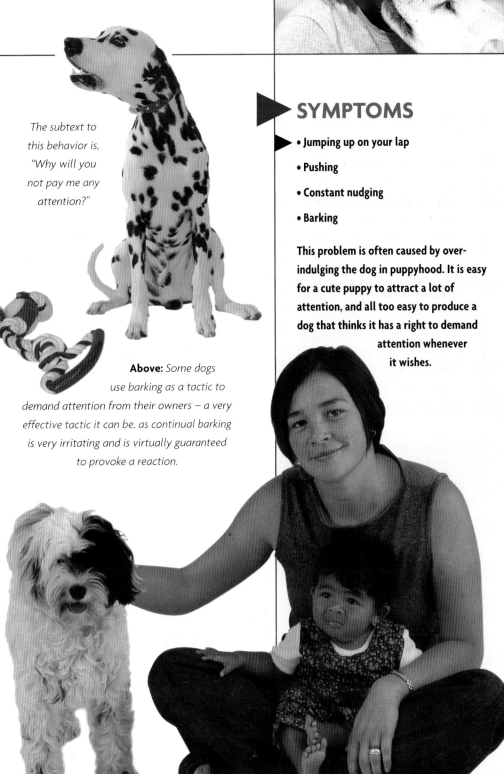

The Doggy Drive

From the day a puppy is born, it has an instinctive drive not only to survive but eventually to become pack leader, and one of its tools is the ability to get attention. Dogs that demand your attention on cue, by order, by stealth, or by looking dolefully into your eyes, get noticed. Dogs that get noticed get on in life, and that is why dogs seek our attention.

So what's wrong with a bit of attention seeking? Well, the main problem is that when we want our dogs' attention it should be on our terms, not theirs. Most dogs, if allowed to do so, think that it is a better deal when they grab our attention for their use and ultimately dominate our time and lifestyle. Passive dominance it may be, but dogs love to be control freaks!

Anyone who has had the experience of bringing up children will know a great deal about sibling rivalry and attention-grabbing behavior. This habit is pretty well developed in humans as well as dogs. Dogs are even better at demanding attention than most children. If they were not, people like me would not have a job.

The subtext to this behavior is, "Why will you not pay me any attention?"

Above: *Some dogs use barking as a tactic to demand attention from their owners – a very effective tactic it can be, as continual barking is very irritating and is virtually guaranteed to provoke a reaction.*

Right: *Mothers with young babies have incredibly busy lifestyles with plenty to occupy them throughout the day. What they don't need is an attention-seeking dog that butts in and interferes with the daily routine in the house.*

SYMPTOMS

- **Jumping up on your lap**
- **Pushing**
- **Constant nudging**
- **Barking**

This problem is often caused by over-indulging the dog in puppyhood. It is easy for a cute puppy to attract a lot of attention, and all too easy to produce a dog that thinks it has a right to demand attention whenever it wishes.

87

Excessive Attention Seeking

▶ Attention Trip

Excessive attention seeking on your dog's terms simply means that the behavior is so over-developed that it is unbearable. You cannot go about your daily chores without tripping over the dog, which has already worked out yet another way of interrupting your routine, like sitting on your knee. He definitely gets attention and, obviously, it is to his benefit.

Of course, the point at which attention seeking becomes a nuisance rather than a pleasure depends on your character as well as the dog's. Some people simply love and encourage their dog's attention, as it makes them feel needed and

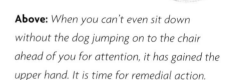

*Left: A German Shepherd on your lap is just what you do **not** want when you settle down on a chair to rest. The best response here would be to stand up immediately while avoiding eye contact and the temptation to shout at the dog.*

Don't push him down to the floor – even that contact can seem like a reward.

Above: When you can't even sit down without the dog jumping on to the chair ahead of you for attention, it has gained the upper hand. It is time for remedial action.

loved. In this case, it actually adds to their well-being – and to their dog's likewise. However, in other cases the dog's attention seeking has a negative effect, disrupting the owner's lifestyle, and at that point the dog/human relationship is on the rocks.

The majority of dogs presented to me for excessive attention seeking are in fact the toy breeds like Yorkies or Pekingese. Their small size makes it very tempting to pick them up and cuddle them all the time, with the result that they become over-attached and never learn to stand on their own feet. Problems are also common with insecure rescue dogs. Here, the temptation

Right: *Toy breeds in particular can develop attention seeking to an undesirable degree because they become used to being picked up and generally pampered by their doting owners.*

▶ TRAINING DIGEST

▶ **The majority of dogs presented to me for excessive attention seeking are in fact the toy breeds like Yorkies or Pekingese. Their small size makes it very tempting to pick them up and cuddle them all the time, with the result that they become over-attached and never learn to stand on their own feet.**

Below: *Attention addicts, whether dominant or insecure, need or want attention on demand. If you give in, the dog will expect to get its way every time until the habit becomes embedded.*

Dogs can be manipulative – rolling over to be pet is a good way of securing someone's attention.

is to compensate for their poor start in life by lavishing attention on them – only to find that the more you give, the more the dog demands.

▶ Tackling the Problem

These dogs basically want to become top dog in the attention department. The rules of the pack are simple: use your brain to get what you want and when you want it. The only way this can be stopped is by a smarter, more consistent fellow pack member – i.e., you – acting like a higher-ranking leader dog. If you have problems with your dog's behavior, you have to act like the boss all of the time.

The end result will be your dog changing into a well-behaved companion – and moreover, a dog that loves and respects you even more because you are an excellent pack leader. Strong leaders lead; they do not fawn over the pack members.

Some people don't like dogs and the feeling is mutual. They don't pay any attention to the dog, and it also ignores them. Those of us who do like dogs can learn from such people what turns dogs off – and use it to our advantage.

Excessive Attention Seeking

What Is Excessive?

While there's little doubt that this behavior problem is learned, there is a lot of difference of opinion as to what is excessive. What one owner thinks is much too much may be quite acceptable to another. Inconsistencies can also occur within families, causing variations in reaction that simply confuse a dog and make it more difficult to alter the behavior.

Right: *If you have real problems with a dog that pesters everyone that comes to visit you, it pays to put the dog on a leash and drop the end of the leash over a hook in another room. The dog should only be allowed to greet visitors once it has calmed down.*

This happens when some visitors encourage your dog's advances with rewards (touch, praise, rough play), while other visitors lose their cool at the sight of a single dog hair on their clothes. The dog is still being intermittently rewarded, so he will continue to try to solicit more attention until all visitors ignore his advances — and continue to do so until the behavior ceases to be a problem. This may even mean your leading the dog into the

Left: *As with so many of the behavioral problems described in this book, inconsistency makes it harder to correct a problem. If some visitors are happy to pet an attention-seeking dog like this while others ignore it, the dog will continue to solicit attention because it knows that it stands a chance of being rewarded with a pat and acknowledgment of its high status.*

house on a collar and leash and popping the end of the leash over a hook or fixture to keep him at bay until he has calmed down after visitors have arrived (see the hook restriction program in Chapter 3).

Of course, most dogs work by stealth — especially when you are on your own. Many owners fall into the trap of petting their dog whenever he seeks attention. When they think they have shown him enough attention, they stop and expect the dog to understand that they have been fair. He doesn't. All he knows is that

Below 1 and right 2: *This is another clever way of gaining attention — the dog heads off and reappears with a favorite toy in its mouth that it wants you to throw for it to retrieve. It may seem like innocent fun, but the dog is trying to control the agenda; ignore its demands.*

1

Right: Learn to harden your heart and turn your back on a dog that is pestering you. By ignoring the dog, it will come to realize that the behavior carries no rewards.

he can demand attention with a fair degree of success. So only pet your dog when petting is initiated by you. At all other times, ignore him and his attention-seeking ploys.

Many clever dogs bring toys for you to throw – and yes, we, being humans, are pleased, impressed, or made to feel important by such cleverness. Don't be deceived. This is indeed clever, but it is just another ploy that the dog has learned to control you and get attention. Don't respond at all. Keep your hands still and your mouth shut, and wait until your dog becomes bored and goes away. Then, maybe later get the

2

Eventually the dog will get bored and give up the game.

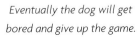

toy, throw it, make him bring it, and release it. When the game is over, put the toy away. Again, your dog will see you behaving like the boss and will respect you for it. In time he can still have fun on your (not his) terms, and eventually his pestering tactics should diminish and eventually be extinguished.

▶ TRAINING DIGEST

▶ Many owners fall into the trap of petting their dog whenever he seeks attention. When they think they have shown him enough attention, they stop and expect the dog to understand that they have been fair. He doesn't.

While showing affection for the baby, the mother could give the dog some food treats in a rubber food toy. This will serve as a pleasant distraction.

Above: *It's times like these that you do not need a dog pestering for attention. The mother wants to spend time playing with her tiny baby, and does not want to have to use her other hand to fend off the attentions of the dog.*

Excessive Attention Seeking

How to Prevent Attention Seeking

Teach your dog that it's normal for him to spend time on his own again – see some of the tips on tackling separation anxiety in Chapter 5. Build up gradually from five minutes to one hour twice daily, over several weeks. Whenever your dog nudges you or looks at you with doleful eyes, ignore him completely. Even if he starts crawling over you, which is unlikely, don't push him off, as the mere physical touch can be construed by the dog as a reward.

Moreover, remember that to **ignore** the dog is your best training device. In the short-term if a dog is impossible and you find it very difficult to ignore him, using some deterrent spray on yourself or your seating area will deter him from coming near you. Orange

Preoccupied on the phone, the woman pushes the dog away.

But the dog enjoys the fact of being touched.

3

2

1

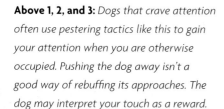

The nudging and pawing are all meant to say: "Why don't you talk to me?"

Above 1, 2, and 3: *Dogs that crave attention often use pestering tactics like this to gain your attention when you are otherwise occupied. Pushing the dog away isn't a good way of rebuffing its approaches. The dog may interpret your touch as a reward.*

or lemon peel rubbed on your hands may discourage the endless nudging with which some dogs seek attention. Large, powerful dogs that literally throw themselves at you may need a set of training discs (see Chapter 2) to dissuade

them from bullying you into giving them attention – but don't use these on very sensitive dogs or young puppies.

Points to Remember

- Make sure that any attention is on your terms: you decide when enough is enough. Always ignore your dog if he requests further attention.
- Make all the family and any visitors follow the same rules. Consistency is important.
- Remember that as far as a dog is concerned, being pushed off could be construed as a reward. To a dog, touch is very potent praise – so what

you intend as discouragement can be interpreted by him as encouragement to continue!

- If your dog tries to get on your lap, simply stand up quickly and allow him to slip off before he gets comfortable. Don't make eye contact, and don't shout. Bob up and down like a yo-yo if necessary until you get peace.

- Obedience-train your dog to get down and stay, then use this when the dog is being demanding. Teach the dog to go and stay in its bed as a fun game – use a reward. When the dog has received the message in a positive way (usually after ten or more lessons), this can also be used to get some relief.

I have found that most dogs respond well to the above retraining procedures. If you remember how your dog learned to get attention in the first place, you will now know what not to do. Eventually you can reinstate a moderate amount of affectionate response on your terms and may be able to relax most of the procedures depending on your circumstances. However, a few dogs are so conditioned to effusive and frequent response from their owners that praise and affection always have to be kept to a minimum.

► TAKING CONTROL – RECAP

► • Ignore attention-seeking approaches – the message is "Don't tell me when to pet you."

• Use deterrent spray on your chair – "Don't approach my seat."

• Rub orange or lemon peel on your hands – "Don't nudge me."

• Use training discs or a deterrent spray – under expert guidance.

• Remember that friends and family must treat the dog in the same way. Consistency is important.

The provision of a treat gets the dog used to the idea that going to its bed is a rewarding thing to do.

Below: *A gentle pet rewards the dog for behaving as you want it to do.*

Above 1, 2, and 3: *Obedience training is helpful in dealing with a determined attention seeker. Once your dog has gotten used to the idea of being sent to its bed from time to time – a treat reward helps to encourage this behavior – you can command the dog to go and stay there when you want some peace and quiet. In other words, attention is given when a command is obeyed.*

8: Destructive Behavior

Why Are Some Dogs Destructive?

Coming in to find your dog munching on your favorite slippers is not everyone's idea of the ideal owner-dog relationship. Of course, from the dog's point of view there's nothing wrong with chewing tasty leather or soft material — it's only natural to investigate objects by smell and taste, and anyway, it's great fun. We can accept that, but it's also only natural for us to become upset when our dog chews something that we value. We need to remember that dogs don't share our sense of values. For your dog, there's no difference between an old slipper and a new one, or between a soft toy and the fringes of an expensive rug.

Most destructive behavior is caused by one of three factors:

- **Normal puppy behavior.** It's natural for a puppy to investigate the exciting new world, often by chewing or tasting as much of it as possible.

- **Boredom.** When a dog is insufficiently active or stimulated, as it grows from puppy to adult dog, it specifically targets certain items in the house to play with (in its view) or damage (our view).

- **Separation anxiety.** This is the most common reason for destructive activity. A dog that has not learned to spend time alone becomes stressed when separated from its family, and may seek relief in frantic action, often causing drastic damage. This behavior may be accompanied by urination, defecation, barking, and whining. If you believe this is your dog's problem, see Chapter 5 for the way to tackle separation anxiety.

Prevention is the best remedy, and even though many people coping with this problem will have adult dogs in whom the behavior is already well ingrained, it's worth starting by looking at prevention.

Prevention Advice

(for puppies and newly acquired dogs)

It is important to have a dog who can be left unsupervised. From an early age, gradually accustom your dog to being left alone; aim to work up to periods of one hour. Don't encourage him to be under your feet all day. Instead, allow him to spend time by himself in the yard, on the patio, in a dog pen, or in another room while you're elsewhere. This encourages self-reliance and prevents a dog from becoming overly dependent upon its owner's presence — this is especially important in a one-person-one-dog relationship.

A new dog or puppy should never be allowed to roam the house freely for the first few months until you are able to judge its all-around behavior. Most chewing takes place in your absence, so by curtailing your dog's freedom you limit any damage to a single location, which is easier to deal with. Moreover,

Right 1–3: This sort of destructive behavior can be a sign of separation anxiety.

1

2

3

Above: *If you come home to a scene like this, it's no good punishing the dog after the event. The dog will not associate your displeasure with his earlier act of chewing the cushion.*

in the kitchen, for instance, you can implement preventative actions to teach the dog what it can and cannot chew. Eventually you can open up the house to the dog if that's your desire.

Exercise and Food

Exercising your dog before you leave him can help to burn off pent-up energy. He will be more likely to curl up and go to sleep than rampage through the house. Tired dogs chew less!

Consider feeding your dog before you leave the house (but make sure he's had ample time to evacuate his bowels before you go out). Satiated dogs become sleepy and lethargic, and are less inclined to chew.

Cage Training

Puppies should become accustomed to an indoor cage from day one. Ensure that your dog sees the cage as a refuge rather than a prison by providing marrow bones, toys stuffed with treats, or hide chews to keep him occupied in it while you're out. But when you return, make sure you collect the chews and keep them for the next time you go out; otherwise your dog will not find them interesting. Feeding the dog in the cage once or twice daily also helps condition him to accept it as a positive amenity.

If the destruction takes place in your absence, it may be for the reasons mentioned above. Dogs that have not become gradually accustomed to your absence may become anxious when left. These dogs are the ones that follow you around the house or seek eye contact with you no matter what you're doing. They must be taught that being alone is not the end of the world (see also Chapter 5 on separation anxiety).

▶ RECAP

• **Accustom your dog to spending time away from the family.**

• **Restrict access to rooms within the home until your dog has learned how to behave.**

• **Don't leave him alone and full of energy – tire him out first.**

• **Feeding him before you go out will leave him more inclined to have a post-dinner nap than be active.**

• **Consider using an indoor cage, but make it attractive to the dog and large enough for him.**

Above: *It may look rather forbidding but, if properly introduced, a dog will start to view its cage as a familiar refuge in which it can enjoy pleasant experiences.*

95

Destructive Behavior

Direct Action

Punishing destructive behavior can be difficult because we're often not at home when the destruction takes place. Punishment after the event is useless. If you come in and find your house trashed, with the perpetrator peacefully asleep among the wreckage, it's only natural to feel angry with him. But it doesn't come naturally to him to link your immediate anger with something he did earlier. All punishment will achieve is confusing him. All you can usefully do at this stage is clean up and resolve to begin a retraining program immediately. However, if your dog is destructive in your presence, or you catch him in the act, then there are a couple of measures you can use.

Have several ready-filled water pistols around the house. When you catch your dog chewing, squirt water at its head, simultaneously commanding "No." (Alternatively, you can simply use the squirt without the command.) As the dog comes to associate chewing with an unpleasant squirt, it is less likely to enjoy

Below 1, 2, and 3: Frequently this sort of destructive behavior will take place when you are out of the house — a hapless toy bears the brunt of the animal's feelings of frustration and anxiety at being left on its own.

Above: *"Who, me?" Try not to give way to your anger and punish a dog when you come home and find a trail of damage around the house. The dog will be pleased to see you and will not associate a rebuke with its earlier actions. Harsh words at this time will only confuse the animal who expects a greeting from you.*

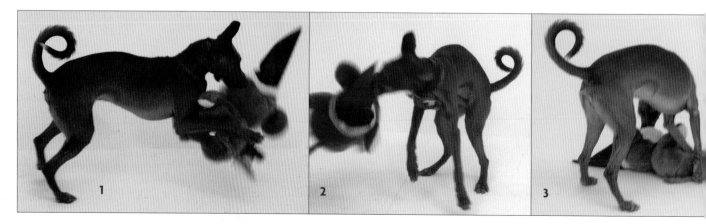

Left: *If you actually catch your dog in the act of chewing, you can use deterrent measures such as a squirt of water or the clatter or training discs employed in conjunction with the command "No."*

Do not physically hit the dog, take hold of it, or shout at it, as this is less effective. In some cases, it even encourages bad behavior, such as chewing. After all, for some dogs, attention of any kind is better than none.

this activity. However, this approach is effective with puppies and dogs in the early stages of destructive chewing only, and will not affect dogs exhibiting anxiety-related destructive behavior.

A more direct means of training by association is to throw a bunch of training discs or a bunch of large metal keys that jangle near the dog's legs when you catch it chewing, so that the noise distracts it and interrupts its actions. Most dogs realize you are the thrower, so don't bother trying to disguise the fact. (See also Chapter 2 on how to use training discs.) When using the water pistol or training discs, remember that it's vital that all correction takes place at the time of the incident.

See also Chapter 2 on how to use training discs.

► **DETERRENT MEASURES – RECAP**

► • **Keep a water pistol or training discs handy for when you catch your dog in the act. All dogs should learn the command "No."**

• **Don't punish by grabbing or hitting the dog or shouting at it.**

• **Don't punish a dog after the event.**

Above: *A quick squirt with a water pistol can be a very effective way of interrupting destructive behavior. It works at long range and is essentially harmless to the dog.*

Left: *Use a firm tone of voice to reprimand a dog that has misbehaved, but don't resort to shouts or smacks. It is counterproductive. Don't expect instant results with a destructive dog – you will need patience.*

Destructive Behavior

Bitter Experience

(for puppies and sensitive adult dogs only)

If you have a dog that primarily chews specific objects, say the kitchen furniture or a particular item of footwear, first try and use a deterrent spray. In this way, the dog learns from its own experience that chewing these things is an unpleasant sensation, which leads to a bitter taste in its mouth.

When I have a new dog, I spend the first two weeks spraying the knobs on the kitchen furniture with deterrent spray daily, sometimes twice a day. This means that on every occasion that the dog attempts to chew, it experiences an unpleasant taste. Dogs don't repeat unpleasant experiences too often; they will remember repetitive bitter experiences. The weakness in this procedure is often with the owners. They forget to keep up the spraying, or think that an occasional squirt is enough. It

Above: *Another useful tactic when dealing with a destructive or scavenging dog like this is to leave a chew or food-filled toy as a distraction; the dog finds it is more fun to chew the treat than the furniture.*

isn't – you need to fix it in the dog's mind that these items always taste bad. It is wise to spray the objects when your dog is not in the room, and leave a window open for ten minutes before allowing the dog back in. This ensures that the dog can distinguish the spray scent on the objects to be avoided, rather than sensing its presence throughout the room.

Simultaneously, leave the dog a chew and interesting toys – the kind designed to be stuffed with food that the dog can extract a bit at a time is ideal. This means that, while the deterrent spray steers him away from forbidden objects, he has

Below 1, 2, and 3: *Sometimes destructive behavior around the kitchen will also involve scavenging for food from a trash can. In such cases regular applications of a deterrent spray can stop the dog from nosing around the trash can.*

1

2

3

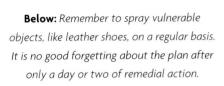

Below: *Remember to spray vulnerable objects, like leather shoes, on a regular basis. It is no good forgetting about the plan after only a day or two of remedial action.*

something that is permissible and pleasant to chew. The longer it takes the dog to extract the food (real wet food is preferable), the more the dog will use the toy as an object on which it can exercise its curiosity and desire to chew.

When dealing with puppies at the chewing stage, I spray all electrical wires, plugs, and sockets daily to deter the puppy from even considering them as chewable. Ideally, with puppies, all wires should be out of reach or left unplugged. The same technique can be used on other items that your dog chews, like slippers or children's toys.

If in certain extreme cases your dog's behavior is resistant to discouragement, you may need to consider using an outside pen and kennel for a few months until the problem can be dealt with

properly. Your dog will need to be gradually accustomed to using the pen, working up from five minutes, two to three times daily. Remember to leave him some interesting toys filled with treats. Then when you're not at home you can leave your dog knowing he is quite safe – and so is your home. Don't over-use the kennel, however.

USEFUL TIPS

▶ Dogs are intelligent creatures – keep their minds occupied with fun games.

Don't tell a dog off after you have discovered damage. It has no effect except to teach the animal that you are oddly unpredictable.

If damage is intolerable, use an appropriately sized cage if you need to leave the dog alone – but only for short periods not exceeding two hours.

If a particular deterrent spray doesn't work, look around for different types. Something should be effective.

Secure or lock away all trash cans.

Above: *Items of furniture, electrical wiring, slippers and shoes, baskets, and even oven gloves can appear on the menu of a dog that is determined to ease its anxiety by chewing something.*

9: Play-Biting

Most dog owners have experienced that little nip on one or more of their fingers as they try to play with the new puppy member of the family. Because the new puppy arrives with the most adorable expression of innocence, the exuberance and accompanying mouthing are often forgiven. We also know the hurt is not intentional. Yes, puppies appear to have been designed to bring the most stoical and resolute person to their emotional knees, despite the pain of a bitten finger.

Puppies develop sharp, needlelike teeth that appear to be rather excessive for such small creatures. Though the teeth are for eating food, another use is to help other littermates learn bite inhibition and how much pressure to use on one another. Sharp puppy teeth hurt, without causing real damage. So when a

Above: *Unless corrected, puppies that mouth people can turn into habitual play-biters.*

litter of puppies are play-fighting, they quickly learn how hard they can bite without upsetting a playmate. If they bite too hard, the other puppy will respond by becoming aggressive or will cease playing. Puppies instinctively wish to dominate their littermates, and biting is also a part of their defense. The puppies learn how and when to use

Above: *Rough and tumble games and tug-of-war contests over a prized toy are all part of the way in which one dog seeks to assert its dominance over a fellow pack member. Puppies practice play-biting in the same way.*

their teeth with their littermates, one useful set of social rules for future canine relationships. They also use games of strength to assert their pack positions. If one watches very young

children at play, one will learn a similar set of rules: over-aggressive children are avoided by the others, so moderation promotes inclusion, the basic tenet of pack behavior.

▶ Why Dogs Play-Bite Us

When puppies leave the litter and arrive in our homes, they bring with them their experiences, one of which is using their mouth – play-biting, mouthing, nibbling, and play-growling. Investigative mouthing behavior is exhibited at a very young age in puppies for a number of different reasons. But when humans take the place of littermates, puppies can become confused. Without correct training, continued mouthing can develop into habitual play-biting. Though it is termed "play," what we are really talking about is dogs and puppies actually biting people, which hurts!

A common scenario occurs when a puppy wishes to initiate play or attention. The puppy nips the owner who reacts, either by pushing the puppy away – which he interprets as joining in the game – or by encouraging rough play games. Either way, the puppy learns that play-biting is acceptable. Early dominance behavior like growling or snapping can also be a problem, though this is less common in very young puppies. But whatever is happening, it should be discouraged and stopped immediately.

Dogs use their mouths for all sorts of purposes including affection, touching, and testing, which are expressions of

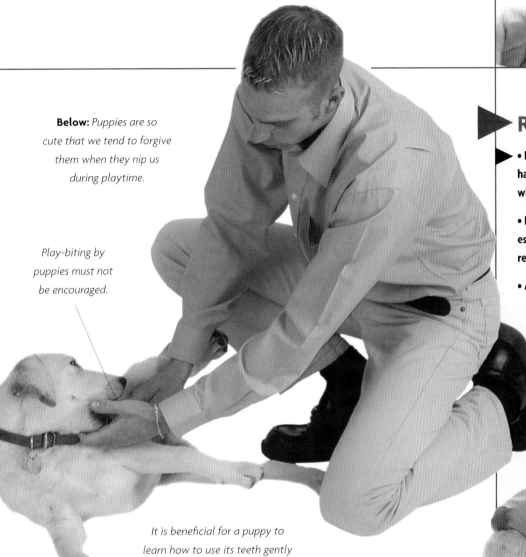

Below: Puppies are so cute that we tend to forgive them when they nip us during playtime.

Play-biting by puppies must not be encouraged.

It is beneficial for a puppy to learn how to use its teeth gently when interacting with people.

▶ RECAP

• **Puppy play-biting can escalate into habitual nipping by the adult dog – who has bigger teeth!**

• **Play-biting among puppies helps to establish rank over other puppies or in relation to their human owner.**

• **Among themselves, puppies deter rough play-bites by biting back harder. But they also deter this behavior by refusing to play with the biter, and this is a useful tip.**

Here, the mouth is used to express affection.

Above: Dogs use their mouths for more than just eating and barking. Their mouths are part of the sensory equipment with which they investigate the world around them, other animals, and their owners.

play. If we watch dogs at play, we see a great deal of play-biting and mouthing, especially around the neck area, as rough and tumble games ensue. Dog trainers and breeders who watch their dogs interacting will have seen many times that sudden aggressive outburst in a game between two dogs, when one of the dogs bites too hard and the recipient becomes angry and bites back, generally bringing the game to a close. The bitten dog no longer wants to play and is now ignoring its friend. If play is to continue, the biter will have to learn to use its teeth more gently.

Dogs have their own natural response mechanisms to various interactions with fellow canines, and innate skills like pressure sensitivity, speed, and timing that help them fine-tune their reactions. We don't. Therefore, it is not a good idea to begin imitating dog behavior to deter play-biting. Instead we can use our understanding of canine psychology, which is obviously a more subtle approach than biting back!

Play-Biting

Play-Biting Is Painful

I know many dogs that play-bite or mouth gently, or take their owner's hand into their mouths. Their owners don't find this a problem, and the behavior has not worsened. Personally, I believe that no dog should be allowed such familiarity if it is to be a safe companion – especially with children. Moreover, if you have young children, even gentle play-biting or mouthing can be frightening to them. It can also lead to more serious rough behavior, including later dominance aggression in a few cases. If it is never allowed to develop, there is little likelihood of it getting out of hand. You must make the choice.

Most people genuinely don't like being bitten, in fun or otherwise. Our reactions are often sufficient to teach the puppy that we do not like what they are doing, and the game is over. Un-

Above: *The way this terrier is shaking the toy reminds us that dogs like this are hunters by nature – this is how it kills rats.*

Right: It may seem fun when a puppy nips and tugs at your pant leg in play, but if you let the behavior go unchecked, the situation can get worse. The puppy gets bigger and the habit harder to stop.

fortunately, some people – and especially children – react in an animated, defensive manner that encourages the puppy (or dog), thus making the episode into a game from the pup's viewpoint. Instead of learning not to bite, it learns to bite more. As time goes on the puppy can become even more dominant and it finds this behavior rewarding. It bites, you pull your hand or clothing away, and then a tug-of-war ensues, which is even more fun.

A typical scenario goes like this. The puppy grabs a pant leg; the owner hears the little growls from this tiny pup and thinks it is charming. The owner moves his leg and makes a little game of it – the puppy responds to the prey-like movements and really starts to enjoy the game. Many weeks and games later, when the puppy is now four times the size and weight, it gets out of hand and the owner responds with shouting, slapping, and eventually, when this no longer works, shutting the dog in another room.

The pup or adolescent dog has learned that it dominates the rough game and that it normally wins, and that's what being a dog is all about. As the dog gets rougher, the owner's shouting and anger may increase – all very rewarding in terms of canine play. By this stage, of course, young children are hopelessly unable to deal with the dog and also begin to avoid its rough play-biting. Unfortunately, the dog has now been conditioned to play-bite. Shutting the dog in another room only makes it frustrated, hyperactive, and keener than ever to enjoy its dominant playtime. The next stage is that the dog is brought to my center for retraining with children who are frightened of a puppy that was acquired to enhance their lives.

Toy or Prey

Many toys on the market are designed for human/dog fun, for example tough fabric ropes made for tug-of-war games.

Right: *Only play tug-of-war games with your dog if it observes the ground rules – ultimately you must always win the game.*

If the dog starts to react aggressively, it's game over.

The dog must release the toy when it is told to.

> ## TRAINING DIGEST
>
> ▶ **If play-biting is never allowed to develop, there is little likelihood of it getting out of hand. You must make the decision.**
>
> **Tug-of-war toys are safe when used with a strict set of rules – notably that the owner always wins.**

Above: *Children love playing with a dog, but don't allow play-biting to be part of the game. It may frighten the child and lead to worse aggression or very rough play.*

They are safe when used with a strict set of rules – notably that the owner always wins and that the dog allows you, on command, to take the toy away at any time without a fight or any grumbling. Thousands of dogs enjoy the exercise and the mind-stimulating game, and so do their owners. However, it is inadvisable to allow children under the age of twelve to play tug-of-war games with dogs unless supervised, and important to insist that they play by the rules above.

If you notice the dog beginning to growl and become over-stimulated and aggressive, take that as your signal to end that type of tug-of-war game, maybe for good. Many dogs growl as a normal expression and it's not a sign of aggression. However, the average owner cannot recognize the differences in canine vocalization so the games that produce them should be discontinued for good, especially around children. Many of the terrier and guarding breeds also need to be monitored, as they tend to inherit dominant characteristics. The terrier likes shaking toys as he would a rat, and the tug-of-war rope is an outlet for that natural behavior. It's perfectly harmless as long as it isn't your finger that's involved.

Play-Biting

Prevention Advice

This advice will apply mostly to puppies, but is also worth using with any newly acquired adult dog. From day one, avoid playing any games that involve mouthing, i.e., teeth on skin. If your puppy tries to solicit attention from you by play-biting, ignore him. Just get up and walk away. Alternatively, take hold of the puppy by the scruff and say "No" firmly, looking directly into his eyes for about two seconds. The command must be delivered sharply and crisply. Then

Above: *Use the firm command "No" and then ignore a dog that pesters you and tries play-biting to gain your attention. If the dog persists, get up and walk away.*

If you don't have a hook on the baseboard, the valve of a radiator works just as well for a small dog.

Below: *Play-biting can be a problem with dogs, whatever their size.*

let the dog go and ignore him. This is normally enough to discourage play-biting in the very early stages, say between six and eighteen weeks, and it teaches your puppy the useful "No" command.

If the puppy or adolescent dog has already developed play-biting to a high degree, and resistance to its owner's countermeasures is severe, holding by the scruff may be seen by the dog simply as more rough play or a dominant threat. It is best just to say "No" and then ignore him.

With an adult dog, leaving a leash trailing behind him — only when you are present — is also an excellent method to stop determined play-biters. By grabbing the leash you automatically get instant control — you can drop the leash end onto a wall hook or radiator knob, and

instantly the dog is prevented from continuing his play-biting when you move out of his reach. Alternatively, with large dogs (not puppies), you can check the dog with the leash, always accompanying the action with the command "No." I call this the "Rapid Check." I will

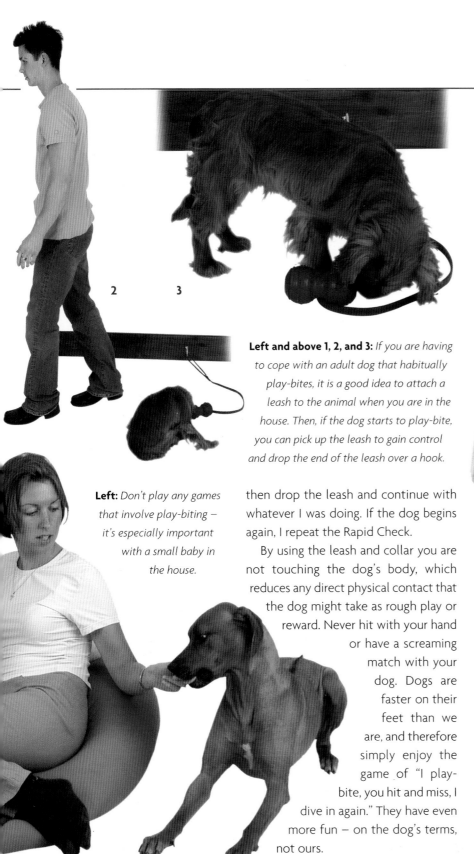

Left and above 1, 2, and 3: *If you are having to cope with an adult dog that habitually play-bites, it is a good idea to attach a leash to the animal when you are in the house. Then, if the dog starts to play-bite, you can pick up the leash to gain control and drop the end of the leash over a hook.*

Left: *Don't play any games that involve play-biting – it's especially important with a small baby in the house.*

then drop the leash and continue with whatever I was doing. If the dog begins again, I repeat the Rapid Check.

By using the leash and collar you are not touching the dog's body, which reduces any direct physical contact that the dog might take as rough play or reward. Never hit with your hand or have a screaming match with your dog. Dogs are faster on their feet than we are, and therefore simply enjoy the game of "I play-bite, you hit and miss, I dive in again." They have even more fun – on the dog's terms, not ours.

UNDERSTANDING THE SITUATION

It is natural for dogs to use their mouths as a tool to help them explore the world around them. We need to learn how to discourage or redirect that behavior when it is inappropriate in a domestic setting.

Above: *A soft toy can be a useful distraction – the puppy learns to have fun with the toy rather than play-biting.*

TRAINING DIGEST

From day one, avoid playing any games with a puppy or newly acquired dog that involve mouthing, i.e., teeth on skin.

Never hit with your hand or have a screaming match with your dog.

► Play-Biting

► How to Discourage Play-Biting

The traditional (and still the best) way to prevent or stop play-biting is to obedience-train your dog. Puppies should be trained from the very first day that they arrive. You'll probably need help to learn how to train such a young pup. Instructional DVDs and books are the best solution at this age. Concentrate on the "Down, stay" position. When this has been mastered, you can command your dog to do this when he tries to play-bite. I realize that it's easier said than done, but owning a

Above: *Dogs do not like the experience of mouthing something that has been treated with a bitter-tasting spray. If your dog mouths your hand while on a walk, spray your hand and the leash before you leave.*

dog is inevitably time-consuming. Once you have put in the early work, you will enjoy your dog's company more – and he will love you even more for

behaving like a leader. The first six months of quality education provided for a dog on a daily basis is without a doubt the crucial factor in helping you to enjoy a lifelong positive relationship with your pet.

► Redirecting the Play

Throwing a toy or a ball is another distraction method that I use – especially in the park and yard, but in the home as well. Squeaky toys are ideal. Directing the dog's attention to a toy instead of your hand is a very safe and effective way of reducing play-biting and

Below 1: *One of the most effective ways of stopping a play-biter from persisting with the habit is to obedience-train it to a high standard from an early age.*

Below 2: *This dog is being taught the "Down, stay" command. Once a dog has been conditioned to behave correctly when it hears the command, you have a powerful tool at your disposal to interrupt unwanted behavior and gain control over the animal.*

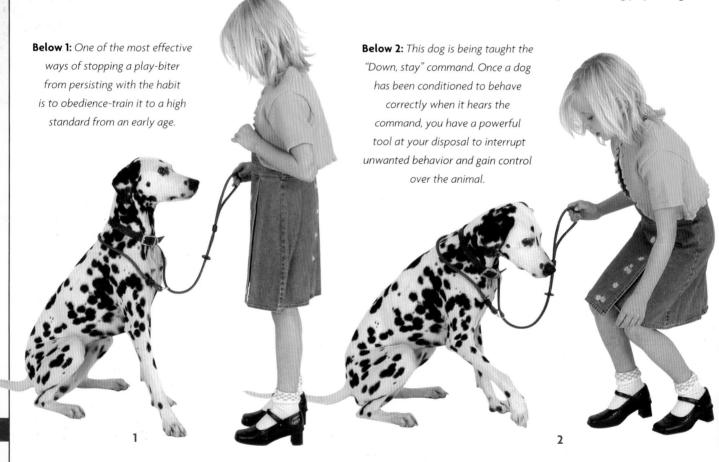

1

2

Above: *It is great when a family and their pet develop a close bond, but it must be on the right terms – the dog must respect its owners and not be indulged when it shows signs of wanting to play-bite humans.*

Below 3: *A treat is given when the dog has obeyed the command as a reward to reinforce the desired behavior.*

3

at the same time teaching the dog what it can use its teeth on.

Some puppies mouth their owner's hand when being walked, as they are attracted to the dangling leash, which can become a target. And your hand is in line too. You can also try using a deterrent spray. Spray your hand and the leash just before embarking on the walk. Taste deterrents work on most dogs, especially if used for many weeks to ensure that the lesson is well implanted.

In the home your dog may be what I call an armchair mouther, who is constantly reaching for your hand when you are sitting down. Again, a deterrent spray applied to your hand each time you settle down will discourage this behavior.

▶ REDIRECTION – RECAP

▶ • Don't reward mouthing by responding – ignore it.

• Distract a play-biter with a favorite squeaky toy.

• Use deterrent spray to make mouthing an unpleasant experience.

Above: *Lively children and an inquisitive puppy – potentially a volatile mixture.*

▶ USEFUL TIPS

▶ • Deterrent sprays on vulnerable areas – clothing or children's arms – make mouthing a distasteful experience. Do check that the deterrent used is harmless to dogs – and children.

• Consider using training discs with dogs that have been conditioned to their use (see Chapter 2).

• Ignore undesirable approaches from the dog – don't respond to them.

10: Jumping Up

Dogs seem to be obsessed with face-to-face contact, wanting to lick and nudge our faces and mouths with theirs. This is rather like our preoccupation with shaking people's hands when we meet them. Between dogs this is an important social action, serving as a greeting, a plea for an older dog to regurgitate food, and even a sign of submission. When it's directed at a human, the height difference means that they learn to jump up to reach our faces. Since we're not dogs,

Sharp claws can inflict painful scratches as the dog scrabbles for attention.

face-licking is a habit we don't normally like. The associated practice of jumping up is even more of a nuisance. It can also be dangerous, especially when big dogs and small children or elderly people are involved.

Like most habits, this one starts in puppyhood. Puppies are small, so we naturally bend down or lift them up, giving them the perfect opportunity to lick our faces. As the puppy grows, it's natural for him to try to continue the behavior by jumping toward faces.

Prevention Advice

While following this advice it's important that everyone the dog jumps upon partakes in a retraining program. Everyone must use identical commands and actions, or the dog will become confused and even less responsive. No half measures, please! Young children should always learn in the company of a capable adult.

Four Paws on the Ground

If you have a puppy, don't allow him to lick faces, especially where children are involved. Hygiene is one factor, but it's also dangerous – a

Left: *When we are not down at their level, dogs that are prone to jumping up bridge the height difference by getting up on their hind legs. With big, strong dogs, behavior like this can be quite a problem – it's easy to be caught off balance.*

Above: *Puppies and young dogs love it when they can lick our faces and thrust their noses toward our mouths. This may be an inheritance from wolf behavior, where pack members solicit in this way for morsels of regurgitated food as a treat.*

grown dog can easily knock someone over. When you greet your dog, command "Sit," and only offer praise when your puppy has all four paws on the ground. If he does jump up, stand absolutely still and say

Retraining your dog will require patience and a calm disposition.

1

nothing. To the puppy this is boring, and he'll quickly learn that there's no fun or reward to be had by jumping up. All the family and any visitors must participate in this program consistently if the behavior is to be stopped.

When your dog jumps up on people indiscriminately in parks and in the street, this can be more difficult to control. It's often difficult to stop dog lovers from petting your dog when it jumps up on them – but only in this way can you hope to prevent this behavior. Many people, especially children, find puppies

irresistible, and here an extending leash can be useful to control a puppy's exploration of a new world full of people who love puppies and unwittingly love teaching them just what you don't want – to jump up.

Owners often try to deter their dog by hitting it or pushing it off, to no avail. Unfortunately, for most dogs any kind of touch is a strong reward, so they can interpret what is intended as a corrective measure as encouragement – a rough kind of game. Over time, the dog's resistance to its owner's efforts builds up, wearing the owner down.

Below: *Four paws are on the ground – good! The dog can have a treat as a reward.*

Left and below 1 and 2: When training a dog to stop jumping, everyone in the family must adopt the same commands. Adults may have to monitor children.

The use of a leash confers an extra degree of control.

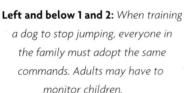

2

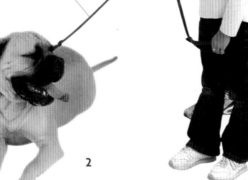

PREVENTION ADVICE – RECAP

• Don't respond to jumping up by shouting, smacking, or pushing away – step back, turn away, and ignore.

• Ignore a jumping puppy; praise a puppy only when all four paws are on the ground.

• Use an extending leash in the park to control jumping at passing dog lovers.

While following this prevention advice, it's important that everyone the dog jumps upon partakes in a retraining program. Everyone must use identical commands and actions, or the dog will become confused and even less responsive.

Jumping Up

▶ Initial Triggers That Teach Dogs to Jump Up

When we are sitting down and a little pup jumps up, placing its front paws on our knees, it's a natural response to lean forward (trigger one) and either stroke the puppy (trigger two) or, even worse, lift it onto our lap for a cuddle (trigger three). Three reinforcements have taken place, laying the foundations for a dog that jumps up in the future. Even if you then put the dog back on the floor, he has learned an important association: jumping up brings rewards. Dogs that are lifted onto a lap obviously enjoy the contact, but it's unfair to do this with a puppy and expect him to understand when he is bigger that you no longer want him on your knees. It's even more confusing to him if you let him jump on you, but not on your friends. Dogs need black-and-white rules, not complex "sometimes do, sometimes don't" situations. Teach what you want for the long-term, not for the immediate moment.

It may be wiser to play with the puppy on the floor.

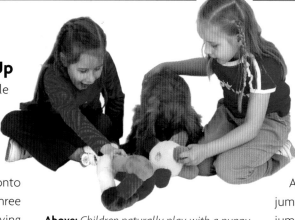

Above: *Children naturally play with a puppy on the floor, and we can all learn from that. If you also get down on the ground to play games with a puppy, it will not feel the urge to jump at you to gain your attention.*

Such play is far more interactive, and coincidentally removes the pup's need or wish to jump up. Of course, many readers will have dogs who are already expert at jumping up and getting their own way. Whether the motivation is dominance, demanding attention, or seeking affection, let's look at some methods to counter the dog's expertise.

▶ I'm Home, I'm Ignoring You

Aim to eliminate whatever excites the jumping up. For example, if your dog jumps up when you return home, then stop greeting him when you come in. At each homecoming ignore him for the first fifteen minutes. Keep your hands still, and don't even say hello. Ensure that all family members do the same. At first it will be difficult. Because your dog is used to an effusive greeting, he will probably be somewhat confused at first. However, as the reward of being pushed off, pet, or praised is no

Jumping up has not brought any rewards.

Right 1, 2, and 3: *If your dog jumps up when you are sitting in a chair, avoid petting him and simply stand up, forcing him to drop on to all fours again. Ignore him until he stops acting in this way.*

1   2   3

Right 1 and 2: *Praise the dog when it responds obediently to your command to "Sit," You must only reward correct behavior.*

1

2

longer forthcoming, the reason for jumping will have gone. Your dog should soon learn that there's no point in continuing to jump up. After the first fifteen minutes, you can call him to you, tell him to sit, and give a reward that does not over-excite him. You have now simply reorganized the time and manner of greeting to suit you. Dogs adapt with no hard feelings.

The "Ignore" exercise is also useful around the home when your dog suddenly jumps up at you. As soon as he jumps up, pivot away from him, with no eye contact and no commands. When he gets the message, tell him to sit, praise him, and maybe offer a small treat. Ignore him again if he becomes excitable. The dog will learn that his action does not get the reaction he wants, but that staying calm and quiet is rewarded with the desired attention.

Dog Training

Obedience training, especially when combined with the "Ignore" exercise described, has the highest chance of success. If you train your dog to a high

standard, through a reputable club or through your own efforts, you will have a dog that listens to your commands.

If your dog learns to sit on command, whenever he's about to jump up, instruct "Sit." When he sits, praise him verbally. Make sure that jumping up is always ignored, never rewarded. Once he realizes that, he'll soon try sitting to achieve the desired praise. But remember that consistency is vital.

Now is the time to offer praise, when the dog is sitting quietly.

TRAINING DIGEST

► The "Ignore" exercise is useful around the home when your dog suddenly jumps up at you.

Below: *It looks like the cold shoulder, but it does pay to ignore a dog that jumps up at you in a frenzy when you return home. The dog will start to learn that jumping brings no rewards.*

Jumping Up

Redirect Unwanted Greetings

If your dog loves retrieving games with toys or balls, take one with you to the park. For the first ten lessons, make sure the dog does not have access to any of his retrieve toys at home. Lock them all away for awhile, and only take one out with you during his walk. As soon as you see that your dog is about to pay unwanted attention to a passerby, call him and throw his ball or toy. This is a good distraction method for dogs that like retrieving. Timing is vital, so attract your dog's attention before he jumps on someone, not afterwards.

If your dog is difficult to control, tell him to sit when he brings the ball back, and at once connect his leash. Then briskly walk off, away from his target person. Show him the ball as you go, exciting him a little. After about 50 yards (45 m), unclip his leash and throw the ball again for him to retrieve. This also teaches the dog that having the leash clipped on him does not necessarily mean the end of his walk. He cannot predict your actions, therefore you stay in charge.

Water and Sound Deterrents

(for determined dogs only)

This method is best suited for dogs that have long-established jumping up problems, very big dogs that can hurt people by jumping up, and dogs that need to be retrained quickly because children or old people are involved. You will need a water pistol or a dog-repellent sound alarm. To back up this method, it is important to deal with the root cause of the behavioral problem by following the Intelligent Leadership programs (see Chapter 3).

Right 1: If you have difficulty when out for a walk in the park because your dog tends to jump up at passing strangers, try taking a ball or favorite toy with you. When the dog is about to jump up at someone, throw the toy and encourage the dog to chase after and retrieve it.

Right 2: Praise your dog when it brings the toy back to you. This tactic redirects the dog's attention away from the passerby and onto the toy instead.

1

2

Have the device handy wherever the problem occurs. For example, if the dog jumps up when you return home, have the water pistol by the door. As you come in and see him about to jump up, command "No" and squirt water in his face. Repeat this as many times as it takes to stop the dog. Eventually he will come to associate jumping up with an unpleasant squirt of water, and this will discourage his bad habit. Again, it's important for all family members to take part if your dog is to learn. Some dogs find a sound alarm more off-putting than a water pistol.

Smell and Taste Deterrents

(for determined dogs only)
Bitter apple and other safe

Right: *If you plan to use the toy or ball retrieve method described on the opposite page, it makes sense to lock away all similar toys in the home. The dog will be very excited when the toy is taken out for the walk.*

non-toxic dog repellent scents are also useful to dissuade dogs from jumping up on us. This I find especially helpful with children or the elderly. Of course, children also need training not to confuse the dog and not to teach him to jump up in the first place. It's often hard for a child to understand why some canine actions are undesirable, and patience is needed all around.

If the dog jumps up on the child when you are nearby, spray the air around the dog (or the child can do this himself if he is old enough to follow instructions). The dog discovers that instead of the reward of being fondled or even pushed away, he has the unpleasant experience of reaching toward a target that stinks to high heaven. This interrupts his learned behavior pattern. Most dogs learn quickly that jumping up is no longer enjoyable, as long as the humans involved act consistently.

Left: *A water pistol or plant spray is an effective deterrent measure that will take even large, pushy dogs by surprise. When the dog makes you the victim of its unwanted attention, a quick squirt of water accompanied by the command "No" should cause it to get down quickly.*

Above: *Special collars that emit a sound or an alarm can be used to stop a dog that wants to jump up.*

Jumping Up

▶ Collar, Leash, and Hook

Though dog owners accept the need to use a leash and collar in the outside world, they rarely think of using it in the house. But most dogs are highly conditioned to the use of a collar and leash, which has pleasant associations for them. Your dog will normally be happy to allow you to connect his leash and will follow you.

This powerful conditioning can be used to control dogs jumping up at visitors to the home. Ensure that the dog is wearing his collar beforehand. Hang the leash on an easily accessible hook on a wall or near the front door. When the visitor arrives, as the dog starts jumping around excitedly, clip his leash on, then choose one of the next steps, depending on your level of control.

1 Tell the dog to sit well away from the door. If he jumps up at the visitor, snap the leash and command "No." Now make him heel as you escort the visitor into your house. If the dog has calmed down, drop the leash on the floor, but leave it attached in case you need to exercise further control. After about fifteen minutes, if all is well, disconnect the leash. Make sure the visitor does not over-fuss the dog.

2 If the dog is uncontrollable, attach the leash to a designated hook on the wall for about fifteen minutes. Only release him if he calms down, and ask the visitor to ignore him initially.

Above 1:
The Ignore response acts as a powerful deterrent to stop this type of behavior.

Right 1: *Training discs can also play a valuable part in discouraging a dog from jumping up.*

Left 2 and right 3: *Just as the dog gets up on its back legs to paw at your pants, throw the discs sharply onto the ground next to it while commanding "No." The clatter of the discs will startle the dog and should cause it to drop down onto all fours again.*

1

2

3

Arms folded, no eye contact – classic Ignore tactics.

2

Be consistent – inconsistency breeds uncertainty in the dog's mind.

3

Above 2 and 3: *The dog is deprived of any touch or voice reward when it pesters you on its hind legs. Behavior that is not rewarded ultimately loses its attraction and the dog should eventually stop acting like this.*

Other Methods

Once a dog has been conditioned to training discs, these can also be used to discourage jumping up. See Chapter 2 on how to introduce the discs. The hook method (see Chapter 3) is also a very good training routine for dogs that dominate the house and visitors' arrivals.

In Conclusion

Whatever method you choose, remember that your dog is the product of his upbringing, and of your understanding of his basic natural instincts. Obedience training, when carried out properly, is the solution for most behavioral problems. A dog that lies down or sits on command simply cannot jump up at the same time.

Different methods work for different dogs, so try experimenting. For example, use the leash and collar (my favorite method) and combine it with the use of training discs if necessary. Asking another person to help is equally useful at times, giving the owner a high chance of succeeding in a controlled environment. Wherever possible, try to predict your dog's likely actions and be prepared. You lead; he's led.

DISCOURAGING JUMPING – RECAP

▶ Methods to stop your dog from jumping up at visitors include:

DETERRENTS:

- water pistol
- sound deterrent
- spray deterrent
- training discs

PREVENTION:

- Collar and leash attached to hook

USEFUL TIPS

▶ If you wish to praise the dog for getting down, do so in a calm, gentle tone, not one that reactivates the dog's excitement. Alternatively, say nothing and carry on with your routine.

Petting the dog when it jumps up, and then expecting it to stop jumping again, only confuses it.

Be consistent – all people the dog encounters and wishes to jump up on need to behave in the same way and to use the Ignore action.

11: Aggression Toward People

Below 1 and 2: *It's fun to play tug-of-war-type games with an energetic dog, but there is a danger that an incipiently aggressive dog will treat the game as a challenge that it plans to win.*

1

2

▶ Dominant and Fear Aggression

In this section we will deal with dominance aggression and fear aggression displayed toward people as they are the most common problems presented to me. Dogs are natural predators, and if not socialized and habituated to people and other dogs they can and do use many types of aggression to communicate their personality, mood, and status. Beneath the endearing, lovable exterior of our dogs beats the heart of an animal with natural drives inherited from the wolf, however moderated they may be through domestication. The behavioral training programs I recommend generally apply to both types of aggression, with a few minor adaptations.

People's domestic circumstances vary greatly but the training programs I suggest are, of necessity, general in application. You must read carefully and select from the information provided that you consider is most applicable to your dog and situation.

This chapter will be split into various sections dealing with the situations where aggression commonly shows itself including aggression toward people, dominance toward family members, aggression directed toward other dogs, territorial aggression, possessive aggression, aggression over food, and aggression when being groomed.

Dominant aggression toward people and especially family members is the problem I am most frequently asked to help with – quite rightly people take it very seriously. The second most common problem is fear aggression displayed toward people outside the family. Dogs can display fear aggression toward other dogs and dominant aggression toward their own family members – so identifying the problem can sometimes be a little confusing. So what are the main problems people encounter with aggression and their dogs?

▶ Prevention Advice: Reducing the High-Ranking Attitude

If you have a young dog and wish to prevent him from becoming too dominant with your family, accustom your puppy or new adult dog to the fact that you are in charge by using the method outlined in the Intelligent Leadership program (see pages 44–47). Most dogs do not usurp your authority and position as head of the pack.

Don't play rough games with puppies who appear to be dominant, as this can produce a familiarity that may be difficult to undo at a later stage. Remember what the wild dog desires – leadership and a high secure position, if possible.

Below 3 and 4: *This dog accepts that its owner is leader of the pack and so can take ultimate possession of the toys. A dominantly aggressive dog may seek to challenge this position.*

3

4

Leaders survive longer in times of stress or food shortage than lower-ranking dogs (or wolves). Obedience-train your dog; this is the best known way to control a dog and induce it to defer to your top dog position.

Don't allow play-biting in any form, or pulling on clothing. Allow your dog to play with toys but insist on being able to remove a toy without a struggle. When the game is finished, lock the toys away so that your dog can see that you are the keeper of them and he is not. Your dog must not win. Every game and obedience or feeding routine must have a set of commands and rules that you dictate. This includes a weekly grooming session so your dog learns not to object to your touching him whenever you wish. At some stage a veterinarian will have to handle and examine your dog, so touching, grooming, and close physical inspection should be the norm for a dog from day one.

Rope-type toys are popular, but this particular game of strength should not be practiced with an apparently dominant dog, especially where children are involved. The more the dog wins the tug-of-war, the more it feels confident about challenging the person playing the game. Dogs can then transpose this confidence to other areas of their relationship within the family – aggression may be the end result. I realize that many dogs growl and bark during play behavior without any problem ever occurring, but that simply means that you are accepting the potential risk, and I feel that with children it's unnecessary and unwise.

Above: *It is important that a pet dog should accept handling by its owner without complaints or overt signs of aggression. The dog must learn that you rule the house.*

Aggression Toward People

Circumstances: The Crucial Factor

However you view your dog's aggression, the circumstances in which it manifests itself are the most crucial element that determines how serious the behavioral problem is. A dog that growls at its owners and the occasional visitor but never bites and is generally amiable is a problem dog and should be helped. But take the same dog and now place it in a family with small children who behave impetuously and who are easily within reach of the dog's jaws, and the serious-

Below: *No one wants to own a dog that growls and bares its teeth at members of the family. It is usually possible to remedy the situation, but not always.*

ness increases tenfold. It's still the same dog, but the "triggers" for aggressive responses have also increased tenfold.

Then take the same dog and place it with a single person who lives in the countryside and who has few visitors. It may be the same dog with the same level of aggression, but the problem is now less serious.

So the circumstances in which the aggression is triggered are the key to its seriousness. The breed and size of a dog will also influence the magnitude of the problem: a Yorkie can inflict little damage on an adult with careful handling, but some of the large or giant breeds, like a St. Bernard, can inflict serious injuries, even on the strongest adult.

1

Types of Aggression Toward People – Inherited Dominance

All dogs are born opportunists looking to improve their pack status. Inheritance plays a part in determining how much dominance your dog will exhibit in your family. Very dominant dogs inherit a desire to be the leader, though factors such as upbringing, how you treat the animal, environment, and breed all affect its personality and the intensity of the dog-human relationship. Pedigree dogs often display more clear behavior traits; Border Collies may display an aptitude for aggressive chasing, while guard breeds may display territorial aggression,

1 and 2: *Children are particularly vulnerable to aggressive dogs, but puppies rarely pose a threat unless something scares them badly.*

which is when a dog won't allow people to enter onto its property without imprinting teeth marks on their legs.

Puppies rarely exhibit true aggressive responses to people or other dogs unless unduly frightened. Their innate body language of appeasement seems to protect them until sexual maturity. Of course many dogs never seem to display any problems in this area, but their desire to dominate is still present, although it runs at a very low level. However, change of circumstances can alter that pattern.

Dominantly aggressive dogs appear confident with a positive body carriage and the look that says "I'm ready for you."

2

This dog looks like it wants to run, but the fear may be channeled into aggression.

The lowered head and insecure demeanor are characteristic of a dog displaying fear aggression.

FEAR OR DOMINANCE AGGRESSION

▶ How do we determine the type of aggression our dog is exhibiting? Body language is often helpful here. With dominant aggression, your dog will appear confident (tail erect, ears held high, body displayed as large as possible, and generally he moves forward to challenge at a steady pace while eye contact is maintained). With fear aggression, the dog will look frightened and skulking (lowered head and body, ears down, tail curled under bottom – shifting eye contact and lip-licking, which is indicative of unsureness). Alternatively, movement can be a sudden darting to and fro. However, some dogs may display both types, being fearfully aggressive with visitors but dominantly aggressive toward their owners.

Aggression Toward People

▶ Dominance Aggression Toward People

So why are dogs dominantly aggressive to the hand that feeds them? Dogs are born with set instincts that prepare them for living in a wolf pack that is based on rank positions. Even when they're in a human family, dogs still assume their pack role and try to establish a niche through interaction with the other pack members, namely you and your family.

Dogs also inherit a predisposition toward dominance from their parents. Because the pack is very important to a dog, most dominant aggression is directed at other pack members. The way you handle and generally interact with your dog deeply affects the dominant dog and its view of you. Good socialization and early handling greatly reduces the dog's willingness to try it on.

▶ Specific Triggers

Many people are confused by dominance aggression because their dog can be the most wonderful, kind, and gentle creature most of the time, but not when he's eating, or resting, or whatever. They are describing a dog that has learned to be dominant in some, but not all, situations. In other words, the dog accepts your leadership in certain areas of the relationship, but not in others. Most dominance aggression is directed at a family member or occurs within the family pack. An example is the dog that only growls when you go near him when he's on his bed or is eating. No other aggression may be displayed. That is what the dog has learned and has gotten away with over time, so he holds on to it for dear life. It's not personal; it's just a dog behaving as dogs do. But it is still aggression, and that's unacceptable in a harmonious and trusting relationship.

▶ Dominance Aggression in Public Places

In public places dominantly aggressive dogs generally do not react to other people unless that person starts to impose on the dog by trying to pet it. Joggers and people performing other unusual actions, like games, can sometimes activate the dog. People who come too close to their owners to pass the time of day can also be perceived as a threat to the pack.

I find it best when implementing the Intelligent Leadership program to concentrate on training the dog to obey my commands entirely, removing from it this element of choice. It must not be allowed to make its own decisions on how and when it can become aggressive.

Right 1: *The body language of this dog says it all – the head and body are lowered, the ears are down, and the tail is coiled under the animal's hindquarters. This is a classic example of a fearful disposition.*

The dog's weight is shifted to the rear, showing that it would like to back away.

1

Above: *Displays of aggression directed toward people constitute one of the most serious problems that a dog owner ever has to face. If uncorrected, such behavior can become a positive danger.*

▶ Fear Aggression Toward People

Though fearful aggression can be inherited, it mostly occurs as a result of poor early socialization or an early trauma in puppyhood. Most fearful dogs become aggressive as they mature, though not all do. There are still too many breeders who do not like letting puppies go to other homes at seven or eight weeks of age, even though there is plenty of evidence to show that it helps prevent temperamental problems from developing, especially fear aggression.

▶ POSSIBLE CAUSES OF FEAR-BASED AGGRESSION

▶ Lack of early socialization during the sensitive period between five and twelve weeks of age, meaning your dog has not been allowed to socialize with people other than your own family members.

Early in its life, it has probably experienced trauma(s). This means that as a puppy it has been traumatized, perhaps by a stranger. The cause could be something as innocuous as a person tripping over the puppy and accidentally hurting it.

It may have inherited a predisposition toward fear of people linked to breeding lines. Some breeds and breed lines do have a greater propensity toward developing a fearful temperament.

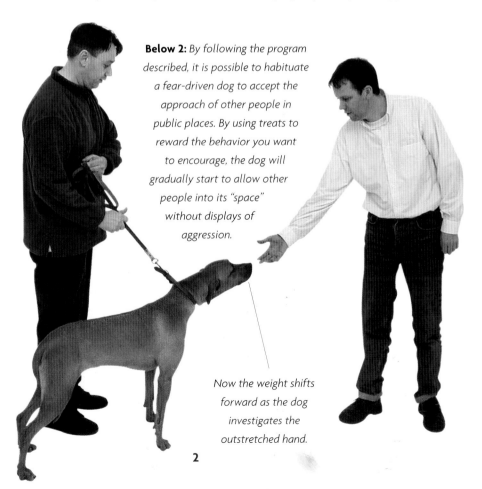

Below 2: *By following the program described, it is possible to habituate a fear-driven dog to accept the approach of other people in public places. By using treats to reward the behavior you want to encourage, the dog will gradually start to allow other people into its "space" without displays of aggression.*

Now the weight shifts forward as the dog investigates the outstretched hand.

Above: *The ears are back, the head is lowered, and there is tightness around the muzzle — this dog is fearful.*

2

Aggression Toward People

▶ Fear Aggression Toward People in Public Places

Fear-aggressive dogs are very dangerous in my view because of their unpredictable nature. Common triggers are numerous: pedestrians that walk with a limp, animated children, well-meaning people in the park who

Left: This is a cage-type muzzle. The dog can pant freely while wearing it, and treats can be fed through the mesh. This is helpful when you need to reward your dog for behavior that you wish to encourage.

try to befriend your dog by petting it and thus imposing on it. They may believe that this will rid the dog of its fear; in general it has the opposite effect. Children, of course, are often attracted to pretty dogs, so you need to be firm

and polite in explaining to the inquisitive child that they must not touch the dog.

At this point in the chapter I should mention muzzles. It is best to use a muzzle if you feel that in the early stages of training your dog may bite, or if you have not yet gained the upper hand in controlling it. The caged variety are best because the dog can still pant, and treats can still be eaten through the gaps in the muzzle. It is imperative that the dog is taught to accept the muzzle in your home and yard for at least one week before walking the dog in public places. To understand how to get the dog used to a muzzle, see the training exercise on pages 32–33.

▶ Keeping a Safe Distance

When you're dealing with a fear-driven dog, you'll notice that what triggers or intensifies the fear in your dog is the distance between him and the object of his fear. If your dog remains reasonably calm at 10 feet (3 m), that's the distance you need to start from when using some of the programs that follow.

If your dog is calmer in a larger space, try to arrange for visitors to arrive at your home while you and the dog are in the yard. Always control the dog with a leash and collar or a Flexi-type leash. The space reassures your dog that it can escape if necessary. Everybody should

act normally and ignore the dog, for it is direct eye contact or physical approach to the dog that often triggers the fear reaction. If your dog remains relaxed, your visitor can slowly throw a treat near it. The distance between your visitor and the dog can be gradually reduced until your dog is taking the treat from their hand. This will take many sessions and perhaps require many months of habituation.

▶ Do Not Impose on Aggressive Dogs

One of the most important rules when dealing with fear or dominance aggression is to move slowly and to not corner the dog or try to befriend it in the normal way. In fact, acting calmly and ignoring the dog completely is often the best way of reducing the dog's fear. Many people who enter a house as

1

visitors feel embarrassed when a dog is aggressive, especially if they are dog lovers. They react by trying to win the dog over with kind, reassuring actions or soothing words. Of course, these actions exacerbate the fear, causing more embarrassment all around.

When I visit homes with an aggressive dog – fearful or dominant – people often expect me to perform magic and go straight into a hands-on relationship with their problem dog. Most quickly notice how I barely even acknowledge the dog. That is why I don't get bitten or provoke their dog's aggressive behavior.

The atmosphere becomes relaxed and

Below 1, 2, and 3: *It's a good idea to invite children to your home so that they can play with a new puppy. Socialization at this early stage of the dog's life helps it grow up into a well-adjusted and pleasant pet.*

Right: *During the vaccination period recommended by veterinarians, puppies are more or less insulated from the outside world. They can miss out on the valuable experiences of socialization.*

calm and I can observe the owners, the dog and its environment, and what is going on. People often say that their dog is unusually relaxed with me and better behaved than usual – that's because I am better behaved as a human and don't impose on the dog or owner.

VACCINATION PERIOD

Another factor that can contribute to the development of fearful dogs is the recommended vaccination period. This occurs at one of the most crucial times of a puppy's life between five and twelve weeks, which is the critical window of opportunity for socializing the puppy to the world it will live in – there is no second chance. At seven weeks of age I take all my puppies on short car trips. I park the car in a busy spot and just sit with the puppy on my knee (or in a cage) with the car door open, allowing it to see all around, habituating the pup to sounds, smells, and sights. I don't let other dogs contact it physically.

There is a mild health risk, but I believe it's the only way to ensure that my pups develop well temperamentally. It is your choice. Check with your veterinarian if canine diseases like parvovirus are endemic in your area.

I also invite people, especially children, and dogs that I know to be free of ill health to my home to accustom the puppy to them from day one. Again, there is a small risk – however the risk of aggression developing later on is a greater worry to me, as it might mark the dog for life or end up having to be put down.

Aggression Toward People

How to Remedy the Situation

Now we have a better understanding of how and why some dogs behave in an aggressive manner toward people, we need to adopt a program to demote the problem dog psychologically, and at the same time implement practical training routines that quickly teach the dog that it will have to change if it wants our time and attention. From now on, it's you who should lead.

If you implement the training program that is outlined below, remember not to slack off when you see signs of improvement. This is a mistake and only teaches the dog to wait patiently to reestablish its alpha, or near alpha, position in the pack as far as dominance is concerned.

The following programs, either

The main aim is to:
1 Remove endlessly repeated commands of "Stop it," "No," and excited voice tones.
2 Use silence effectively to increase the impact of commands delivered that are clearly heard.
3 Stop owners from panicking or becoming upset by their dog's aggressive responses.
4 Take complete control of all situations.
5 Train the dog to accept you as leader at all times.

Ignore the dog when it pesters you like this.

Above 1 and 2: *Showing him who's leader. No longer respond to your dog's nudges by petting him; that's now history. Rewards will come when you say so.*

pursued individually or in combination, will improve your dog's behavior. The more methods you implement, the better the result is likely to be.

Redefining Who's Leader

Psychological demotion is the key to all the behavioral changes we wish to achieve — it sets the ground for the practical training lessons to follow. Whatever the type of aggression you are dealing with, fearful or dominant, this program should be implemented for at least one week before you attempt to deal with the specific type of aggression. Safety is paramount in all retraining programs.

Get the whole family together and agree upon a consistent approach. This speeds up the behavior change and

reduces your chances of failure. All the adults and older children should occupy the top dog positions in the pack. The person whom the dog already respects most should implement parts of the program to which the dog is very resistant, until all family members can join in.

The dog has to be psychologically demoted; this is a non-confrontational approach and is safe even with children. Most people who follow this program notice a change within days. As you begin to implement the changes, some dogs' bad or boisterous behavior may worsen due to changes in routine, but

this is a temporary blip and as the week progresses the dog should begin to respond positively. Other dogs appear (in their owners' words) sad or miserable. Don't misinterpret these visual signs. This is simply the dog taking the cautious approach while the pack is re-arranged. So now let's follow the program.

Days 1–7 Begin to deprive your dog of attention on its own terms. Take away every contact with you that he takes for granted or that you may have inadver-tently given him. For instance, when you are reading a book or watching TV, the dog may nudge your hand and most peo-ple automatically respond with a stroke. Don't! That's now history. This means no more petting or free treats. From now on, every treat or reward your dog receives will be for doing something that you want. I call this the reward link train-ing. Every reward is attached to a link (action) or training exercise. No longer

will the dog receive any attention from you on demand.

Psychological Demotion

These methods are not punishments. They are ways of initiating a new regimen in which you are the leader and your dog is led so that it can learn how to behave. I find that even fear-driven dogs become more obedient and less aggressive when this program is implemented without dilution. It is best to introduce the pro-gram over a two-week period.

Firstly, embark on a strict obedience course at a reputable club or preferably with a one-on-one trainer in the neigh-borhood. This has an enormous effect on your dog's perception of who is boss and your future relationship. All members of the family should take part. Then put into effect the psychological demotion program described in Chapter 3 (see also box right).

Right: *The dog must occupy the lowest position in the family pack's hierarchy if your will is to prevail. Aggressive dogs need to be demoted psychologically.*

> ## WARNING

> When young children are present, you should always seek help from a professional dog behaviorist or specialist dog trainer.

> ## PSYCHOLOGICAL DEMOTION – RECAP

> • Ban the dog from your bedroom.

> • Around the house, make the dog get out of your way – do not walk around him.

> • Give no unearned treats.

> • Remove all toys and balls. You decide when the dog has them.

> • Stop petting your dog "for free." Petting is now earned.

> • Ban the dog from any rooms/areas of the house that he treats as his own territory.

> • Don't let your dog though a doorway ahead of you.

> • Teach your dog that he will only get his food when you are ready.

> • Ignore any nudges or solicitations while you are reading or watching TV. Leaders ignore lower pack members.

> • Only let the dog into the living room by invitation, and make sure that he leaves the room when commanded to do so.

Aggression Toward People

▶ How to Take Charge

As mentioned above, the first step is to embark on a training course, teaching your dog to obey "Sit," "Down," "Come," and "Stay" in all situations. The "Down" can present a problem for dominant dogs, as this is a very submissive position. Take it slowly. If you are following the guidelines outlined in the psychological demotion program explained in Chapter 3, your dog will probably be delighted to receive any praise. Use this fact to help you when training, and you'll find your dog will look forward to being trained.

Below 1 and 2: Obedience training with the assistance of a collar and leash is not some arcane discipline that can only be practiced at obedience classes – get used to doing it at home, too.

▶ House Obedience Training

Few clients realize that obedience training should be practiced using a leash and collar in the home. The home is where many of the problems with dominant dogs crop up, yet people will happily go off to a club once a week to learn training and may even practice in the park, but few teach obedience in the home. Practice three times daily using a collar and leash always. The dog can now see you asserting your authority in the place where it often feels more dominant – the effect can be immense.

Having trained your dog in basic obedience, you can then extend this control to influence its bad behavior. For example, when it will not move off the couch or when it growls when you try to move its food bowl, you can command "Come," then "Down," and then "Stay." Your dog will obey and will accept you as leader. This will take time, but it does work provided you are consistent and patient and are prepared to put in the necessary long-term effort.

The next step is to implement structured training routines that alter your dog's ability to behave badly; in other words, stopping repetition. You will now decide how your dog will behave in your house.

Below 3 and 4: When you have taught your dog to respond obediently to basic commands such as "Sit," "Down," and "Stay," you have a powerful set of tools at your disposal that you can use when you need to assert your authority in any situation.

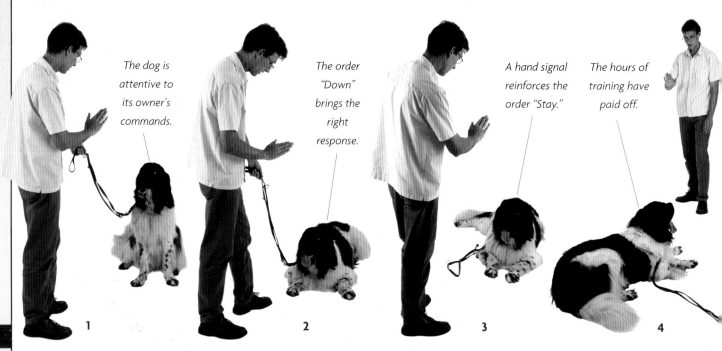

The dog is attentive to its owner's commands.

The order "Down" brings the right response.

A hand signal reinforces the order "Stay."

The hours of training have paid off.

1   2   3   4

Controlling the Dog in Your Home

The first action is to stop your dog from using the entire house as its own territory with the right to roam anywhere, anytime. You will now decide when and what will happen – in simple terms like a child the dog has to learn and be aware of your rules, but you also have to rediscover how to teach them. Patience for the first five days is important; no anger, no shouting, no rough-handling of the dog.

The equipment required is the same as that described in the chapter on the dominant dog (see pages 48–49); again, you will employ the hook restriction program.

While you are at home, place your dog on the hook using his leash and collar for about fifteen minutes at a time, three times a day. Condition your dog that you will only release him when he is quiet and relaxed. After fifteen minutes, approach him; if he becomes over-excited, barks, or jumps up, walk away immediately. He may continue to bark or yelp. Say nothing. Ignore all remonstrations. Repeated many times over a week or so, the dog learns that you release him only when he is quiet.

The dog is now partly conditioned to a new set of rules that will help with visitors and on other occasions when you want to curb boisterous behavior.

The Food Toy Reward

It is very difficult to leave a dog restricted on a hook and leash and simultaneously provide a reward that he associates with that restriction. By using his daily diet packed in a rubber food toy, you can achieve this most powerful reward. The end result is a dog that associates being placed on the hook with a pleasurable reward.

You will have to alter the type of food he is given. He will now only get his food through this toy. For several months no food will be delivered through the food bowl. In fact you can lock it away – but not his water dish.

I begin by dividing up the food into enough portions to match the number of times I plan to restrict him on the hook daily, three times in this case. Always use healthy dog food. Foods that contain chemical additives may be influencing your dog's behavior. Do not use heavily processed foods; we need real meat, which is sticky and of a nice texture that gels to the toy.

On the Hook

Each time you take the dog on his collar and leash to the hook and secure him there, place the food toy on the floor. The more the food is jammed tight into the toy, the longer it will take the dog to extract it. That uses up energy, occupies his mind, and keeps him quiet. Over time the dog will learn to associate the restriction with a powerful reward. He's also being conditioned to accept being tethered as a norm – just the same way he once accepted being restricted by a collar and leash as a norm when a puppy. After several weeks most dogs happily accept the training lesson.

HOOK RECAP

Once your dog has learned to accept time spent while tethered to a hook with equanimity, you now have a good way of controlling your dog without conflict.

Only practice the hook method when you are in your own home. Do not leave the dog unattended. Once the dog accepts the hook restriction method, we can now progress to dealing with dogs that show aggression toward visitors.

Above: *By combining time spent tethered to the hook with the reward of a toy stuffed with succulent meaty food, the dog grows to accept and even enjoy this very effective method of controlling him.*

Aggression Toward People

Aggression Toward Visitors

Dogs that are fear-aggressive to visitors see them as a threat to their safety – they often feel trapped or view a visit as an intrusion on their territory. Dominant dogs often push forward to inspect or bite or nip the visitor; fear-driven dogs can react with a façade of ferocity while inside they're trembling. Some dogs simply hide behind their owners' legs, watching as if transfixed by the visitor.

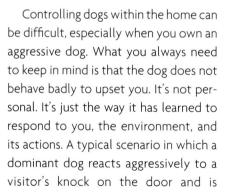

Below: *Over a period of time, dogs that are restrained with a collar and leash can be acclimatized to the approach of a visitor, and eventually come to accept being pet. The use of treats to reward placid behavior is a good idea.*

Left: *A dog that cowers behind its owner's legs when a visitor comes to call may nevertheless behave aggressively through fear if closely approached.*

Controlling dogs within the home can be difficult, especially when you own an aggressive dog. What you always need to keep in mind is that the dog does not behave badly to upset you. It's not personal. It's just the way it has learned to respond to you, the environment, and its actions. A typical scenario in which a dominant dog reacts aggressively to a visitor's knock on the door and is "rewarded" with attention from both the visitor and owner is described and analyzed in Chapter 3. The remedial training method is also explained there. To recap, the stages to follow are these:

1 If your dog displays aggression near the door, place your dog on the hook ten minutes before your visitor's arrival (if the visit is pre-arranged).

2 Answer the door, invite your guest in, and tell him or her not to acknowledge the dog at all.

3 If your dog starts barking, just ignore him. Make no fuss and behave as if everything is normal.

Peace at last! The dog is concentrating on the toy.

Left: *A meat-filled rubber food toy provides the perfect diversion. Your visitor can roll it to your dog across the floor and, once the dog has settled down to nuzzle out the food, the two of you can also settle down to enjoy an uninterrupted chat.*

The food is packed in here.

COMMON MISCONCEPTIONS

▶ **COMMON MISCONCEPTIONS**

▶ **When people give you the following advice, ignore it:**

- **It's only a stage he's going through.**

- **Dogs have the right to guard their toys.**

- **He's only protecting you.**

- **He's just a bit moody.**

- **It's just the way the breed is.**

Above: *Dogs are very territorial, often sniffing around to pick up scent markers. They consider your home as their patch and may react aggressively when visitors "intrude" on it.*

4 Use the food toy packed with a part of his daily food ration. Get your visitor to roll the toy toward your dog. If your dog is not interested in the food, he's not hungry. When the visitor leaves, don't offer more food.

5 Your visitors should not walk toward your dog or bend down near him. They should remain in their chairs. All visitors, whether children or adults, should avoid moving quickly in your dog's presence. Practice this routine with as many friends as possible. In this way you should be able to establish a good association of calmness, safety, and reward.

6 If your dog growls or barks at the visitor, never throw your arms around the dog to show disapproval. Do not pet him or use a praising voice – also don't constantly say "good dog" – this diminishes real praise. Otherwise you will embed the aggression more deeply. If your dog sees that you are calm, its attitude will eventually be influenced.

7 Dogs that have bitten before or that may bite should be muzzled, at least twenty minutes prior to the visitor's arrival. After five such meetings, bring your dog in on a leash and collar and allow him as near as is safe to your visitor's outstretched hand containing a treat. This action will have to be repeated many times if a good association is to be formed. Eventually your dog should look forward to a visitor's arrival. However, always be watchful in case your dog bites.

Aggression Toward People

Training Discs

As explained in Chapter 2, training discs are used to imprint the following ideas:

- The dog learns a sound and associates it with whatever it is doing wrong.
- It associates the sound with the command "No."
- Eventually it responds instantly to the command "No" without the discs being used.

Timing is of the essence with regard to the command and the action of the discs being thrown. Eventually you will be able to stop using the discs and continue only with the verbal command, with the word "No" having the same effect as the discs being thrown.

Above: *The loud clatter of training discs thrown onto the floor at the same moment that you order "No" helps to imprint the command in a dog's mind.*

Many people read that you should never use any admonishment when your dog attempts to attack, bite, or growl at strangers, as the dog associates this with the stranger. This is nonsense. If your dog has been pre-conditioned to pay attention to the discs and the word "No," this association is already firmly established in its mind.

The discs and the command "No" work best when the dog is about to perform its aggressive routine. Once the dog is calm, you should, if possible, ask the stranger or helper to throw some treats on the floor near your dog. The dog is an intelligent creature and has no problem in discerning when you, the leader, are displeased by its aggressive actions. It will also realize that meeting a stranger can be a pleasant experience with the food reward.

Once you have reached a stage where your dog looks forward to visitors in your home or is at ease with people you meet on daily walks, you can begin to relax the hook method after about fifteen minutes and release the dog in the living room. Still allow the visitor to offer the toy with food in it and/or the odd game with a toy – this is risky but that's the way it is.

If you are still very unsure or not confident, and if your dog has been previously conditioned to wearing a muzzle, fit a muzzle to the dog while on the hook and then release it into the room. The guest can use pieces of chicken that can be fed to the dog through the gaps in the muzzle to maintain and continue the reward association training. In the park you can also use the muzzle and food reward training with whomever will cooperate. Enlisting helpers unknown to the dog to meet you in the park to offer the food rewards is of great benefit.

Cage-type muzzles should be used whenever you feel your dog may bite people or while you are still trying to impose your control over your dog. Muzzles, contrary to the opinion of some ill-informed writers, do not make dogs aggressive. They do, however, make a dog look aggressive to the general public – that is a price you have to pay until a muzzle is no longer needed.

Changing Canine Attitudes

At the end of your behavior training programs your dog will have learned some new ideas:

- That you are the leader in and outside the home.
- That it will obey you, the leader, even in situations where it has become used to acting independently of you.
- A new language of training that has appropriate rewards and/or punishments when necessary.
- That people are not to be feared or attacked, and that many people have tasty morsels of food waiting to be given out as rewards.

As time passes and your dog changes for the better, you will become more confident as you see results – the dog will notice you acting like a leader. Your new precise training language will be clear and consistent and the relationship should flourish as both dog and owner respect the new pack hierarchy. As the pulling, panicking, and shouting cease and clear praise and rewards take their place, the dog's mind will become more settled and calm – I call this lifting the relationship fog. The result is a well-mannered dog, or at least a very well-managed dog, even if not always one that behaves perfectly.

Above: *After releasing it from the hook, it's a sensible precaution to fit a muzzle to any dog that has previously bitten or seems liable to bite a visitor. The old axiom "better safe than sorry" should guide you here.*

 ## Euthanasia

This is the taboo subject for many dog owners. However, some dogs are just too badly damaged temperamentally for true rehabilitation to take place. As usual, it is not the dog's doing. I don't believe dogs are born bad. They may have strong innate drives that can run counter to human wishes, but that is still a dog behaving normally. We choose to own the dog – it has no say in the matter or how it will be brought up – so responsibility is ours.

Most people will go to extraordinary lengths to avoid destroying their dog. Emotions run high and facing reality is hard to do – to many people it's like considering killing one of the family. Often people will do anything to avoid accepting reality and prefer to pass responsibility on to others – they may give the dog to a rescue center that can only offer it a pen and kennel for life – not much quality of life there.

If a dog has been assessed by at least two canine behavior practitioners and the consensus is that the behavior is not manageable or cannot be remedied and is dangerous, euthanasia is the responsible and truly considerate avenue to take. Your veterinarian will explain the procedure and he or she should be shown the behaviorist's report. Any assessments you obtain from canine behaviorists or a veterinarian should be in writing.

Above: *Training discs help to discourage certain actions. This is the other side of the coin. Small treats of food offered as a reward for good behavior serve to encourage the dog to repeat the actions that have elicited the reward. By repeated use of reward and reprimand, unacceptable behavior can be modified.*

Aggression Toward Other Dogs

Dogs that are aggressive toward any other dog, irrespective of sex, size, or breed, tend to be motivated by a sense of fear. Specific aggression toward dogs of the same gender usually tends to be of the dominant type and can

Always make safety your first concern if you meet an aggressive dog when out on a walk.

be stimulated by competition coupled with a strong inherited drive to be in charge. Either type can be caused or fueled by lack of early socialization with other canines, which helps to moderate competitive drives. Alternatively, fear aggression can be caused by a traumatic experience when young. It may even be inherited – certain breeds are more predisposed to inherit a sensitive temperament, and so need much more frequent socialization when very young. Fearfulness in dogs is quite variable too: some dogs are afraid of certain other dogs but not all, and some are apprehensive of certain places; others may have a combination of these traits. Some dogs are more aggressive when in a restricted area, on a leash, or in a car.

Fear Aggression

When your dog starts growling at or attacking dogs that it perceives as a threat and the other dogs back off, your

dog interprets this as a success and the aggressive behavior is reinforced. Most fear-aggressive dogs are worse in restricted spaces and on leashes, especially short, tight ones. This is because your dog senses a lack of space for escape and consequently feels more threatened. Conversely, some dogs are more aggressive because they are on a leash knowing they cannot reach the other dog.

I often find that if I suddenly detach a fearful dog from its leash while it's being antagonistic, it will look at me in surprise and its aggression will subside. Of course it's difficult for the average owner to know why their dog is being aggressive, so **I don't advise anyone to follow this example.** Safety is always paramount, so use a muzzle on your dog if it's aggressive. It is also sensible to seek expert advice before progressing further, as it may be difficult to identify precisely the underlying cause of aggression.

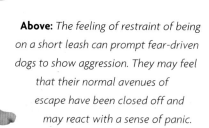

Above: *The feeling of restraint of being on a short leash can prompt fear-driven dogs to show aggression. They may feel that their normal avenues of escape have been closed off and may react with a sense of panic.*

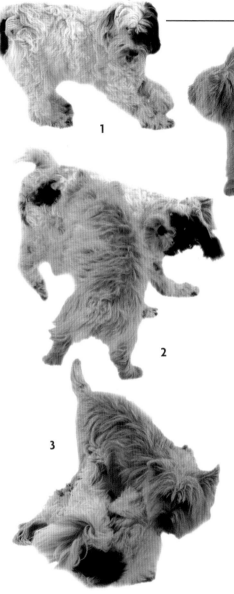

Above 1, 2, and 3: *Aggression between dogs may be caused by fear or by a desire to show dominance. It's not always easy to distinguish between the two motives.*

Some fear-driven biters can learn to appear to behave like dominant dogs, and often people have difficulty deciding whether the aggression is fear-triggered or not. These dogs, in fact, have learned through experience how to remove the threat by attacking first. They seem dominant by their physical posture but the underlying problem is still fear-generated. These are often the aggressive bullies of the dog world. A good dog trainer or behavior practitioner can identify the subtleties of behavior in these dogs.

▶ The Dominantly Aggressive Dog

Many dogs that display dominance aggression have been brought up in well-balanced homes and were socialized correctly, but they still go on to become dominant and aggressive. These dogs may have been allowed to bully other puppies when they were young, or the owner may have an older dog that allowed the dominant puppy too much rough play without any corrective retaliation – in other words, lack of dog discipline! Many dominant dogs seem to actively enjoy the cavalier action of bullying their way around the park and challenging other dogs. Fortunately, this type of problem behavior is not as common as fear-driven aggression.

To cope with it, you must assert your alpha status by following the Intelligent Leadership program in this book and training your dog in basic obedience. Following much of the advice on how to deal with the fearfully aggressive dog in this section will also help a great deal in remolding your dog's antagonism.

▶ WHEN TO ACT

▶ Sometimes people instinctively know what they have to do but they hesitate to do it because they lack confidence, knowledge, or determination, unlike their dog. Often many people are worn out by their dog's antics, or just give up. Giving up can also mean eventually giving up the dog and passing on its problem to others. A quick consultation with a behavior practitioner can sometimes help bolster their confidence so the problem begins to be dealt with effectively.

I think the hardest step to take in dealing with an aggression problem is to admit its existence and ask for help. I really do respect such dog owners. It takes courage; by accepting the problem, you take on the responsibility of trying to correct it by carrying out advice which, though essential, might cause emotional stress in the short term to all involved.

If you don't follow this advice, it may indicate to a dominant or adolescent dog that you are not in control. This may encourage it to assert its dominance further, and eventually it will consider its position in the pack to be higher than yours. The result may be that your dog will stop listening to you and will no longer care about your displeasure.

Aggression Toward Other Dogs

Next let's look in more detail at the many factors that can contribute to or exacerbate aggressive behavior in dogs.

▶ Lack of Socialization

This cause of aggression is very common. It's comes about because of poor socialization between six and twelve weeks of age and thereafter. This is the time when all puppies need to learn how to interact with other dogs and humans. If the experiences of contact are limited, the puppy becomes an outcast to its own kind – it does not learn the canine communication skills it will require to deter or defer to other dogs. Like children, dogs learn what they can and cannot do from play and general social contact. When these experiences are lost at the critical or sensitive period, they can become fearful and then develop the aggression that is the bane of so many dog owners' lives. Though dogs continue to learn throughout their lives, it can be most difficult to correct lack of early socialization.

This dog is tensed for action.

He now crowds the other dog's space.

His weight has shifted forward.

Above and right 1, 2, and 3:
Here, a dominant dog is showing aggression toward a companion. Such attacks can traumatize younger animals. Dogs that have suffered an upsetting incident like this in the formative months of their development may store up their fear and redirect back at the outside world in the form of aggression.

1

2

3

Traumatic Experience

Being bullied or attacked by an aggressive dog can produce a strong imprint on a puppy or adolescent dog. Though many puppies can shake off such an incident, providing most of their initial experiences with dogs are friendly and pleasant, some individuals retain the unpleasant association for life. A very severe attack can create a similarly long-lasting impression on even the most stable dogs.

Some dogs can be traumatized by what appear to us as minor incidents. The fact is, it is the dog that reacts to the incident, not the owner. If a dog decides another dog is aggressive and is to be feared, the result can be the beginning of fearfulness of its own species. Moreover, many of these damaged temperaments often do not reveal their own aggression until some time later — even into their second or third year. I call this latent aggression. But when it happens, they can grow more and more aggressive with each successive attack as they learn that attack itself can become a successful defense tactic.

Cyclical Aggression

Probably the most common reason that dogs become aggressive is as a result of being attacked by another. It angers me that owners ignore the issue and walk aggressive dogs in places where they can

Above: *It's important that dogs learn the skills of socializing with people and other dogs at an early stage of their lives. Play is a powerful teaching aid.*

attack others without control. The majority of dogs that I see have an early history of being attacked or set upon by such dogs. I have seen the same people walking in the same parks month after month watching their dogs repeatedly attack good-natured dogs, many of which will themselves become aggressive because of the trauma they suffered. These same people usually proffer so many lame excuses to explain away their dog's behavior or to absolve their guilt. What they don't do is address the serious problem. If your dog is aggressive, you have a responsibility to muzzle it first and seek professional advice immediately.

POSSIBLE CAUSES OF FEAR AGGRESSION – RECAP

- • Lack of socialization when a puppy.
- • Behavior influenced by a traumatic experience.
  - • An inherited predisposition.

Above: *Young dogs that are attacked by others in their formative months and years can be mentally scarred by the experience. As a consequence, they themselves may start to display aggression toward other dogs later on in their lives.*

Aggression Toward Other Dogs

▶ The Rehabilitation Plan

How should we start to cope with the problem? At my center we follow these procedures to test and assess the suitability of socializing dogs that are aggressive for whatever reason. If you can find a dog trainer or a canine behavior specialist who can show you by example how to do it, this is a good start. It may work right away and it also allows you to learn the

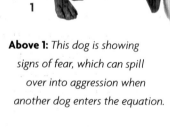

Above 1: *This dog is showing signs of fear, which can spill over into aggression when another dog enters the equation.*

introduction skills required. I use a large yard that has a tall fence around it and enough shrubs to allow dogs to hide if they tend to feel insecure when loose.

There is normally a dog trainer and myself present. The owner brings their dog on a leash into the area and relaxes for ten minutes as we all chat about the procedure. Sometimes we just sit in a relaxed manner on lawn chairs a little distance apart to create a

calm atmosphere. Next we carefully select an assessor dog with a stable temperament that will ignore the aggressive dog completely. We release it and then monitor the reaction of the antagonistic dog. If it is mild, we then perhaps use a muzzle and walk it around at a discreet distance until the dogs are reasonably relaxed. Sometimes we ask the client with the antagonistic dog to perform obedience training exercises to take their dog's mind off the test dog. This often works.

Above and right 2 and 3: *By getting the problem dog used to the company of a companion dog with a calm temperament, over time it can learn to lose its aggressive instincts and socialize happily.*

If the problem dogs are very large and aggressive and could be dangerous, we always use leashes and muzzles for the first ten or so lessons and slowly work up to the socialization system described in the previous paragraph. Over time, if progress is made, we go on walks with the dogs on and off leashes. Other times we simply sit in a room with both dogs on leashes to discuss the training procedures. The antagonistic dog becomes bored or starts to relax.

We have now reached a foundation level of harmony that can be built upon over time. The overriding factor is that the fearful dog realizes that it is not attacked and experiences the close proximity of other dogs in a positive way. Dominant dogs come to realize that they no longer decide when and how to

approach other dogs. They also learn that we humans lead and so are to be obeyed.

Time and practice is always the mainstay of these methods. In our fast-paced world we often want quick results, but remember dogs are not instant – they move at their pace, not ours.

If you follow my advice and work hard, the following results should occur. I make no promises – but equally I tell it as it is. This is not a problem for which easy solutions are to be found – despite what you may read in other books and magazines written by so-called "experts" often with precious little experience of the real world.

1 You will solve the problem and your dog will begin to socialize with other dogs.
2 You will improve your dog's behavior enough to be able to enjoy a fair degree of normality. But always be watchful and ready to control the situation if your dog shows aggression.
3 You will stop your dog from attacking others while on its leash and prevent it from making your walks a misery, but you will not be able to remove its desire to attack entirely or allow it to run freely with other dogs.

Left: Leave the park immediately if your dog is attacked during training; one bad experience can ruin all your good work.

4 In a few very stubborn cases, and especially if you live an area densely populated by dogs, you may have to re-home your dog due to the poor quality of its lifestyle with you, combined with the danger it continues to present to other canines.

That is the reality of owning an aggressive dog for most people. The problem when trying to rehabilitate aggressive dogs are the dangers involved in a fight. There are no quick and simple solutions.

Above: With patience and sensitive handling, a problem dog's behavior should improve – but it takes time.

GENERAL TIPS

Don't take a fear-aggressive dog to places where there is a high concentration of dogs, like dog clubs or play areas, if you're trying to socialize it. This will increase your dog's anxiety, not lessen it.

Don't use physical punishment with fearful dogs. It often frightens them more, rather than teaches them. (Distraction devices, like water pistols or training discs, are useful in some cases to put a stop to the aggressive cycle.)

Don't put your arms around your dog to reassure it if it becomes aggressive or shivers and shakes. These actions simply magnify your dog's fear. Taking a no-nonsense, detached attitude is better.

Do find situations that don't frighten your dog and do make use of dogs that your dog knows and doesn't fear. When you begin your retraining program, use confident, passive, indifferent dogs. As your dog becomes more confident, other environments and dogs can be gradually introduced over many weeks or months.

Do leave the park immediately if over-boisterous dogs pounce on your dog and the owners either can't or won't control them. One over-boisterous or aggressive dog could put your training back months.

Aggression Toward Other Dogs

▶ Getting to Know Other Dogs

I will now assume that we are starting with a dog whose belligerence is based on fear, which is true ninety percent of the time. What we need to do is alter the dog's view of other dogs. This won't be easy; in following the program you will need to be methodical and very patient.

Below: Fear-aggressive dogs can be encouraged to accept the proximity of other dogs by a program of walking them together while gradually reducing the distance between them.

A flexible leash allows the small dog to keep a safe distance.

Firstly, find some submissive, possibly small dogs, preferably of the opposite sex. I realize this might not be easy but it's the only way. Start with one companion dog and arrange to meet the handler and dog on loose leashes or flexible leashes in a park or open space. Observe the distance your dog will accept the other dog to approach without showing aggression. Then walk across the park, keeping this distance between you. Repeat this back and forth. If your dog doesn't bark or growl, lessen the distance between the dogs on each walk across the park. Never be tempted to let the dogs off the leash because your dog appears relaxed at this stage. This exercise should be repeated daily until your dog accepts walking on a leash alongside the other dog without displaying any aggression.

Next you should arrange to meet in different parks and places, or in your friend's yard, provided there is enough space to prevent your dog from feeling threatened. Eventually – it may take several weeks or longer – the dogs should be able to walk side-by-side on leashes without any fuss or displays of aggression.

The next stage is to let the dogs off the leash. If you're unsure of how your dog will react, buy a muzzle and fit that to your dog. This will allow you to be more relaxed, which in turn will help relax your dog. Start by walking the dogs on the leash for around 200 yards (190 m), then release them and allow them to say hello to each other. If there's no

Above: Friends at last! There are ways that will help a fear-aggressive dog to accept the presence of others.

trouble, you can build on this until they become good friends.

Your dog can now learn to play, or at least say hello, and interpret canine body language, and this will build its confidence. You will now have completed the first step. You should aim to progress to meeting as many other helpers and their dogs as possible. Eventually your dog may be able to play freely and comfortably with other dogs, or at least begin to experience the fun of being with other dogs as opposed to fearing any threat they pose. If at any stage your dog displays aggression, that simply means it's not ready to move on. Your dog will only improve at its own rate, not at your insistence. The occasional snap (not bite) is not the end of the world. Such reactions can still happen during the program.

Above 1, 2, and 3: *If your dog responds positively and obediently to the basic commands, you can use them to defuse potentially hazardous situations by re-asserting your control over the dog.*

You may well ask what you should do if dogs come up to you uninvited in the park. Ideally, you should try to walk your dog at times when few dogs are around, and when you are walking your dog keep a face collar on it. You could also try asking other known park users to help by keeping their dog away from yours, especially if they're dominant or boisterous individuals.

▶ The Leader Speaks

Training your dog to a high standard using the sit, down, come, stay, and heel exercises in a variety of locations not only puts you in control but makes you and your dog more confident with one another. Use obedience training to prevent the first antagonistic aggressive displays by your dog and to distract its attention from the other dog. If your dog is heeling, staying, or lying down, it cannot easily be preparing itself for any sort of aggressive action.

By redirecting your dog's habitual actions, you cool down the situation. You can then walk away casually using heeling methods, and maybe give your dog a food reward when it has relaxed. Obedience does not make your dog friendly to other dogs but it does stop the aggressive buildup of tension.

▶ Dogs Visiting You

Fearful dogs can also be very territorial, so bringing strange dogs to your home can be a difficult situation to deal with. I suggest you leave this until you have first corrected or improved your dog's attitude in open spaces. When you have accomplished this, you can use a combination of obedience exercises and food rewards to gently introduce other submissive, non-threatening dogs to your home. Follow methods similar to the introduction techniques described.

When using the above advice and training methods, you will find that all dogs will reach a point beyond which they no longer improve a great deal. It is for you to judge how predictable and reliable your dog has become, but if you are in doubt, a muzzle or a face collar are a sensible precaution.

▶ FOOD-FRIENDLY ASSOCIATIONS

▶ Using favorite treats is a useful way of rewarding your dog for good, non-aggressive behavior. It is best to link the treat to a sit or a stay. This method only works with dogs that love food; alternatively, you could leave out one day's meal and on the following day take a bag full of chicken or ham chunks to the park to reinforce good behavior. This method does not teach your dog not to fear other dogs nor make it like them – it simply teaches him to associate a place where he may otherwise feel threatened with a reward, and that can be helpful.

You can also use food rewards when teaching your dog to walk in company as described above. Again we need to use a loose or flexible leash. However, this time use the food rewards on each occasion that you meet another dog and your dog stays calm. Only give a food reward when your dog is not growling or barking. And remember, repetition over a long period is required, not an occasional effort only when it's convenient.

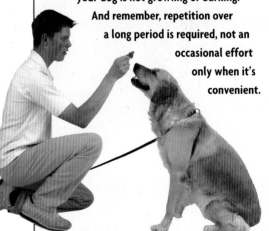

Aggression Toward Other Dogs

What to Do If Your Dog Is Attacked in Public

Every park user, whether a human or a dog, has a right to go for a walk without being bothered by unsupervised or un-controlled dogs. A dog coming wildly toward you might be friendly and have nothing more fearful in mind than saying hello, but its bulk and speed can be quite intimidating. However, you may be dealing with a fierce brute intent on terrorizing you and your dog. I've met people who have such a phobia of dogs that the prospect of walking across a park causes them misery. Though these are extreme cases, they're indicative of the fear that uncontrolled dogs can inspire. Badly behaved dogs ruin the reputation of the rest. If you fear being on the receiving end of an attack by an aggressive dog, read on for advice on how to deal with the situation.

When dogs are about to attack other animals, they normally go through a three-stage process:

Stage One: Predatory Aggression, identify prey. Potential victims are sized up and one is singled out.

Stage Two: Predatory Aggression, pursuit. Suddenly they take off at full speed toward their target dog.

Stage Three: Predatory Aggression, the kill. The final stage is the actual attack. That's the wolf ancestry in your dog revealing itself.

Practical Attack Avoidance Techniques

If you or your dog is attacked, here are some suggestions on how to deal with the situation and defuse the crisis.

Before you adopt any of the defense methods that follow, do be certain that the approaching dog has aggressive intentions before you act, otherwise you could precipitate a fight when otherwise there would not have been one – your dog might be simply and correctly displaying appeasing behavior. An example is when a very assertive, bold dog approaches yours, and your dog appears frightened. You may feel that you need to rescue your dog from this humiliating or dangerous situation. By misreading and interfering, you can cause a fight. Sudden movement or shouting can activate the fight-or-flight mechanisms of the dogs. If you notice how dogs normally meet, sniff, and say hello to one another, their movements are deliberate, synchronized, and slow so that neither dog gives the impression of aggression. Dogs use a wonderful variety of body language signals that generally defuse tension and identify rank, sex, and age. Nothing bad happens and they will

Below: If you own a small dog that is threatened by another in the park, you naturally want to spring to its defense. Stay calm and keep your dog under control. Your presence next to it is quite likely to deter the attacker from doing anything more than barking.

Fortunately, noisy displays of barking are often more about bluster than serious aggression.

Don't always assume that big, fierce-looking dogs have bad intentions. Big dogs often have placid natures.

happily go on their respective ways or play together.

Passive Defense

However, if you or your dog are attacked in the park, this can be a very frightening experience, especially if your dog is small or timid and the attacker is large. In cases where the aggression is mostly vocal, simply telling your dog to sit and keeping your body between the two dogs will stop the situation from becoming worse. It is amazing how the aggressive dog will not come too close to a human to get at his canine target – circumnavigating an owner takes more courage than normal. (This will not work if your dog is also barking aggressively.) The antagonist might be expecting your dog to flee so the chase can begin. By keeping your dog calm, disappointment will be his reward.

1

2

Above right 1 and 2: *When dogs meet, they usually go through an introductory ritual, moving slowly and inquisitively around one another, sniffing and sizing one another up. It's their way of establishing relative status without resorting to aggression.*

ATTACK AVOIDANCE AND SELF-DEFENSE

Do be certain that the approaching dog has aggressive intentions before you act, otherwise you could precipitate a fight when otherwise there would not have been one – your dog might be simply and correctly displaying appeasing behavior.

In cases where the aggression is mostly vocal, simply telling your dog to sit and keeping your body between the two dogs will stop the situation from becoming worse.

If the dog is very aggressive and is attempting to bite, or if you believe from its body language that it will bite, try holding a solid object like a stick, bag, or opened umbrella in front of your body with an outstretched hand.

Alternatively, you may have to let go of your dog's leash if you feel that your personal safety is in jeopardy.

Aggression Toward Other Dogs

Object Defense

If the dog is very aggressive and is attempting to bite, or if you believe from its body language that it will bite, try holding a solid object like a stick or bag in front of your body with an outstretched hand. Don't be threatening or wave it. This display will normally distract the aggressor's attention and, if a bite does take place, the object is normally what is bitten. You need to appear calm and make few sudden movements when adopting these defensive actions.

Alternatively, you may have to let go of your dog's leash if you feel that your personal safety is in jeopardy. In the final analysis I can advise but not anticipate every possibility. It's your decision.

The aforementioned actions are not applicable to children when walking dogs. They really have to try to get help. Children should carry a screech-type alarm for summoning assistance.

Umbrella Rescue

The most successful method I have found to stop dog attacks on you or your dog is a telescopic umbrella. It's called Defense Enlarge or DE. This method is now standard defense advice at my behavior center. The basic idea is that most aggressive dogs are not as confident as they appear. By carrying a telescopic umbrella with you, you are equipped with a superb, quick-action device.

If you believe that a dog is about to attack your dog, simply activate the umbrella release button as the tormentor approaches, also pointing it in the direction of the attacker. The sudden pop of the umbrella will take the dog by surprise; keep your dog either on a leash adjacent to your body or hold him by one arm. During tests in more than 300 practical situations of aggressiveness, only two dogs did not either run off or just bark until their owners arrived and controlled them. The other two dogs snapped at the umbrella, but never quite figured it out and did not pursue the attack further.

1 **2**

Above 1 to 3:
An automatic collapsible umbrella is perfect for the Defense Enlarge tactic. At the press of a button, the spring action unfolds the umbrella until it pops into position with a perceptible snap.

Below 1: *When confronted by a dog with apparently aggressive intentions, the handy umbrella can prove a surprisingly effective defensive aid. By opening the umbrella and using it as a shield for you and your dog, you change the dynamics of the situation.*

Right 2: *Most dogs stop in their tracks and just bark at the umbrella – only a few try to pursue their attack and get around the edge of the shield.*

1

2

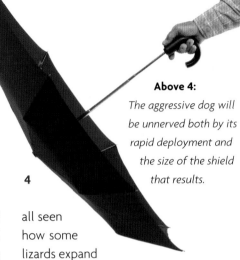

Above 4:
The aggressive dog will be unnerved both by its rapid deployment and the size of the shield that results.

3

4

As the aggressor begins to bark, stand still and place the fully extended umbrella with its outer edge touching the ground. Then roll the umbrella clockwise or counterclockwise according to which way the aggressor is circling you. The antagonist will find it difficult to bypass the defense.

The behavioral principle involved is based on the bluff principle familiar in the animal kingdom. We have

Right 3: *If the dog dodges left and right in an attempt to get around the umbrella, simply roll it along the ground in the appropriate direction to maintain the shield.*

all seen how some lizards expand their ruff around their necks when threatened by a predator in order to makes themselves look larger than they are in life; this trick works for them, and the good old umbrella can work for you and your pet dog.

CASTRATION

In about half the cases where dominant aggression (not fearful aggression) is the problem, male dogs can be helped by castration. You will have to consult your veterinary surgeon for his advice if you think this might help. If the veterinary surgeon does castrate, this physiological change, combined with a strict obedience and a socialization program, should further improve your control over the dog.

WHAT'S THE LAW?

In the United States, it can be an offense to own or to allow a dangerous dog into a public place. Judges can place a restraining order against a dog specifying that it must be muzzled, kept on a leash, or excluded from named places. Alternatively, a control or destruction order may be placed on the dog.

Aggression Toward Dogs in the Same Pack

Many people own more than one dog and, of course, where there are two dogs there is a pack, and two animals who may well compete with one another for position within that pack. Packs are not democracies. A pack is a hierarchy with clear demarcation lines. Most people who own two or more dogs have relatively few problems, as dogs are naturally conditioned to living in a pack. Dogs don't spend their lives worrying about rank; they enjoy playing together and feel secure in one another's company.

However, I frequently see clients with two or more dogs who complain that one has begun attacking the other "out of the blue." The situation can become serious, and severe injuries can and do result. So why do dogs become aggressive toward one another?

Below 1, 2, and 3: *Owners should set aside human notions of evenhandedness and ensure that the higher-ranking dog in the family pack receives their attention first.*

▶ Hidden Currents

Firstly, the situation rarely develops out of the blue and secondly, an issue has generally been rumbling away in the pack for some time. Unfortunately, people don't always see the early signs of a dispute until there is a marked increase in snarls and growls, especially when the dogs congregate around you. In most cases the aggression relates to you, the pack leader, and the privileges that one dog feels the other is enjoying. Jealousy is a good term to use as a general description, but it is not wholly accurate. With children, one could simply make sure that both received identical care and rewards and domestic peace would then reign.

With dogs, on the other hand, such evenhanded treatment is normally the underlying cause of the dispute. Instead it is desirable, for the sake of harmony, that the higher-ranking dog should receive extra attention and that the lower-ranking dog is aware of this. Dogs are not interested in human ideas of fairness; pack instincts dictate that they all have a relative position. Even within households where the dogs seem to be in harmony, there are subtle rank hierarchies that the dogs understand clearly. For example, one dog may quietly get up and move to a different spot when the other comes into the room. This one may then take up the vacated higher-ranking position. Toys and their possession is another indicator of who ranks above whom.

▶ A New Dog in the House

One of the most common reasons for dogs fighting in the home is when a resident dog is suddenly presented with a new companion. Normally, when strange dogs meet in the home a fight or similar altercation may take place, much to the owners' consternation. It is not a good idea to introduce a new adult dog this way – even if it's a bitch being introduced to a male resident dog, aggression can still take place.

1

2

3

Tug-of-war can become a test of strength.

When dogs live together in a family group, they have to establish a pecking order. This is normal and in most cases they can achieve their pack position by dominant play or by serious tests of strength, ritualized threats of aggression, or the odd growl or snap. There are incredible subtleties going on wherever two or more dogs live together – most people do not notice the body language and vocal signals being exchanged between the pack members. Alliances can form between two dogs that gang up against another, but usually there is little friction.

However, as a young dog or bitch grows and becomes stronger, it may decide to challenge an older dog or dogs within the family group. This often happens between about twelve months and three years of age. If the challenged dog decides to resist the pack climber, aggressive fights can occur. There is natural flux in the dog pack, just as wolves in the wild reshuffle the pack order occasionally. Instinctively they solve disputes in their own way using ritualized body language and without external interference. Our bad timing and propensity to interfere is probably another reason why such domestic canine disputes can escalate.

Above: *Toys and their possession is often an indicator of who is above whom in the pack's pecking order. Fights for ownership can break out.*

Most puppies try it, too, but this is not a serious challenge and older dogs treat it for what it is – bluff and impudence. Occasionally the older dog will reinforce its position with a snap, growl, or evil glare, which is often sufficient to deter the most ardent pup from pursuing its goal. In such circumstances we should not interfere unless undue aggression is displayed.

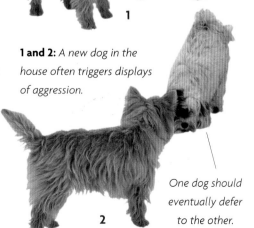

1 and 2: *A new dog in the house often triggers displays of aggression.*

One dog should eventually defer to the other.

1

2

CAUSES OF INTER-PACK AGGRESSION – RECAP

• **Higher-ranking dogs may become jealous if they see their owner, the pack leader, granting privileges to a lower-ranking pack member.**

• **A new dog introduced into the home can create rivalries and pressure on the established pack hierarchy.**

• **As young dogs mature, they may seek to challenge the existing pack order of seniority.**

Above: *Although well-intentioned, our tendency to interrupt when we spot early signs of aggression between pack members may actually enflame the situation instead of calming it down.*

145

Aggression Toward Dogs in the Same Pack

▶ Wolves in the Wild

It is worth taking a look at how wolves deal with pack hierarchy. Packs are started by a bitch and male meeting, breeding, and rearing a family. The yearlings stay on through the next year and help rear the next generation of puppies. As time goes on, the pack grows, numbering on average six to eight members and sometimes as many as forty. The younger wolves tend to challenge the higher-ranking males, their brothers, and their sisters for rank, and in time a stable order is established. Peace reigns most of the time and the high-ranked wolves are the enforcers as they remind the lower-ranking wolves of their place. Most flux in wolf packs occurs annually near the breeding season.

Wolves act out these complex behaviors without human interference. Your dog, on the other hand, lives in domestic circumstances that are alien to pack realignment and peaceful coexistence. I'm amazed how dogs actually do get along so well together, especially when, quite often, little thought is given to their natural behavior. An owner brings in another puppy or older dog and expects them to love one another and be the best of friends. Very deferential resident dogs, especially some bitches, do immediately take to another dog, but that is quite uncommon.

In the wild some wolves are so harassed by other pack members that they leave or are ejected from the pack and peace is again restored. Very few dog owners see this as a viable option because they want their dogs and themselves to live as one big happy family. That's a human desire and has no effect on what the dogs think. Honestly, you cannot force dogs to like one another. But this does not mean that we cannot help to create the circumstances whereby any tension decreases and the dogs do get along. There are no guarantees but most people do succeed.

Most inter-pack aggression in the home takes place when the owner is present – for example, when leashes are being attached for a walk or when the dogs are being pet. At times like these, the dogs vie for your attention and one may feel that the other is pushing in – remember the dog that feels highest ranking next to you, the alpha, is not likely to allow another pack member to usurp its position. Generally, most inter-pack rivalry ceases the minute you leave the dogs on their own. This puzzles many owners; why should their dogs live, sleep, and eat together without conflict when they are not around? However, it does actually pinpoint the root cause, which is you and how you behave.

The look says it – "I'm top dog."

Left: *Dogs are conscious of their status within the family pack, and whenever two or more dogs live together in a household, one dog will achieve a dominant position.*

Above: *Strokes and tickles bestowed by the alpha pack leader are coveted rewards, and the dominant dog in a family will expect to be granted these privileges first. We often don't sense the undercurrents of tension and aggression that can affect the relationship between two dogs.*

Restoring Peace and Order

How should you set about solving this problem of domestic aggression between dogs? First, get the whole family together and agree on a consistent approach. This speeds up the behavior change and reduces your chances of failure. Identify which dog is dominant — sometimes this can be difficult, especially when the dogs are in the transitional stage (i.e., the challenger is about to become top dog). Generally the older dog will be protecting its position, although the younger dog may well be in the process of usurping that position, which means that you will have to show preference to him or her. You may well have more difficulty with this change than the dogs, who understand pack hierarchy, but there may have to be a change if life is to be peaceful. Remember, in such cases it may be better to seek the opinion of a canine behavior practitioner.

Right: *If you do decide to introduce a second dog to the household, it makes sense to choose one that is not similar in size and breed to the resident dog. This helps to prevent struggles for status between evenly matched animals.*

ADVICE ON INTRODUCING A NEW DOG

▶ Ensure your puppy or adult dog receives adequate socialization with other dogs; puppy classes present a good opportunity for this to take place. This prevents many problems of maladjustment from arising. If you're about to purchase another dog, look for one that is not similar in size or type to the resident dog. The greater their difference in size and weight, the less chance there will be of the dogs fighting and creating a competition. There are exceptions to this rule: for example, many small terriers rule the house despite having a big dog as a companion.

One dog loves this attention....

....the other is looking jealous.

Aggression Toward Dogs in the Same Pack

► Removing Friction

Once you have established which dog is dominant and senior in rank, you need to treat it as such. Whenever you are giving the dogs attention, make sure that the dominant dog always receives it first. This may seem unfair by human standards; however, dogs have no sense of equality and applying our rules will only produce friction. The same applies when handing out treats. In everything you do you need to ensure that the dominant dog never feels his position is threatened.

Follow these tips:
1 Always pet the dominant dog first whenever both dogs approach.
2 When taking your dogs out for a walk, connect the dominant dog's leash first and give him plenty of praise.

Below: The dominant dog in the household should be fed and given any treats before the more submissive animal. You should not rock the boat where pack position is concerned.

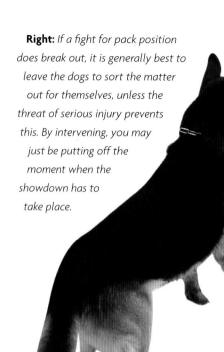

Right: If a fight for pack position does break out, it is generally best to leave the dogs to sort the matter out for themselves, unless the threat of serious injury prevents this. By intervening, you may just be putting off the moment when the showdown has to take place.

Young dogs will often challenge an older partner.

Be careful when powerful dogs come to blows.

3 If the challenger attempts to push in, ignore him and continue with what you were doing.
4 Feed the dominant dog first – this includes treats.
5 Avoid stirring up excitement in confined areas, e.g., doorways and in the car.
6 Games with toys can be continued unless there is constant fighting over such possessions. In this case, remove all toys, bones, and chews for good.
7 If the dominant dog growls at the approaching pack member, don't shout at or smack him. By doing this you only encourage the other dog to feel important because you will appear to be supporting his challenge. You might even encourage fighting to erupt.
8 When young children are involved, you must teach them not to over-excite the dogs. If a fight does break out, there is obvious danger to the children.

► What to Do If a Fight Takes Place

If a fight occurs, you should, in theory, allow the protagonists to sort it out themselves, provided the aggression is at a fairly low level. I realize this could involve injury and veterinary costs, not to mention the stress of watching it occur. However, dogs do eventually sort themselves out and when we interfere, we unintentionally prevent a pecking order from being established. Another fight is then required to resolve the

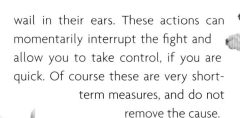

dispute. Very few dogs fight for fighting's sake. If there appears to be no end to the repetitive fighting, this normally means that the two dogs are evenly matched in size, dominance, and determination. One dog will have to be re-homed. That is being kind – keeping them both just because separation would hurt your feelings is selfish and not the behavior of somebody who loves dogs.

If you cannot bring yourself to allow the dogs to fight it out or if, for safety reasons, (e.g., the presence of children) you wish to stop the fighting, then a clean plastic bottle filled with water can be used to squirt a jet of water in the dogs' faces. Alternatively, a dog-stop alarm can be used to screech a loud

wail in their ears. These actions can momentarily interrupt the fight and allow you to take control, if you are quick. Of course these are very short-term measures, and do not remove the cause.

Below: *Preferential treatment should be given to the dominant dog when it is time to attach leashes to go for a walk. These little actions send signals to the dogs that you are aware of their relative status.*

Left: *When two dogs approach you in the home to be pet, be sure to make a fuss of the dominant partner before acknowledging the more submissive animal.*

TRAINING DIGEST

▶ Whenever you are giving the dogs attention, make sure that the dominant dog always receives it first.

▶ If a fight occurs, you should, in theory, allow the protagonists to sort it out themselves, provided the aggression is at a fairly low level.

Aggression Toward Dogs in the Same Pack

▶ Canine Divorce

Remember that in a wild dog pack, any individual that is bullied or attacked can move a considerable distance away from the antagonist until the perceived threat is removed or the passage of time reduces the tension. House dogs cannot follow this behavior, so the dominant dog may feel constantly challenged no matter how many times it puts its fellow dog down.

Equally, if a wild dog is continually picked on and decides enough is enough, it will reluctantly leave the pack's security for good and take its chances. Again, domestic dogs do not have this option of removing themselves from the scene, which explains why the fighting is often so intense.

Depending on the severity of your dog's aggression, you may need to consider whether keeping him is fair to other dog owners and to your other dogs. Re-homing is a possibility, though we find it emotionally difficult. Permanently muzzling your dogs is not a solution. When most of the recommendations in this section are followed, with regard to reassuring the dominant dog of his or her position, and provided you fully understand the reasons for inter-pack aggression, peace can in most cases be restored within a few months.

Left: The dominant dog will naturally seek reassurance from its owner that it is number one in her eyes. Make sure that you respond in the appropriate way.

Remember – treats go to the senior-ranking animal first.

Above: *By following the recommendations in this section, you can help your dogs settle down amicably in one another's company.*

A fight involving a dog this size is likely to be a serious matter.

Above right: *Constant challenges to its position in the home can wear down even the largest and most powerful-looking dog.*

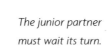

The junior partner must wait its turn.

The Pros and Cons of Neutering

Two males in the same house: castration

I have found castration to be of assistance in about half the cases I have dealt with. Alternatively, your dog can be injected with progesterone, a hormone that can lessen aggression. However, this is a hit-and-miss affair and not one I recommend, although many vets are keen on it. If you are considering either of these courses of action, contact your veterinary surgeon for his advice. It is not wise to castrate the dominant dog in the group.

Always castrate the less dominant dog – you may achieve peace by widening the dominance gap between the combatants. Take professional advice from a vet or canine behavior practitioner on which dog is the dominant one if you are uncertain, as the operation cannot be reversed.

Females: spaying

Recent evidence suggests that spaying bitches tends to produce more dominance rather than reduce it. Again, consult your veterinary surgeon for further information.

ADVICE ON REDUCING INTER-PACK AGGRESSION – RECAP

• Establish which is the dominant dog in your household and treat it as the senior-ranking animal accordingly.

• If a fight breaks out, if possible let the animals sort out their struggle without your interference.

• If you have to step in to a fight to prevent serious injury, use a water pistol or dog-stop alarm to interrupt the fighting so that you can take control.

• In bad cases that just do not respond to correction, one of the dogs may have to be re-homed.

• In some circumstances, neutering can offer some assistance by widening the dominance gap – seek professional advice about this.

Left: This is the sort of scene that we want to encourage in the home – the two dogs are happy in one another's company and look alert and content. On occasions, however, displays of rivalry and competition do not resolve themselves and a continual battle for dominance is the result. In these circumstances, unfortunately, it may be necessary to re-home one of the dogs.

Possessive Aggression

Wolves in a pack spend a good deal of time collecting bits of carcass and bones and playing around with them. The odd bone will be taken and apparently treasured by members of the pack because ownership of the object can be used as a signal of higher rank. In domestic circumstances, toys are used by many dogs for the same purpose of declaring ownership and status. This is especially true of dogs that have been allowed to usurp leadership of the family pack. We may regard it as a game when dogs try to keep possession of

Right 1 and 2: *It's fun to play tugging games with your dog, but watch out for signs of possessive aggression. If you cannot take the toy away at the end of the game, the dog is asserting its dominance.*

1

toys, but to the dog it's part of a display of dominance.

If your dog growls at you, snaps, or is just plain unapproachable when in possession of an item like a toy, you must understand that the dog has taken its dominance to the final stage and now uses aggression to signal its rights of ownership and status. This behavior is not acceptable in the pet dog for obvious reasons. Every time your dog gets its own way when it displays possessive aggression will add to its feeling of dominance and superiority when it has the object between its paws. This can take the form of the dog growling when you pass nearby.

In the wolf pack, the frequent arguments over food are generally resolved through a set of ritual threats of bared teeth, growling, put-downs, or stares. The pet dog also uses the same forms of communication with owners, but we don't necessarily see the more subtle signs or pick up the behavioral undercurrents. Owners that retaliate or threaten with undue force often exacerbate the problem – this approach is not recommended in the domestic situation. More subtle methods work better.

Possessiveness with Toys

If toys or, as is often the case, a particular toy is the cause of a problem, simply remove it

Resistance is part of the game, but insisting on winning is not!

2

The dog must learn that you own the toys.

1

A collar and leash keeps you in control.

2

The reward of a morsel of food is a strong inducement to let go of the toy.

3

are sole owners. Always using a leash and collar, throw a toy a few feet in front of you, then reel the dog in gently and tell him to sit. Don't drag him in. Have some tasty morsels of cheese, chicken, or ham available. Offer the food simultaneously in exchange for the toy – the dog learns that this

for good. Why make life hard? By following the Intelligent Leadership program combined with leash obedience training, you can alter your dog's attitude psychologically and through appropriate training. This often has a big effect.

You can, if appropriate, then reeducate the dog as to how the possession rules really work – you and the family

exercise has pleasant rewards and often the dominant challenge subsides. In time the dog accepts the routine, and food only needs to be offered occasionally until the new rules are cemented.

TRAINING DIGEST

In domestic circumstances, toys are used by many dogs for the same purpose of declaring ownership and status. This is especially true of dogs that have been allowed to usurp leadership of the family pack.

Every time your dog gets its own way when it displays possessive aggression will add to its feeling of dominance and superiority when it has the object between its paws.

If toys or, as is often the case, a particular toy is the cause of a problem, simply remove it for good.

To reeducate your dog, have some tasty morsels of cheese, chicken, or ham available. Offer the food simultaneously in exchange for the toy – the dog learns that this exercise has pleasant rewards and often the dominant challenge subsides.

Above left 1, 2, and 3:
When training a dog to overcome possessiveness with toys, use a collar and leash. The dog should be encouraged to retrieve the toy, bring it to you, and then surrender it to you without complaint. A treat often helps at the final stage to tempt the dog to let go.

Possessive Aggression

At this stage, the game is just harmless fun. The dog appears to be playful and cooperative.

But if the dog's next action is to grab the toy and make a run for it to hide under a chair, the situation will have changed because the dog will no longer be deferring to the pack leader.

▶ Using Spray Deterrents

Dogs that hide under furniture with a toy and growl when anyone approaches are most difficult to deal with. In the short-term, I simply spray the air above the dog with citronella or some safe citrus-type spray — the vapor gently descends over the dog's olfactory system. This completely ruins the dog's well-rehearsed game of dominance, and it will leave the toy and the spot, allowing you to collect the toy in full view. You are now the alpha wolf. Don't say a word. It is important not to point the spray at the dog in a threatening manner. Imagine you are spraying the air with a room scent, which your dog has probably seen you do many times. Your

Above left 1: *It's obvious that the spaniel is enjoying this game with a cuddly toy, just as the owner is.*

manner should be nonchalant, not aggressive. I've yet to meet a dog that stayed put. Again, it helps to remove any toys of which the dog is particularly possessive.

▶ Do's and Don'ts

• Don't try to take a toy back from your dog if it has adopted a position sheltering underneath a chair, a sofa, or a table, for it is more likely to snap or growl

Above: *If the dog will not release the shoe, spray the item with a bitter spray.*

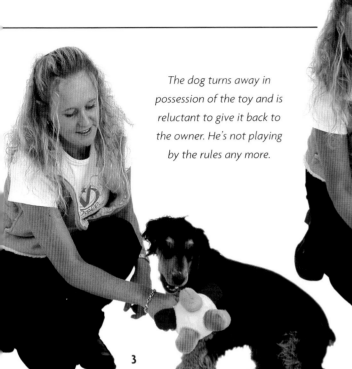

The dog turns away in possession of the toy and is reluctant to give it back to the owner. He's not playing by the rules any more.

3

4

Above 3 and 4: *Now things are getting more intense – the dog makes a grab for the toy and manages to pull it from the owner's grasp. No problem there, you may think, but what if the dog will not let go when it's time for the game to end?*

and you'll be in a relatively vulnerable position.

- Don't smack your dog to make it release any object. Confrontation with very dominant dogs can cause complications or more aggression.
- Don't shout loudly at your dog. Use only clear, concise commands and offer food in exchange for the toy.
- Don't kneel down talking gently to your dog as it growls – this only underlines the dog's dominant status and generally it will growl more.

- Do follow the "Ignore" method, which works with some dogs. By not responding to its growls and grunts, the dog elicits no reaction from you. Some dogs stop defending their possession in the face of their owners' lack of response.
- If you find that the dog likes to take possession of items like shoes or slippers just to make the point that he has them and you don't, spray these items with a pungent-smelling spray every day. The dog finds that when he grabs them the taste is foul. Eventually the dominance possession routine subsides.
- If a dog regularly finds items in the park that he won't let you take from him, read Chapter 12 on food scavenging and employ the corrective techniques suggested there.

DEALING WITH POSSESSIVE AGGRESSION – RECAP

- **Implement the Intelligent Leadership program immediately (see pages 44–47).**
- **Remove any toys or objects of persistent contention if possible.**
- **Spray all children's toys or other items that the dog takes possession of with bitter apple or citronella spray.**
- **Resist the temptation of shouting at the dog – it only reinforces the sense of challenge.**
- **The command "No" given as the dog is about to take possession often helps.**

Above: *Be careful if your dog has retreated under a chair or table with a favorite possession. It may feel cornered and be more liable to snap or growl at you.*

Aggression Over Food

Food is the strongest driving force for animals in the natural world. Of course, most dogs are happy to munch on what their owner provides on a regular basis and occasionally supplement it with what they hunt (find around the home). Unfortunately, many puppies are not taught from day one that you have the right to take away food or place your hand near their food without any dispute.

This type of aggression takes the form of the dog either growling when you walk near him when he is eating or lying near his food, or when you try to remove the food bowl, which he has decided to guard in a display of dominance. In the wild, disputes over food are a daily occurrence, but they are acted out mainly through a set of ritualized threats – bared teeth, growling, or stares. In fact, the pet dog uses the same signals to communicate with its owners. Owners who retaliate or threaten often find that it only causes more aggression, which adds a twist to the vicious cycle. Each confrontation we lose reinforces the dog's belief that he is dominant and that he is the winner. This is the opposite of what we want. More subtle methods work better.

The following program shows you ways of avoiding such conflict and re-directing the dog's attention, plus it teaches him that your approach can mean a reward, not a threat.

Retraining Program

1 Change the food to a dry mix, which is less tasty and less likely to be pro-tected than something more succu-lent and desirable

2 Remove the food bowl when the dog finishes eating. Allow only five minutes eating time daily. This again prevents the guarding routine from developing or getting ingrained.

3 Don't feed the dog in a narrow passage or a room in which you have to squeeze by. This only causes friction and unnecessary tension.

4 Feed your dog in a new area, preferably in the yard. In this way there will be no food bowl for him to defend when you pass him in the house. The new location also stops him from associating food with the place where formerly confrontation took place.

5 Allow no begging at the table and give no treats at any other time.

6 If bones or chews cause problems, stop giving them permanently.

Obedience Training

Using the "Come" command that is part of the recall training program can be helpful in reinforcing good behavior. Use a leash and collar, as most dogs associate the leash with control and are usually more respectful of their owners when attached to one. Then practice recall exercises in the house, repeated twice daily. This may take several weeks to master. The idea is to condition the dog

Possession of the food bowl can lead to disputes between a dog and its owner.

Above: *Dogs that start to guard their food aggressively pose a real problem to their owners. They have to be taught that you, not they, are the master of the food bowl.*

to come to you on command. Always give a treat when calling a dog.

When your dog leaves his bowl on command, you can stop attaching the leash. Your dog is learning to leave his bowl, come on command, and to accept that you control the situation. He also benefits from a food reward, and comes to realize that the situation is not in any way threatening.

Spray Distraction

This method works on most dogs if very subtly applied. If you have a very

determined dog who always growls, and for practical reasons you have to get on with your daily routine and get past the dog, this method will interrupt the dog's guarding behavior. It does not stop aggression, but it stops the incident from worsening or being played out in the dog's favor.

Use a citronella spray or other harmless, bitter-scented aerosol. As you walk near the dog, simply spray the air at least 5 feet (1.5 m) above the dog's food bowl. As the atomized particles descend onto the dog, its olfactory sense will take in this horrible odor and taste. It is critical that you say nothing to the dog. It will generally leave the area, enabling you to collect the bowl of food quickly without a fight.

It's important not to point the spray at the dog in any threatening manner. Simply imagine that you are spraying the air from side to side with a deodorant room scent. Your manner should be nonchalant, not aggressive.

Food Exchange

This technique is used with some success. The timing and how you manage the procedure will determine how effective it is. Though I have used it on all dogs, it is especially good if a dog is in the early stages of food guarding.

First change the dog's diet to a less tasty one – dried dog foods often fall into this category. Follow the hook restriction program (see page 48) and using a 6-foot (2 m) leash, attach your dog to the wall hook by its collar and leash. Prepare the dog's food and place it in front of the dog – just beyond reach. Then place some small pieces of ham or chicken on a plate next to you out of the dog's reach. Push the dog's food bowl within its reach and simultaneously show it the treat. If it smells the chicken or ham and prefers it, the chances of success are high.

Simply offer the treat and remove the food bowl; this is called food exchange. This can be repeated as many times as necessary to teach the dog that far from being a threat, you are a source of tasty treats. Be watchful and have some help nearby. The tether will help prevent any serious aggressive lunges from reaching you. If your dog takes to this method, repeat it over many weeks.

In Conclusion

Prevention is the best answer, but there are some very aggressive dogs that don't respond to any obedience training when food is present. This is normally because they are beyond mild correction or because their owners were not skilled enough to teach them at the right age using the right methods. With these dogs, the only answer is to feed them away from the house and avoid the situation. You must be very cautious when dealing with this behavior, especially if children are routinely part of the household. I do not think that aggressive dogs and children should mix on a permanent basis.

▶ SOME DO'S AND DON'TS

▶ • Don't try to take a bone from your dog if he is underneath a chair, a sofa, or a table, for it is more likely to snap or growl. You are physically very vulnerable in such situations.

• Don't smack your dog to make it release any object.

• Don't shout loudly at your dog. Use only clear, concise commands and offer food in exchange for the toy.

• Don't kneel down talking to your dog gently as its growls. This usually reinforces the dog's sense of dominance while the close contact makes the aggression worse.

• Do follow the "Ignore" method, which works with some dogs. When the dog sees no reaction to its growls and grunts, it may stop defending its food due to lack of response from the owner.

Below: *If your dog starts to snap when you try to take away its food bowl, don't kneel down to reason with it – it may interpret the gesture as either deference or aggression.*

Aggression When Grooming

Why Dogs Show Aggression

Grooming your dog ought to be very enjoyable – a form of social contact that the dog really loves. Most dogs do indeed like being groomed, but some don't. The problem here is that the dog may be indicating, through growling, that he is high-ranking, you are low, and don't you forget it. Each time you groom him, he reminds you again. Most owners tend to get annoyed, but if the owner becomes aggressive and shouts, that just ups the ante. Expressing annoyance rarely works, especially with older dogs.

In my experience nearly all dominant dogs that grumble when being groomed actually like being groomed. They simply want to reinforce their status in the only way they know how. In the wild, dominant wolves can approach any lower-ranking wolf and demand attention in the form of grooming. However, the converse is not so. Lower-ranking wolves risk being put in their place if they try the same approach on a higher-

Above 1, 2, and 3: *It pays to accustom dogs to human touch from early puppyhood so that grooming becomes an enjoyable activity that cements the bond between you. Be careful if your dog seems inclined to snap when you brush a particular area – you may be hitting a sore spot that needs medical attention.*

ranking wolf. Your dog is simply trying to apply the rules of the pack, but you don't like it and why should you?

Breed Problems

More serious types of grooming aggression occur when a dog has a sore or injury below the fur. This needs to be dealt with by a veterinarian. Moreover, people who choose to purchase breeds that

Left: *When a dog first joins the family, grooming is very much about touch and physical acceptance of its human companions.*

3

require hours of grooming because of the length or texture of their coats can have problems, as knots occur in the hair and pulling at them with a comb hurts the dog. If these dogs are handled by professional groomers from puppyhood, the early conditioning of the dog to accept such handling prevents later clashes from occurring.

▶ Using Muzzles on Very Aggressive Dogs

Some dogs object to grooming by growling or snapping, but few dogs actually bite. However, if your dog does, consider buying a muzzle while trying to reeducate him. You should try to accustom your dog

to wearing the muzzle prior to the grooming sessions. This is especially important with very aggressive dogs and it ensures that your dog doesn't have further irritations to aggravate him at grooming time.

Use a collar and leash to secure your dog to a wall hook and keep some food morsels (ham/chicken) nearby. Also make sure that the dog is very hungry – and I mean very hungry.

Start by grooming a part of your dog that doesn't upset him too much for the first ten sessions. Because he is on the hook, you can use both hands, which makes your effort twice as effective and keeps you very much in charge.

Then slowly progress to grooming the more touchy areas. If your dog stiffens or growls, don't praise or reassure him. However, if he accepts light grooming, praise him and give him a treat. Do not physically pet your dog, as this can be misinterpreted. Eventually your dog may accept grooming and you will have mastered a useful exercise.

Left: *It is satisfying to groom small, compliant dogs on your lap, particularly as the years go by and squatting or kneeling on the floor for prolonged periods becomes more of a physical strain.*

▶ PREVENTION ADVICE

Grooming your puppy daily for the first six months of its life, even if it is not a breed that requires such regular attention, while offering favorite treats (ham or chicken pieces) and making sure the puppy sees you as leader, is the best way of preventing aggression linked to grooming developing later on. In this context, grooming also includes general touch, examination of the dog, or simply lifting it up and moving it around physically.

▶ GROOMING – RECAP

• Use a collar and leash plus a hook on a wall.

• Make sure the dog is very hungry and have juicy treats on a plate nearby for use.

• Use a muzzle with a very aggressive dog and keep using it until you are happy that the dog's aggression has reduced.

• If the aggression comes out of the blue, consult your vet in case of a skin infection or other injury that you are not aware of.

• Only groom the areas that don't upset the dog for the first ten sessions.

• In the early stages, grooming is about touch and physical acceptance, not actual grooming.

12: Stealing Food and Scavenging

Dogs are scavengers by nature. Wild dogs owe their success to their virtually omnivorous eating habits and their readiness to supplement hunting kills by eating carrion and anything else they find. To a wild dog, any food source can mean the difference between life and death. Domestic dogs have their food supplied by us, but they retain the instinct not to waste anything – whether it be an unguarded sandwich in the house or animal droppings in the park.

It follows that dogs don't understand our views on stealing food, or indeed the concept of stealing – they merely eat what they find as their wild cousins do. So they find our reactions quite incomprehensible. Dogs learn by association. If every time a dog finds a delicious piece of decaying rubbish his owner chases him, grabs him, and tries to grab it out of his mouth, what is the dog to conclude but that the owner wants it for himself?

Understandably, the dog learns that the best response is to make a run for it – and since he has two more legs, the resulting victory is a foregone conclusion!

Taste Buds

Dogs have fewer taste buds than humans, and very different ideas on what is edible. Furthermore, they are not bothered by human perceptions of what might be toxic or dangerous. To dogs, therefore, the world is their restaurant. We, however, find it distasteful when our pets vacuum up waste food in the park or on the street. We also know that this is dangerous, since it can cause severe food poisoning.

Equally, it is natural for dogs to gobble up cow, horse, and sheep dung or, in fact, the dung of any herbivorous animal. The dung of herbivores contains many partly digested nutrients, and the canine motto is "Waste

not, want not." Some dogs go further and roll in the stuff for good measure, to help mask their own scent. Again, humans are repelled by this. We understand that dogs can ingest parasites through eating dung. For wild dogs, incurring a parasitic infection is an acceptable risk – but it's a risk we prefer our pets to avoid.

In the Home

Food is the strongest driving force for animals in the natural world. Domestic dogs are fed on a regular basis, but they still have the urge to supplement this occasionally with what they hunt (find). This is frequently provided by neglectful humans who leave cakes, sandwiches, and other treats on temptingly low tables. It would be unnatural for a dog to turn up such an opportunity. Each successful foray reinforces the dog's instinct to hunt down such supplementary snacks.

Often, dogs learn to steal food more out of boredom than from hunger. Dogs that have been left for long periods of time with little stimulation seek to entertain themselves, just as we would if we were stuck in a room for too long on our own.

Following Their Noses

Their acute sense of smell encourages them to explore, and the exciting aromas escaping from the kitchen trash

Above and right: *Dogs are great opportunists, and the hunt for food is one of the most powerful of their natural instincts. It is hardly surprising that a low table and a tasty slice of bread can lead to this.*

Left and below 1, 2, 3, and 4:
Where there's a will, there's a way. Dogs can smell food from afar and will eat what they find, until trained otherwise.

What could be more convenient? An unattended sandwich and a chair to climb on.

1

2

3

4

WHY DOGS STEAL FOOD

• **NATURE** – dogs are programmed not to waste food.

• **OPPORTUNITY** – food is left in accessible positions.

• **BOREDOM** – bored, lonely dogs seek entertainment.

TRAINING DIGEST

Food is the strongest driving force for animals in the natural world. Domestic dogs are fed on a regular basis, but they still have the urge to supplement this occasionally with what they hunt (find).

Dogs that have been left for long periods of time with little stimulation seek to entertain themselves by stealing food, just as we would if we were stuck in a room on our own.

Having found the experience rewarding, a dog is likely to repeat it. To prevent this, it's wise to secure all trash cans, indoors and outdoors.

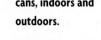

can are irresistible. Tipping over the trash can not only provides a food reward but is also fun in the form of rummaging and investigating. Having found the experience rewarding, a dog is likely to repeat it. To prevent this, it's wise to secure all trash cans, indoors and outdoors.

Some breeds are gluttons in the first degree – Labrador Retrievers are famous for this. Such dogs don't need an excuse to eat what they shouldn't! Gobbling up unattended food comes naturally.

Stealing Food and Scavenging

▶ Obedience Training

At home or in the park, teaching your dog to obey your obedience commands is the only sure way to prevent scavenging. Since dogs cannot understand our views on food, they need to be taught that "No" means "No" and not "Maybe." It's advisable to teach puppies or new adult dogs the word "No" early on. Then walk your dog around the house on a collar and leash. If he approaches any food, check him with the leash and tell him "No." It helps to leave food out in a container, which allows it to be seen and smelled but

Right: *It's tempting to feed a dog from your hand – especially if it's performing tricks like this. Treats are useful reinforcers in structured training routines, but otherwise try to avoid feeding a dog by hand.*

Left: *Learning when "No" means "No." Teaching your dog obedience commands is vital if you are to stop it from scavenging around the house or when out on a walk. The use of a leash helps to reinforce the lesson.*

prevents the dog from getting a reward if he snatches it. This is vital, as one food reward may be remembered forever.

The rules are made clearer to your dog if you never hand-feed him, and never offer food to him from your plate. Few dogs waste their efforts staring and drooling at the plates of people who never feed them by hand. It's natural to hand your dog a portion of what you are eating, as a way of saying, "Let's share but don't take." However, what this signals to the dog is that whenever you have food there is always a chance of a reward, and this simply increases the likelihood that he will start helping himself.

▶ Deterrents

In my experience, deterrents are less effective than prevention. Some people recommend discouraging theft by leaving out food smeared with an unpleasant-tasting substance, such as mustard. This is usually a waste of

time. Most dogs smell the horrible substance and steer well clear of it, but still continue to steal untreated food. Others will just eat anything and look for seconds – treated or untreated.

Above: *Those beseeching eyes and long, doleful stares while you are eating are hard to resist, particularly for people who live alone and rely on their pet dogs for support and companionship. However, when dogs learn that a particular behavior may earn them a food reward, the habit can become ingrained.*

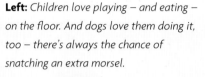

Prevention Advice

Dogs develop the habit of taking food from tables or kitchen surfaces because of careless owners. It only takes one successful foray to establish the practice! The best prevention is never to leave food unattended. Lock every tempting morsel away. This will eliminate the reward and stop the habit from developing – especially important in the puppy and adolescent periods, when bad habits are easily formed.

With a dog already conditioned to stealing, set the dog up regularly so that you control the situation and are not caught off guard. Allowing the dog to dictate training times is a recipe for failure. You must be in control at all times.

The combination of young children, food, and dogs can be a nightmare for you – and a delight for most dogs. Toddlers often drop food down on dogs from their high chairs, and this is a difficult situation to resolve. Probably the best solution is to keep your dog out of the room while the child is eating, and not let him back in until you have cleaned up all crumbs and splatters. If the dog has learned the "No" command, you can use this to restrain him – provided the child does not require all your attention. Alternatively, you can use the hook restriction method described in Chapter 3. It's important to be in control, rather than let the dog dictate his own actions.

Left: Children love playing – and eating – on the floor. And dogs love them doing it, too – there's always the chance of snatching an extra morsel.

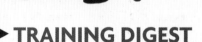

TRAINING DIGEST

▶ Teaching your dog to obey your obedience commands is the only sure way to prevent scavenging.

The rules are made clearer to your dog if you never hand-feed him, and never offer food to him from your plate.

The best prevention is to never leave food unattended. Lock every tempting morsel away. This will eliminate the reward and stop the habit from developing.

Deterrents are less effective than prevention.

Below 1 and 2: A dog has to learn that his food will only be delivered to him through his bowl. You may deliver extra treats, but preferably not from your own plate.

When offering food by hand, make sure that you call the shots.

1

2

Stealing Food and Scavenging

Direct Action

When your dog steals food in your presence, the "No" command can be backed up with various aids, such as a water pistol or training discs. As he reaches for the food, squirt water at his face or throw training discs (or a large bunch of keys) just behind him. The squirt or the clattering noise will put off all but the most hardened thieves.

Alternatively, you can use a remote-controlled spray deterrent collar. (This is not a shock collar.) The device is very effective in interrupting undesired behavior like stealing food, although you will need to learn from a trainer how to use it correctly. The remote control means you can operate the spray mechanism without the dog realizing that you are directly

involved – instead he associates the unpleasant effect with his own action.

Setting Up Your Dog

This "natural learning" method often has the best chance of teaching a dog what is a bad deal and what is a good deal in life. If you wish to dissuade your dog from stealing food when you are out of the room, then "set him up." Tie several tin trays or empty tin cans (make sure there are no sharp edges) together with string, secure the other end of the string to a piece of food such as a tough piece of meat, and place them all on a kitchen table. Then leave the room. When your dog grabs the meat, it will pull off the

Right: *If you catch a dog in the act of stealing food, a well-directed squirt of water from a spray can provide just the sort of sharp, unpleasant shock that is needed to discourage the behavior.*

trays, causing a loud crash.

Most dogs will be put off by the noise. Repeat the exercise regularly, with variations and in different rooms, and a dog soon learns not to take food unless it is in his bowl.

Using Muzzles

In extreme cases where a dog constantly takes food (especially in the street or park, where he may pick up dangerous substances), a muzzle may be necessary. Once a dog is accustomed to wearing the muzzle, he can go out anywhere without being able to scavenge.

Above 1: *Food left unattended is an easy target for a dog, especially a young one like this who has not yet been obedience trained.*

Right 2: *Sometimes smearing food with an unpalatable substance proves an effective deterrent, but it's not infallible. Some dogs eat anything!*

Keep the leash quite short for good control.

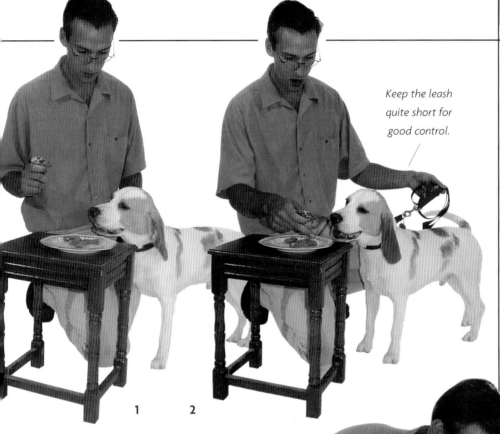

1   **2**

Above 1 and 2: *With the dog held under control by means of a collar and leash, it is possible to work on the "No" command, diverting any lunges toward the plate with a restraining pull on the leash.*

Right 3: *Training discs add an extra deterrent effect. When you spot a dog about to snatch some food, throw the discs on the floor close to him. The clatter of the metal discs sets up an unpleasant association in the dog's mind with the act of stealing the food.*

This interrupts the behavior pattern and eventually, if this is combined with obedience training, he may learn not to eat what he finds. The muzzle can be used in the home for particularly persistent dogs or big, strong dogs that are difficult to manage. Muzzles should not be left on dogs for more than two hours at a time, preferably less.

3

Below : *A spray deterrent collar works by startling a dog that is doing something of which you disapprove. It emits a shrill sound and a burst of vapor with a pungent smell.*

SCAVENGING – RECAP

• **Don't leave food unattended or within the dog's reach.**

• **Work on the "No" command.**

• **Don't offer morsels of food from your plate.**

• **Make stealing an unpleasant experience (use a water pistol, training discs, or "setup" situations with clattering trays).**

• **Dedicated thieves and scavengers may need a muzzle – for short periods only.**

13: Sexual Problems

Very few dogs are genuinely over-sexed. Overtly sexual behavior, such as mounting cushions or people's legs, is not uncommon in puppies and is a natural part of adolescence with its surge of hormones. Mounting another dog can also be an assertion of dominance, and is one of the means by which a pup establishes its position among its littermates.

Most pups will outgrow inappropriate mounting behavior. However, some – most commonly males, but also some bitches – develop this habit to an unacceptable level and continue it into adulthood. Most owners find it embarrassing to own a dog with a sexual fixation on cushions or a favorite cuddly toy. When dogs direct their attention to human arms and legs, this is even more objectionable, and potentially dangerous where children or the elderly are concerned.

Marking Territory

An associated unpleasant habit that some dogs develop is raising a leg on furniture – or even on human legs. Although this may not necessarily be related to sexual behavior, it can be discouraged by using some of the same methods, as outlined below.

Prevention Advice – Water Pistol and Training Discs

One simple deterrent is a water pistol (or a plastic bottle filled with water). As soon as you see your dog start to mount

Above: *This is the moment that many dog owners dread – a visitor has just arrived at the house and your dog decides to relieve its sexual urges on his leg. It is embarrassing when directed at an adult, but potentially dangerous when small children or the elderly are targets.*

a cushion, squirt a jet of water at him, with the command "No." Aim the jet at his face – most dogs' bodies are too well covered with fur for a squirt to have

much effect. If your dog has already been conditioned to the use of training discs, you can use these instead of a water pistol. Repeat the treatment every time the dog indulges in the undesirable behavior, and eventually the verbal command "No" should be enough to stop him in his tracks on its own.

Redirect the Energy

If your dog loves playing with a favorite ball or toy, teach him to fetch it. Reward him with praise each time he brings the ball back and repeat the exercise two or three times daily. Don't overdo it. Keep the sessions short – never continue until he is bored or tired.

When the ball's appearance or the command "Fetch" produces an immediate response from your dog, his training has progressed sufficiently to be of use as a distraction from the undesired activity. Now if you see your dog about to mount somebody or something, call his name in an excited voice and throw the ball for a retrieve. In this way his mind is diverted to the ball game and away from sexual gratification.

Scent and Taste Deterrents

Dogs that mount people's arms or legs can be discouraged by spraying the appropriate body parts with a scent or taste deterrent, like lemon or citronella spray. This is a particularly useful method to protect small children, who are likely to have difficulty controlling a dog by voice. Spray deterrents can also be used

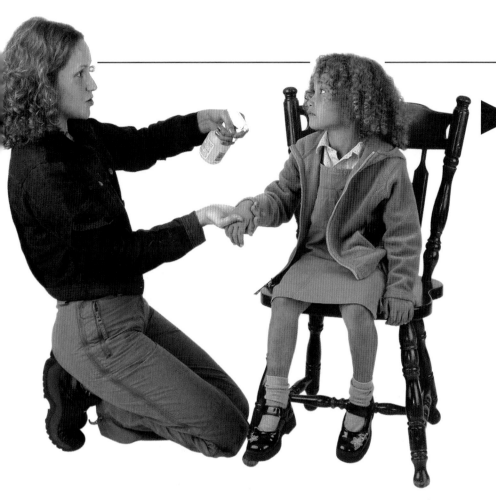

Above: *If you are dealing with a dog that persistently mounts a person's arms or legs, it often helps to spray that person's limbs with a bitter-smelling (but harmless) spray. It's a useful method to use where children are concerned, as they may tend to panic when confronted by an unruly dog.*

to protect objects such as cushions. Re-apply the spray three times a day for a week. The dog will soon learn that his sexual targets offer an unpleasant, rather than a rewarding experience. This method is often very effective.

Obedience Training

Last, but not least, obedience-train your dog. When he is trained to a sufficiently high standard, you can use the sit, down, and stay commands to divert your dog's attention as soon as he starts to mount something inappropriately, rewarding him when he obeys.

Some dogs (especially bouncy, dominant ones) use inappropriate sexual behavior as a means of actively seeking attention. If mounting a cushion results in the owner pouncing, shrieking, or even smacking, it's all attention – which such dogs construe as a reward. In such cases, leaving the room each time the dog starts can result in a cessation of the behavior. So apply your chosen method with this in mind, and stick to the one that works for you.

PREVENTION AND TRAINING RECAP

- **Active deterrent** – a squirt in the face from a water pistol or some training discs thrown on the floor accompanied by the firm command "No."

- **Passive deterrent** – apply deterrent spray to the object.

- **Redirection** – distract the dog by initiating a ball game and/or practice obedience training.

- **Avoidance of reward** – you leave the room.

Above: *Someone tell the dog that this is a cuddly toy, not a mate! Young dogs are prone to act like this as their bodies respond to hormonal urges.*

Sexual Problems

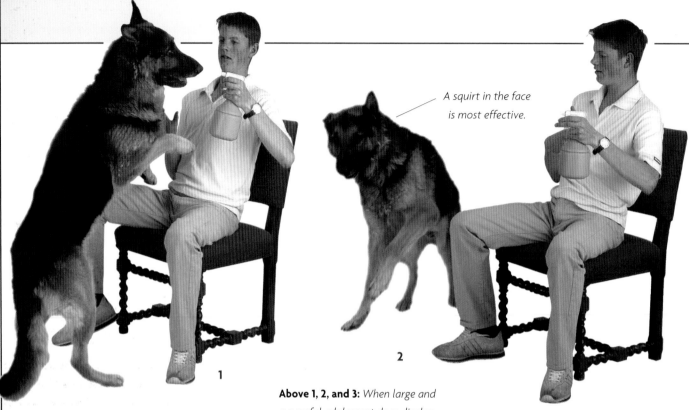

A squirt in the face is most effective.

1

2

Above 1, 2, and 3: *When large and powerful adolescent dogs display hypersexual behavior, they present quite a formidable challenge. The use of a water pistol or spray can be extremely effective in stopping them in their tracks.*

Should I Neuter My Dog?

Many people consider neutering as an option to prevent male dogs from exhibiting undesirable sexual behavior. In serious cases, you should consult your veterinarian regarding neutering, which does in many cases stop or reduce sexual impulses. I am not in favor of chemical castration, as I have seen very poor results from this approach. It's really a hit-and-miss method that carries risks for your dog's psychological and physical well-being.

Castration

Male dogs, like the males of most mammal species, are driven by their instincts and hormones to reproduce with any female in heat (oestrus) in their vicinity. For some reason, it's com-paratively uncommon for owners to neuter male dogs as opposed to spaying bitches. I feel that, provided a dog is not developing any of the problems associated with an entire (unneutered) male, castration is usually unnecessary. It has been argued that if all nonbreeding male dogs were castrated, the amount of dominant aggression displayed by dogs toward people and other dogs would reduce considerably. This is probably so, though much of this type of aggression could be prevented in any case by educating owners on how to socialize young male puppies at the sensitive preadolescent stage.

Prevention of Dominant Aggression

There are circumstances when castrating dogs is recommended. One instance is when a behavior practitioner, in conjunction with a veterinarian, feels that neutering will reduce aggressive or dominant behavior. When the testicles are removed, the amount of the male hormone testosterone in the dog's body is greatly reduced. This consequently reduces competitive and/or related sexually aggressive behavior, though it can take up to six months for the full effects to be noticed. Castrating a dog once it is mature and fully developed rarely works against aggression of this type.

Hypersexuality

Castration may also be advisable for over-sexed dogs. Hypersexual behavior

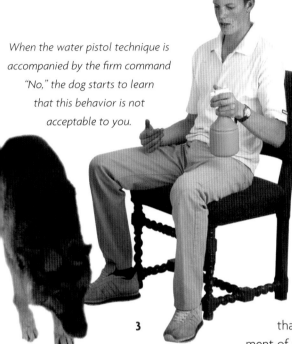

When the water pistol technique is accompanied by the firm command "No," the dog starts to learn that this behavior is not acceptable to you.

3

The effects of neutering are usually not apparent for some time. In my experience, a considerable reduction of sexual behavior usually takes place within four weeks, followed by a further gradual reduction over some months – although this can vary. Castration is not a cure-all for all male bad habits and is often carried out unnecessarily in the hope that it will have an effect, rather than as a result of a rational assessment of the behavioral problem.

The most common question I am asked about castration is whether it will make a dog less masculine and alter his character. My answer to this is yes, his character and behavior will change, otherwise there would be no point to the operation. However, his basic personality will remain more or less the same as it always has been. Probably the greatest change you will see will be the fact that he may not be as investigative or lively in certain situations.

is not uncommon in adolescent male dogs, when it is caused by occasional hormone surges, and will usually settle down with maturity. But when a dog continues into adulthood with an excessive desire to mount anything that moves, this can be a serious nuisance. It may also be accompanied by aggression, especially where children are involved. In such cases it is worth considering castration. Of course, do take advice from your veterinarian, and also from a canine behavior practitioner.

Right: *Castration will often calm oversexed dogs, but seek professional advice.*

► ## CAUSES OF HYPERSEXUALITY

• **Hormonal surges.**

• **Habitual learned behavior.**

• **Sexually driven dominance.**

• **Sometimes redirected behavior caused by boredom/frustration.**

► ## NEUTERING A MALE DOG – PROS AND CONS

• When you buy a puppy, some breeders may request that you do not have it neutered. However, if there is good reason to do so, that should override the breeder's interest.

• Castration has little effect on a dog's aggression if he is already an established fighter with other dogs.

• Castrated dogs are prone to put on weight if their diet isn't carefully watched.

• Neutered dogs may urine-mark territory less often, but castration will not necessarily cure a dog who is in the habit of raising a leg on furniture.

• Castration usually has a calming effect on general behavior.

• Castrated dogs are less likely to roam.

14: House Toilet Training

Most people realize when they acquire a new dog that they will have to invest time in training it. House training comes at the top of the list for obvious reasons, especially where young children are present, and it's critical to establish some rules from day one. Nobody wants to play hopscotch around their rooms while avoiding dog mess!

Dogs usually become house-clean naturally as long as they are given the opportunity to defecate and urinate in the right area. However, we often expect too much too quickly, and that is where problems begin.

Patience is all important. When a puppy messes in the house, it's no use scolding him, smacking him or, even worse, rubbing his nose in the mess. He won't associate the punishment with the "crime" – all he will learn is to be wary of his owner. In fact, repeated punishments, verbal or physical, can make some dogs so stressed that they mess more often than before.

Even if you punish your dog when you catch him in the act, this may only teach him that it is wrong to mess in your presence, since the same deed goes unpunished when you are not there. Alternatively, he may learn that you don't like him messing in one particular room, and respond by selecting a different room or a less conspicuous place – not the desired effect at all. Unfortunately for puppies, teaching owners to "think dog" can be considerably harder than teaching a puppy how to be clean.

The New Puppy

When a puppy enters your home, like a human infant, he has to empty his bladder and bowels frequently, and he has no inborn desire to keep your house clean. When you start teaching him, he still has no idea what it is all about, and his mental and physical capacity to learn, remember, and associate, is limited. By the time he realizes that you are his new pack and the house is his territory, he has often already made many smelly mistakes if you haven't taken the necessary precautions.

Puppies and adult dogs in the wild are naturally clean in their dens – nature's precaution against disease. A wolf cub, for instance, will wobble over to the nearest dung deposit area to leave his calling card. The presence of adult wolves ensures that smell indicators are in place to guide him. In your home, no such natural indications are present – no signposts, just lovely big carpets, linoleum, or floor tiles.

Stage 1 Training

The surest way to teach house training quickly and consistently is to deny the puppy the opportunity to set up smelly "signposts" around the house. Instead of giving the new arrival the run of the house, restrict him initially to a limited area, either using a large playpen or fencing off a set area. If possible, choose a room with a hard, easy-clean floor (no carpets!), and ideally with access to the outside world.

1

Line the whole room with newspapers and put the puppy's pen, with his bed in it, in one corner. While in the pen, he has no choice but to relieve himself on the papers. You can speed matters up by remembering that puppies need to relieve themselves immediately after they wake up and also after each meal. So, if possible, at these times always take your puppy to an outside area for toilet training and wait until he empties his bowels, praising him when he does so. We have now begun a two-area training program. The pup can be placed safely in the pen when you are not around, and roam free outside the pen in the newspaper-covered room when you are present.

puppy. Plastic imitation ones don't have the same fascination as real bone. Don't use any other type of bones, especially chicken bones, as these can splinter and cause internal injury.

This program ensures that the puppy never has the chance to make a mess in the wrong place. He is gradually conditioned to learn that he can defecate on paper, often scented with urine to encourage him, and outside in the yard, where natural smells are in abundance. Eventually he will learn to seek out one of these places when he needs them.

2

Above 1, 2, and 3: *By using newspapers spread on the floor of a specific room when a puppy is introduced to a house, he can become habituated to the idea of relieving himself either on the newspaper or outside in the yard when you let him out. Gradually, the papered area can be reduced and finally moved outside into the yard.*

3

Toys and chews should be made available whenever the puppy is left alone in his pen. I find large raw marrow bones are the most attractive to a

A newspaper-lined toilet area will retain a distinctive smell that helps encourage a puppy to return to it.

Above: *Puppies enter the world with their dog instincts intact, but with no idea of what humans will expect of them. Messes on the carpet are unavoidable.*

▶ TRAINING DIGEST

▶ When a puppy messes in the house, it's no use scolding him, smacking him or, even worse, rubbing his nose in the mess. He won't associate the punishment with the "crime."

Puppies need to relieve themselves after they wake up and after each meal. So, at these times, always take your puppy to an outside area for toilet training and wait until he empties his bowels.

House Toilet Training

Stage 2 Training

When your puppy is about fourteen weeks old (assuming he arrived at six to seven weeks), you can remove the pen or barrier and give him full freedom of the room. Now reduce the newspapers until they cover about half the floor and move the dog's bed to one corner of the room, away from the papers. He should naturally use the reduced paper area on the floor, as that is what he has been conditioned to do in his short life. If he makes a few mistakes in the wrong area, go back to covering the whole floor with papers again for a few more weeks.

Above: Be prepared! Puppies nearly always need to relieve themselves when they wake up and after meals.

After several more weeks gradually move the papers closer to the doorway (if that leads to a yard), and then outside the door (weighted down to stop them from blowing away). Your dog will now look for the papers to relieve itself or have already gained a preference for the yard itself. Most dogs, when given the opportunity, prefer to excrete on soil or concrete areas rather than indoors, where floors often smell of chemical cleaning agents. A dog flap fitted to a door will also encourage the dog to leave the room into the yard if it needs to defecate or urinate.

Remember to praise your pup whenever it defecates or urinates in the right place. A secondary command like "Hurry up" often helps to teach the animal that its action pleases you, and is handy for future use. Many dogs learn through this type of command to toilet on command, which is very handy.

Stage 3 Training

Once a puppy is relieving itself outside the home in an appropriate area – preferably in your own yard so that you can clean the mess up – you can start to open the house up slowly and allow him to investigate the rooms one by one. You may still leave a small area of papers in the original room for emergencies.

Some people ask how they are to form a relationship with a puppy if he is kept in isolation. The answer is that confinement should not equal isolation. Choose a room that you and your family will frequent regularly, and make time to play with the puppy in his special room. You also have visits to the yard and walk

times to bond with your pup. Puppies tend to sleep about eighteen hours a day, so normal contact is available if one makes the effort. As time goes on, the puppy will soon be allowed into more areas in your home.

Indoor Cages

The pen method described previously is useful, especially from a safety and training point. However, for puppies over fourteen weeks or difficult adult dogs that have not successfully learned the paper method, you will have little choice but to use an indoor cage. This should be big enough for your dog to stand and lie down comfortably. This method makes use of the fact that dogs do not like relieving themselves in their own sleeping area. They generally select an area nearby, but not actually where they eat or sleep.

You will need to accustom the dog to the cage first, otherwise he will find confinement stressful and you could

Left: *It is a good idea to praise your puppy when he relieves himself on the newspaper as you want him to do. The reward of your encouragement helps to imprint the behavior that you want to reinforce. Add a command like "Hurry up" for future use.*

have problems with barking and whining. Start by feeding the dog in the cage, with the door open, and encouraging him to take his toys inside. This ensures that his first impression is positive. After a few more days, when he should be comfortable with the cage, try closing the cage door while you are busy around the room. If he whines, ignore him – say nothing and offer no eye contact. The next stage is to leave the dog in the cage with a tasty treat or chew for a short while, building up to half-hour sessions. Repeat this action several times daily. When releasing him from the cage, don't fuss or praise him – we don't want the dog to see getting out of the cage as a rewarding experience, rather than regarding the cage as something normal.

▶ The Cage Solution

When the dog fully accepts half-hour sessions in the cage, begin your toilet-training program within it. If a dog only messes indoors during the night, then use the cage only at night. Remember that puppies cannot last all night without relieving themselves, so make sure the cage is big enough to place newspaper in one half. This should not apply to adult dogs, as they have mature bladder control.

Each time you feed your dog or he wakes up, allow him immediate access to the designated toilet area, either the yard or the newspaper area. At night, or when you are not there, place your dog in the indoor cage. He won't want to soil his sleeping area, so remember when you let him out that he will probably want to relieve himself at once.

In this way your dog will learn to hold himself for set periods of time, and to form a routine of going to his toilet area when he is released and being praised for doing so.

Right: *An indoor cage can be useful in toilet training. Dogs do not like to soil the area in which they sleep, so they will learn to contain themselves until let out, when they can be directed to a chosen toilet area.*

▶ POINTS TO REMEMBER

▶ • When cage or pen training, accustom your dog to the item gradually.

• Feeding the dog his dinner in the cage causes positive associations.

• Take the dog to the toilet area as soon as he has eaten or woken up.

• The dog will need to spend all night in the cage or pen if that is the time he defecates or urinates (puppies can't last through the night, so provide papers for them in a pen).

• Schedule meals so that the dog doesn't need caging straight afterwards.

• Adult dogs should be exercised immediately before being placed in the cage or let into a room and upon release.

• Dried commercial dog foods produce more fecal waste than natural meats.

House Toilet Training

If Separation Anxiety Is the Cause

Separation anxiety can cause house-training problems, especially in adult dogs. Dogs suffering from this often pace the room. They sometimes chew or bark and exhibit other displacement behaviors. This activity and the stress of being separated from their owner can make them defecate and/or urinate in the house.

If your dog is one of this type, you need to consider reducing the amount of attention he receives, including petting and play, by at least half, especially if the dog constantly follows you around or solicits excessive attention. Just before leaving your dog, withdraw all attention to help prepare the dog for your departure. Do the same on your return, taking a "no big deal" approach, and do not respond to your dog's displays of wild excitement. If you can gradually reduce the dog's anxiety during your absence, this will tackle the house-training problem. See Chapter 5 on Separation Anxiety for more detailed guidance on dealing with this problem.

Territory Marking by Male Dogs

Dominant dogs sometimes mark their territory by squirting urine around the house, especially on furniture. This has nothing to do with any need to urinate; it's just an instinctive territorial habit, and the more dominant a dog, the more it may happen. They often do this if new people or other dogs visit their territory

Left: This dog is anticipating that its owner is about to leave the house and is saying, "I don't want to be alone." Separation anxiety can lead to a number of nuisance behaviors including incontinence around the home. You must accustom the dog to periods of solitude by ignoring its attention-seeking strategies.

Ignore his pestering.

Above right:
Dogs respond to the scent of urine that is sprayed around their "patch" by other dogs who want to assert territorial dominance. Dominant dogs sometimes take to spraying items of furniture around the house in the same way.

The dog wants your attention.

(home) or when they themselves visit other people's houses — leaving a calling card is what wild dogs do when roaming around. I've even had several urinate on my leg in the blink of an eye while I was talking to their owners. It's not personal. They are just letting you know that they are important and here. The dog cocks its leg high to leave the scent at general nose level for other canines to smell and take notice.

This is quite a difficult problem to eradicate because, unlike other house-training problems, it is instinctive. Using a small water pistol to squirt your dog in the face as you command "No" each time you catch him may discourage him. However, it will not stop him from carrying out the action in

174

Above: *You will inevitably have to clean up dog mess while house-training your dog. Pooper-scoopers make the job less unpleasant.*

Right: *Puppies must learn the meaning of the command "No," but don't punish them physically when they make a mess in the house. Try to be tolerant until the puppy learns your house rules.*

Puppies are very receptive to careful and sympathetic training in the formative weeks of their lives.

WHAT'S MY DOG'S PROBLEM?

Dogs make a mess indoors for one of the following reasons:

• **House training was not carried out correctly.** Start again from scratch.

• **The dog suffers from separation anxiety.** Tackle the source problem.

• **A dominant male is territory-marking.** Try deterrent sprays on furniture, and consider castration.

USEFUL TIPS

• Use several layers of newspapers on the floor so that the bottom layer stays more or less dry.

• There are some commercial sprays that help direct a puppy to the paper. I find blotting a little of the puppy's own urine on to the paper just as effective.

• Never punish a puppy physically for urinating or defecating – all this achieves is spoiling his temperament.

• It is better to reward a puppy for messing in the right place than to scold it for wrongdoing.

your absence, nor will it remove the cause. Commercial deterrent sprays applied to his favorite sites may help, but you will need to keep spraying three or four times a day for a long time.

Castration appears to have the greatest chance of success because it reduces the need to mark territory. So a visit to your local veterinarian for his or her advice is worth considering.

15: Stopping Your Dog from Pulling

The bane of many people's lives are dogs – especially large ones – that drag them to and fro. A casual observer in any park is likely to see lots of dogs pulling their unwilling owners along. This book is concerned with behavioral problems rather than dog training, but I will refer to some dog training methods here to help with dogs that pull on the leash. Next to not coming when called, heel training is the most common problem presented to a dog trainer or behavior practitioner. Amazingly, ninety-five percent of all dogs brought to me for pulling on the leash have attended a dog training class. And most of them have been awarded a certificate of competence by the club, even though the dogs pull. Figure that one out!

In this chapter I will introduce some training equipment that really does stop dogs from pulling and that is quite simple to use. However, in the long-term, you may need to receive one-on-one training from a professional trainer if you wish to have a dog that infallibly walks along with you without pulling.

▶ The Language of Command

Few owners understand dog language, but even fewer dogs understand English. They do, however, learn to associate different voice tones with different situations, so commands should be delivered in a short, crisp voice. You may choose your own commands if they are short, preferably just a single syllable. Praise must be given in a very soft tone

Right 1, 2, and 3: This is turning into a walk on the wild side. The combination of a big, powerful dog that pulls on the leash can turn a pleasurable activity like a walk in the park into a nightmare. Such a dog is also liable to knock into other pedestrians.

Even on a short leash, the dog is out of control.

1

of voice (whispering is ideal – as we do with babies) for the dog to distinguish commands from praise. Equally, the dog should understand the word "No," and this should be delivered in a very sharp, commanding voice. Do not mumble or forget to use the same command for an exercise. In other words, make sure you know all the commands and are consistent with them before starting training.

▶ Collar and Leash

For control, make sure you have the correct leash and collar. All puppies

should be trained using a fixed collar and a leash about 4 to 6 feet (1.2–2 m) in length. Face collars, choke chains, and slip collars are not for use with puppies.

When trying to control adult dogs, many people buy a choke chain thinking that somehow the dog will learn not to pull because the collar chokes the dog's neck when it does so. This is rarely the case, however, because a dog's natural gait is faster than ours and it cannot make the connection between the choking action of the collar and what you want it to do. I have yet to meet a person who can use a choke chain

Already the owner is being pulled off balance.

2

3

correctly without having a skilled trainer beside them. Don't think of using one on your own.

You may wonder why we have the dog on our left but hold the leash

Below: Be consistent and employ a firm tone of voice when teaching your dog basic commands. Praise in a softer voice so the dog can distinguish between the two.

in our right hand. This simply leaves the left hand as a working tool closest to the dog. The right hand controls the leash. Although I teach my dogs to walk on my left and at my heel, it's not essential that all dogs walk in this position. In my view it helps a dog to know on which side it is consistently walked, but whether it is two feet ahead of you or by your side is only important if you feel it is. That's why some dogs walked on a long leash that move slightly ahead of you do not seem inclined to pull any further. Of course in town this may not be compatible with busy pedestrian traffic.

Begin your heel training in a yard, a quiet part of the house, or any other quiet place with no distractions where you are unlikely to be disturbed. Continue to practice there for the first few weeks, until you have reached a standard whereby the dog responds to your "Heel and Sit" commands.

TRAINING DIGEST

▶ **All puppies should be trained using a fixed collar and a leash about 4 to 6 feet (1.2–2 m) in length.**

I have yet to meet a person who can use a choke chain correctly without having a skilled trainer beside them. Don't think of using one on your own.

It helps a dog to know on which side it is consistently walked, but whether it is two feet ahead of you or by your side is only important if you feel it is.

Below: When heel training, it helps if your dog gets used to walking consistently on one side of you.

Stopping Your Dog from Pulling

Puppies and Less Determined Pullers

When one trains a puppy on a leash and fixed collar (not a chain or slip collar), it quickly becomes clear that these little creatures are incredibly malleable and can learn to walk next to you in a matter of weeks providing there is enough motivation in your handling. This chapter is primarily concerned with adult or young adult dogs that already pull, but I will give some basic training information for puppies here because that's the ideal time to train a dog.

A puppy has no idea of what you want or why it is that walking on a leash and collar should not involve pulling. However, once a puppy has been habituated to the collar and leash in the home, we can begin heelwork. I always use a cue link in all dog training, which means that I motivate the dog by some action that gives me its attention and then I give it a corresponding reward. In that way, pleasure is imparted to the puppy.

Walking to Heel

Holding a treat and/or a squeaky toy – puppies are easily distracted by our actions – I walk off, commanding "Heel." When the puppy surges ahead of me, I turn to the right, simultaneously bending down with an outstretched left hand that is either holding a squeaking toy or proffering a (very tiny) tasty treat. As the puppy takes a cue and follows my hand, I command "Heel" and give the treat or let the puppy mouth the toy. After repeating this action ten or more times,

I throw the toy for the puppy, making a little game, and finish the exercise. I begin a new lesson later. The puppy has now begun to pay attention, is learning the command "Heel," and realizes that being beside me brings fun and rewards.

The next stage is to practice the heel exercises in different training locations, i.e., the street, park, and other public places. (Note: when near a road or on a public pavement, all exercises must be carried out on a leash – **no exceptions**). At first the dog or puppy will be distracted; this is normal, so now you have to work harder. The dog may find the distractions more interesting than you, which is why this is often the time when a number of owners give up, because their dog appears to be regressing.

When walking to heel down a street, it is natural for your dog to display curiosity toward other dogs when they pass by. Don't stop – just carry on walking, praising your dog to bring it back to your side. At this point you can offer a treat or a favorite toy as a greater distraction to regain the dog's attention. Equally, you can snap-check the leash on an adult dog if he stubbornly pulls toward them. Sometimes I start to run for about 15 feet (5 m) and most dogs find this exciting, wanting to follow me rather than pulling toward the other dog.

1

Stay in Control

Your dog must not be allowed to think that every time it sees another dog in the street or park, it can stop listening to you. Obviously, you might want your dog to play and socialize with other dogs as and when you choose. This is perfectly acceptable, as long as your dog is under your control at all times.

I use the same training methods for adult dogs but add another component. If the dog really surges ahead, I stop in

178

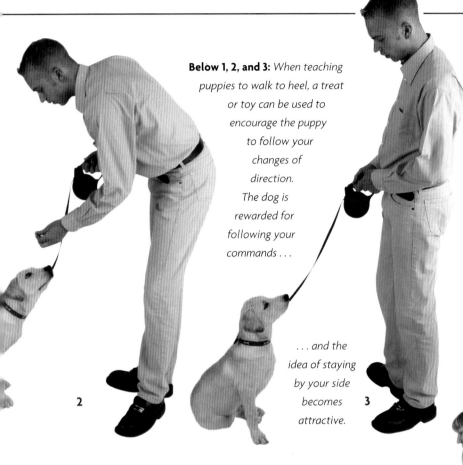

Below 1, 2, and 3: *When teaching puppies to walk to heel, a treat or toy can be used to encourage the puppy to follow your changes of direction. The dog is rewarded for following your commands . . .*

2

3

. . . and the idea of staying by your side becomes attractive.

Above: *To help train a puppy to walk to heel, you can use the lure of a favorite squeaky toy to keep the dog following your hand while walking alongside you.*

HEEL TRAINING – RECAP

- • "Heel" means a change of direction.

- • Food and/or a toy presented to the dog connects the command to a reward.

- • Throwing the toy adds another reward, as does a quick, fun game at the end of the session.

my tracks, command the dog to sit, and don't move again until it calms down and has obeyed the "sit" command. Patience is required, perhaps over many weeks of training. If your dog lags behind you, under no circumstances pull it along, just use praise to encourage it back to your side.

Below: *The appearance of another dog can cause your dog to strain at the leash in its eagerness to say hello. Don't let this habit become established. A snap-check on the leash can be used with adult dogs to draw their attention back to you.*

Stopping Your Dog from Pulling

Using Face Collars with Determined Pullers

(for determined and dominant dogs only)
Face collars fit over the dog's muzzle. They work well on most (but not all) dogs, and I have found that determined or difficult dogs do settle down and learn not to pull.

Unfortunately, as they are only made in about six sizes and dogs' faces vary in size greatly, they can sometimes rub, causing some minor irritation to the surface of the skin. Fitted properly, they are without a doubt the best way to stop a skilled puller from stretching your arms. Once adopted, most dogs walk alongside you and their face collar remains loose. However carefully they are introduced, face collars do cause some stress to a dog – that's a fact. The best you can do is to make the experience less stressful by establishing good associations with the wearing of

the collar, e.g., with food treats (see below).

How to Fit a Face Collar onto a Dog

It's very important to introduce the face collar to your dog slowly and to let the dog develop good associations with wearing it. Most people rush the introduction and then become upset at their dog's stressed reaction to it. Avoid this by following my advice.

Firstly, get your dog to sit with a leash and collar on. Have several juicy treats at hand. Then place the face collar on your dog and reward him with a treat. Leave the face collar on your dog for a few minutes; give a food reward intermittently. Your dog should now associate having the face collar fitted with receiving a reward. This needs to be repeated three times daily for

Left: *A face collar should only be used with a strong and determined adult puller – they are not suitable for puppies and sensitive dogs. When used properly, they can achieve excellent results.*

DOG TRAINING AND PSYCHOLOGY TIPS

1. Before you start to train your dog, make sure you fully understand the exercise you are about to teach. Do not attempt any exercise if you are in doubt.

2. The motivation for your dog to learn is praise, delivered in a pleasant tone of voice. Very few puppies need physical correction – just patience and repetitive training with an enjoyable play period allowed at the end.

3. You can be sure that if the dog appears to be making errors, the fault lies with the trainer who is not communicating clearly enough with the animal.

4. When training, the dog may begin to lose interest, or apparently understand and preempt your commands. Get him to perform an exercise he likes, praise him, finish training, and play a short game. Then try again later in the day.

5. Remember that different breeds, bred with different working instincts, progress at different rates in training.

6. Some dogs are compulsive sniffers. In this case don't walk near walls or bushes that harbor smells. Try and walk in the center of the pavement. This makes training easier.

Above: *An anti-pulling harness uses straps under the dog's front legs that exert pressure if it pulls.*

about ten minutes each time over a period of three days. Next, attach the leash to the face collar and walk your dog a short distance in the house or yard; reward your dog at short intervals. If your dog panics or attempts to rub his head on the floor (which is normal), distract him with the food and use your leash to make him sit.

Most dogs resent the face collar at first but quickly adapt as they come to associate it with food rewards and walks. Once you can walk your dog without adverse reaction around the house or yard, you're ready for normal outdoor use. Do persevere and don't give up or feel sorry for your dog, otherwise you'll be back to square one.

▶ Using a Body Harness

(for determined and dominant dogs only)
There are also harnesses to help stop dogs from pulling. This is a device that uses a thin cord that passes under the dog's front legs (armpits). When the dog surges ahead, the cords pull tight on the dog's "armpits," causing discomfort.

When the dog stops pulling, there is no discomfort. The dog dictates the comfort measure it experiences and in this way many dogs quickly learn to stop pulling. Like the face collar, it is a simple, straightforward training aid that works well.

Left and right: *A dog needs to become accustomed to wearing a face collar – food rewards are useful during the introductory period.*

▶ RECAP

▶ • With puppies and less determined adult dogs, practice heel training using rewards to reinforce good behavior.

• Determined and strong adult dogs can be trained by the intelligent use of face collars or body harnesses.

▶16: Introducing a New Dog into the Family

Introducing a new dog into the family is usually a smooth operation with few major incidents. However, the ease with which a new dog settles in depends on several factors. Any dogs living with you – even if it's only one – view themselves as being in a pack with a set hierarchy. So any new-comer will be regarded as com-petition and will be watched and sized up carefully. Some dogs will just consider a newcomer a nui-sance while others may become aggressive and try to intimidate the per-ceived threat. How your dog reacts depends on its dominance levels and/or relationship with you.

To begin, we need to understand what goes through your dog's mind and through the mind of the new arrival. If the new dog is a puppy, this will present different problems and will require an alternative introduction method. The sex of any resident dogs and of the new arrival (excluding puppies) will also play a significant role in how smoothly the first few days go.

▶ A New Puppy

I always purchase an indoor pen and sometimes a cage for a new puppy. This allows the puppy freedom while the resident dog can enjoy some peace. Also, like a child's playpen, it is a place where a new puppy can be placed out of harm's way when the household is very busy.

When the puppy arrives, the resident dog will be most inquisitive or even a

Above: *Jealousies can arise when a resident dog has to share its home with a newcomer. The status quo of the pack hierarchy is being challenged.*

little aggressive to the newcomer depending on how well socialized the resident dog is. Place the puppy in the pen and allow the resident dog into the room so they can sniff one another through the bars and become ac-quainted. I never leave a puppy alone with a resident dog for the first three weeks and after that only if I am sure they get along well. Resident dogs should always be able to get away from a puppy when they want to – this alone will prevent most confrontations in the early stages of introduction. If you do experience aggression from the res-ident dog, read the section on inter-pack aggression (Chapter 11) to understand the dynamics of the situation more clearly.

A new puppy will slowly adjust to its new environment; it will view any

resident dog as a playmate and friend whether this is appreciated or not. Adult dogs seem to know instinctively that pups are trouble and tend to growl when approached or jumped upon, especially if this playfulness is accom-panied by sharp teeth. The resident dog may growl as a warning to the puppy if it's being impudent, and even the odd bite should be allowed because it is given more as a warning than an act of aggression. If possible, leave the dogs to sort themselves out without your inter-ference. After about a week or so the new puppy will generally be tolerated and in time it may even become liked.

The puppy will want to play with the resident dog and will soon become attached to it and learn from it. So if your resident dog has any bad habits,

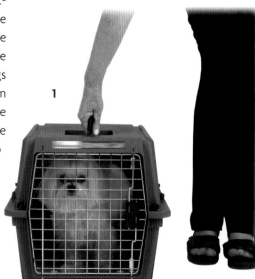

1

like being aggressive to other dogs or jumping up on people, try to prevent the pup from copying these from the beginning. If possible, gently obedience-train the puppy from six weeks of age keeping it away from the older dog during lessons; also walk the puppy on its own once or twice a week and concentrate on the puppy's obedience.

Above: *He looks adorable to us, but a resident dog will view him quite differently. In general, you should try to allow the two to establish their respective pack positions without undue interference.*

Maintain Pack Position

A common problem when a second or third dog arrives is that owners lose control when the puppy becomes too attached to the resident dog and insufficiently mindful of you. You must keep control. Though it's necessary for the

Below 1, 2, and 3: *When any new dog is introduced to a household, it is bound to be inquisitive and want to investigate its surroundings. You should allow this, but also be aware that a resident dog will need its own space.*

dogs to develop a healthy relationship, it should not be at the expense of your being accepted as pack leader.

Enroll in puppy socialization classes when possible. Because of vaccination requirements, you won't be able to take your dog when it is very young but you can use this time to read about training and perhaps visit the different clubs in your area to watch and learn. Then when you do bring your puppy, you'll already be acquainted with other members' dogs and you'll have judged which is the best club for you and your dog.

TRAINING DIGEST

Any dogs living with you – even if it's only one – view themselves as being in a pack with a set hierarchy. So any newcomer will be regarded as competition and will be watched carefully.

I never leave a puppy alone with a resident dog for the first three weeks and after that only if I am sure they get along well.

The resident dog may growl as a warning to the puppy if it's being impudent, and even the odd bite should be allowed because it is given more as a warning than an act of aggression.

You must keep control. Though it's necessary for the dogs to develop a healthy relationship, it should not be at the expense of your being accepted as pack leader.

2

3

Introducing a New Dog into the Family

Below 1: *It is sensible to use an indoor training cage when introducing a puppy to a dog.*

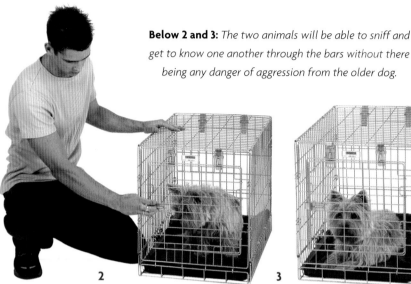

Below 2 and 3: *The two animals will be able to sniff and get to know one another through the bars without there being any danger of aggression from the older dog.*

1

2

3

Do's and Don'ts with a New Puppy

At the beginning **don't** leave the new puppy unattended with the resident dog (unless the puppy is safely out of harm's way in an indoor training cage).

Do ensure the resident dog has somewhere to escape to away from the puppy if it so chooses.

Do consider buying an indoor pen or cage for a new puppy, especially if it shows signs of over-boisterousness; the cage also allows for short periods of peace and helps in toilet training.

If the adult dog reprimands the puppy, **don't** intervene unless the adult dog will not let go or continues biting as opposed to administering a snap, a single bite, or a warning growl. They will sort themselves out.

Don't pay too much attention to the puppy at the expense of the resident dog. When the two approach you for greeting, always show preference for the resident dog first (not equal affection) – otherwise jealousies may occur.

If the breeds are of very different sizes, for example the resident is a Yorkie and the new dog is a Labrador puppy, **do** try to avoid bullying by the puppy. Use obedience control if the smaller resident dog cannot defend itself.

Do feed the dogs separately for the first weeks and then, if the resident dog doesn't seem to mind, slowly bring their bowls nearer while encouraging good manners.

Don't allow the puppy or adult dog to gobble up all the food. The resident dog has the right to growl or bite the puppy if it tries to take its food. Sometimes it will learn from this warning; sometimes it will not.

If the children wish to play with the puppy – as they normally do – **do** make sure it's done in another part of the house or yard to prevent jealousies. This is especially important in the first few weeks. Remember to tell the children to show more affection to the resident dog when both dogs are present.

Introducing Adults of the Opposite Sex

(Two handlers are required during socialization)

Warning: If a fight breaks out when the new dog and the resident dog meet for the first time (this is especially likely if it occurs on one or the other's home territory), this can be a very serious setback to future harmony. First impressions are important to dogs, so avoid this circumstance if possible.

If you haven't chosen the new dog yet, do take time to select a dog that is different from your resident dog in sex, temperament, and size. If you choose dogs that are similar in terms

of temperament and strength, you could be creating trouble in the future. If you introduce dogs of the opposite sex to each other on neutral territory this makes life a lot easier – though some dogs will not even entertain a new friend on these terms. Have the dogs on leashes and try to introduce them on a walk. If this goes well, release them; if they play, that's a good sign.

Below: *Feeding time can be the occasion for displays of aggression if one dog tries to muscle in on the other's bowl. Feed dogs separately until you have seen that they are getting along and will tolerate one another's presence.*

Getting Acquainted

If there is no obvious aggression, the next step is to allow both dogs to meet in your yard and eventually in the home. One dog may be bodily dominant and one may be submissive; don't be distressed if one dog appears to dominate the other – it's their way of sorting out who's boss.

Right: *Always greet a resident dog first and show it preference while it remains at the top of the dogs' pack hierarchy.*

If either dog displays aggression (by biting or attacking), then on their next meeting they should be kept on leashes and both dogs should be given a food reward as they come into sight of each other. This should build up a good association with meeting. Repeat such meetings and food rewards until a good rapport is established.

Don't play any ball games or games that involve competition between the dogs; this could create friction and cause possessive or dominant aggression. When the dogs have fully accepted one another, normal chase and retrieve games can be introduced if no real problems are encountered. As with puppies, always show the resident dog preferential treatment when both dogs approach you for praise or greeting – don't think you can treat them equally. Also bear in mind that the new dog may eventually become the dominant dog and preferential treatment will then have to be given to it whether you like it or not. The dogs should be fed separately until you have established their compatibility and tolerance of one another during feeding.

▶ TRAINING DIGEST

▶ Take time to select a dog that is different from your resident dog in sex, temperament, and size.

▶ Always show the resident dog preferential treatment when both dogs approach you for praise or greeting – don't think you can treat them equally.

Children shouldn't dote on a puppy at the expense of the resident dog.

Introducing a New Dog into the Family

Introducing Adults of the Same Sex

If the adult dogs are of the same sex, they must be socialized before they start to live together unless you have a very submissive resident or new arrival. Do this as described in the previous section. There is definitely more chance of fighting for pack position and rivalry between dogs of the same sex, and when it happens the fights can be terrible.

Don't leave any new adults alone night or day in case of fighting. If the dogs are going to get along happily, then after an initial week or two of mutual appraisal they will begin to relate and play with one another or show affection. They may just ignore one another, but that's quite unusual. The governing factors are how dominant the dogs are by temperament and how you treat the dogs during the initial weeks of acclimatization. It is a hit-and-miss affair with dogs of the same sex, just like humans.

If the resident or new dog seems over-protective of toys and bones, remove them from the home. If the new dog is insecure and needs extra reassurance, then make sure that you have periods alone with it at first. This stops the resident dog from becoming jealous of it; out of sight, out of mind.

Don't create too much excitement when it's time for a walk or when visitors arrive; any sudden excitement can trigger excitement in the dogs, causing one to snap at the other. These are potentially explosive trigger points. It can also cause the dogs to try to dominate the situation by getting the first greeting from the visitor. Be watchful for any strange behavior like staring at each other or constant avoidance of one another. Even after many weeks the occasional growl, lack of play between the dogs, or one dog seeming to be constantly fearful can be signs that things are not working.

In Conclusion

Only dogs can decide whether they like each other, regardless of what we may feel. But we can help to prepare the best environment for that to happen. Don't force two dogs together

Above: *Any new arrival in the home is likely to be viewed with some suspicion by a resident dog, particularly if it is of the same sex and evenly matched in size. You can't force the issue – the dogs will decide for themselves if they are compatible.*

This play bow is a non-threatening posture.

Above: *Be careful when introducing dogs of the same sex – apparently playful behavior can change, and violent fights may break out between them quite suddenly.*

Tug-of-war games can turn into assertions of dominance.

who are obviously incompatible. Happily, ninety percent of adult dogs and puppies do eventually sort out their position and status within the family pack and learn to live together with little fuss or trouble.

INTRODUCING ADULT DOGS – RECAP

- **Try to choose a dog different in size, sex, and temperament from the resident dog.**

- **Initially introduce the dogs to one another on leashes on neutral territory.**

- **Use rewards to help develop a good association in the dogs' minds with meeting one another.**

- **Avoid competitive games.**

- **Show the resident dog preferential treatment at first when the two dogs are together, but be prepared to change if the pack order changes.**

Above: *It may take some time for dogs to become accustomed to one another, but eventually most dogs will settle down and happily accept one another's company. Many even become close friends.*

Above: *Competitive games that encourage the dogs to pit themselves against one another should be avoided. It is also advisable to choose dogs that are dissimilar in size, sex, and temperament when you decide to introduce a new dog to a resident dog that is already part of the household.*

17: Phobias and Fears

A phobia is an abnormal and irrational fear of something. Dogs can suffer from phobias just like people and, like people, they need help to overcome them. Of course, humans who want to tackle a phobia can discuss the irrationality of their fears with a therapist. Dogs can't, but communication on some level is essential.

Phobic animals are among the most difficult cases presented to a behavior practitioner. Essentially, the remedial approach focuses on creating a situation in which the animal's desire to obtain a reward outweighs its fear.

1, 2, 3, and 4: These are some of the physical signs of a phobic reaction. A dog may look fearful (1), have bulging eyes (2), start shaking (3), or hide and cower (4) in an attempt to get away from the cause of the fear.

What Causes Phobias?

Some dogs simply inherit a predisposition to fearfulness. Fears that are apparent at a very young age, prior to twelve weeks, may well have been inherited, unless there has been a very obvious bad experience during that early period. Such inborn fears are almost impossible to cure, which is why gundog trainers usually give up on pups that are "gun-shy" (sound-phobic of gunfire without apparent cause).

However, in my experience most phobias are caused by a traumatic experience. In some cases, this can be so minor that the owner was unaware of it. For example, the seeds of a full-blown phobia might be sown when a dog is alarmed by the owner casually turning on a food mixer or shaking out a plastic bag. In other cases, the original frightening experience can be identified – a crack of thunder, a fireworks display, low-flying aircraft, or simply a black plastic bag blowing down the street.

Prevention by Socialization

The best safeguard against the development of phobias is socialization for puppies between six and twelve weeks. It is at this age that your dog needs to be introduced to a wide range of environmental and social experiences to enable him to develop into a well-adjusted adult. However, it is also at this age that puppies are most acutely susceptible to developing fears. So it's vital at this stage to think about this

Loud Noises

Many dogs are frightened of sudden loud bangs – fireworks, thunder, gunshots, etc. On a leash, they may become hysterical with fear; off leash, they may bolt. The fear may even extend to apprehension of being in the area where the sound was first heard. Surprisingly, even dogs that have accepted loud noises for years may develop noise phobia later in life. Certain breeds also appear to inherit a predisposition to this type of phobia.

Overcoming the Fear

First of all, make a clean start. Don't force your dog back to the area that he already associates with the frightening noise. Once the association is fixed in the dog's mind, it is almost impossible to break. I call this location fear.

Introduce a new regimen by buying pre-recorded sounds of thunder and loud bangs for a desensitization program. Using a small tape recorder, play one of the sounds at a level (very low) that does not cause panic in the dog. It may cause some fear, but a low-key reaction is fine. Whenever you do this, at the same time provide a positive distraction from the fear-sound being played. For example:

- Offer food rewards in the form of favorite treats. (Make sure the dog is very hungry beforehand.)
- Start an exciting game with a toy.

bewildering new world from a dog's point of view. For example, if you walk behind a parked car with the engine running, you might be startled when exhaust fumes hit your legs. Now imagine being a dog in this situation. His head is at exhaust height, so the fumes will blast straight into his face. This is much more frightening, and of course the dog cannot understand what has happened as we can. Most dogs, like people, will adjust and shrug it off. Others, quite understandably, may develop a phobia related to the back of cars.

The Wild Animal in a Dog

Wild dogs and wolves can deal with frightening experiences by running away. Their territory is vast, and any threat (real or perceived) can be left miles behind. Domestic dogs have the same built-in reaction to frightening experiences, but often cannot deal with fear in the way their instincts tell them to. We constrain them with doors, walls, fences, roadways, and leashes. Denied the flight option, puppies need to develop the confidence to cope with an unnatural environment.

TYPICAL SIGNS OF PHOBIA

- **Leaping into owner's arms**
  - **Hiding**
  - **Shaking**
  - **Whimpering**
  - **Urination and defecation**
  - **Bulging eyes**
  - **Salivating**
  - **Panting**
  - **Bolting**
  - **Growling**

4

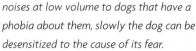

Above: *By playing tape recordings of loud noises at low volume to dogs that have a phobia about them, slowly the dog can be desensitized to the cause of its fear.*

Phobias and Fears

Ignore any negative behavioral response, i.e., if the dog shows fear, don't reassure or pet him but demonstrate by your own behavior that nothing frightening is happening.

If you are carrying out this exercise outdoors, use an extending leash to ensure that your dog cannot bolt. If you can persuade a friend to help, one of you can walk the dog (on an extending leash) while the other walks a parallel route some 20 yards (18 m) away, playing the tape recording – at a very low level to begin with. Over time, decrease the distance and/or increase the volume gradually. It may take many months and

Left: You should avoid petting a dog that shows signs of phobia – act as if there is nothing to worry about.

dozens of practice sessions, but that is the only way to progress.

If there is any particular game or situation that really excites your dog, use that as a distraction to the recorded sound and see which wins the day. For example, you can offer fanatical retrievers a choice between playing a retrieve game or giving in to the fear, the treat being heightened by reserving the ball or other retrieve toy for desensitization sessions only. I have found that most will overcome their fears and go for the ball, providing the audio sounds remain moderate in level.

Household Noises

Some dogs develop phobias about certain household noises, such as wine corks popping or even sheets of kitchen foil rustling. In such cases, try combining the particular sound with your dog's mealtime. While you prepare the food, start making the problem noise – as quietly as you can. Then quickly get a helper to place your dog's food on the floor well away from the noise area, maybe in the next room.

The dog now has a choice to make: panic or eat. At first he may be hesitant, but if he goes for the food, however cautiously, you are on the way to success. If he ignores the food and flees, take up the food bowl and try again later in the day or even next day, when hunger will be on your side. (This method won't work if you feed treats at other times – food must be linked only with the key noise.)

Tranquilizers

Tranquilizers can be used for one-time alarms like fireworks at night, but please first seek your veterinarian's advice. Such drugs should only be used on a temporary basis and not permanently or over long periods.

Do what you can to calm the dog without adding to his panic. If he needs to seek shelter in a dark room, let him have it. If he wants to lean against your leg or follow you from room to room, accept this. But don't comfort him, either verbally or by petting him, because that will only confirm his sense that there is something to be scared of. A matter-of-fact, no-nonsense attitude on your part gives him much more real reassurance.

Taping the Trouble

If your dog is afraid of a specific noise – a vacuum cleaner, motorcycle, etc. – a tape recorder can again help. Record the noise in question. Pick a time when there is a pleasant distraction for your dog, like a fun game or a meal, and play back the noise at a very low volume for ten minutes. Repeat this exercise three times a day for ten weeks. When your dog is comfortable with the sound, raise the volume slightly, gradually working toward the normal level that the dog would encounter in reality. This method has a good success record.

Below 1 and 2: Food can also be used as a way of encouraging a dog to accept the presence of an object that normally would induce an attack of panic. Gradually reduce the distance between the two as the dog is eating. It is likely to be a slow process, but over time the dog should learn that the object does not pose a real threat.

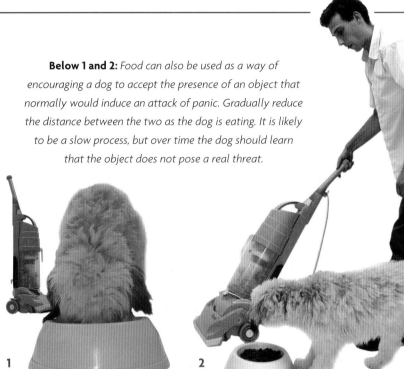

1

2

▶ BEATING FEAR REACTIONS – RECAP

- • Use tape recordings initially at a very low level and/or at a good distance from the dog.

- • Don't reward a fear reaction by offering comfort.

- • Use an extending leash to stop the dog from bolting.

- • Provide positive distractions – food or play.

▶ HELPFUL TIPS

- • Never force a frightened dog to go near to the source of its fear.

- • Don't bend down and cuddle a frightened dog – this only makes matters worse.

- • Ignoring the dog's fear demonstrates that you know there is nothing to worry about.

- • If the dog is scared of something you can easily avoid, avoid it!

- • Long-term use of tranquilizers is not a solution.

- • Some dogs are reassured by the company of other, more confident dogs. Try borrowing a calm dog from a friend.

- • Always ensure that your dog has a strong leash and secure collar so that if panic sets in, he cannot bolt.

Fear of Objects

If your dog fears specific objects, such as cars, vacuum cleaners, animals, children, or people in general, get him to confront these fears at a distance he can tolerate. When he remains calm, reward him on the spot with a treat or a portion of his daily dinner. Gradually reduce the distance and continue to reward your dog with treats. It also helps to try to vary the circumstances, as this can help to build up a pleasant association with the problem.

Right: If your dog develops a phobia about a household noise, you can try preparing its food at the same time the noise is being produced. Often the dog will perk up at the thought of food and will tuck into its bowl rather than fleeing the room in fright.

Slow introduction many times a week over a long period of time has the best chance of success. Do not force your dog, shout at him, or threaten him at any time if he becomes frightened. Equally, never praise or reward him while he is displaying signs of fear, but only when he relaxes.

18: Car Sickness

Some dogs become car sick in the same way that people do. They feel queasy and may even throw up. Dogs can also drool profusely and may appear soaking wet at the end of a short trip because of salivation caused by the journey. Some dogs learn to anticipate a car journey, reacting to cues like the car keys being taken out by the owner, or the car doors being opened. These dogs may start to drool prodigiously even before they have been put in the vehicle. Other dogs can shake with fear – these are all symptoms of car sickness in its various forms.

Causes

Most dogs love traveling by car because they like the proximity of people that they experience in a car and they know that often they are going somewhere exciting, like a park. However, some dogs find the experience upsetting. This is caused by a

Above and right: Try to accustom a dog to car travel so that it comes to associate it with fun activities, like walks in the park. Then the jangle of your car keys will be greeted with eager anticipation.

combination of the disconcerting motion, and the lurching of the car under braking and subsequent acceleration. The usual symptoms of car sickness are excessive drooling, a dull facial appearance and, in more serious cases, actual vomiting.

Prevention Advice

From the start, accustom your dog to car travel. This can take place as early as six weeks when the chances of forming positive associations with the car are highest. When the puppy has an empty stomach, take it for short trips lasting no longer than five minutes. If these trips are frequent, they will quickly create a positive attitude and your dog will associate car travel with the rewards of attention, companionship and – when it is old enough – shopping and walks in the park. These end rewards are what make dogs love the car.

For puppies and older dogs who have already reacted badly to car journeys, we need a strategy to make car travel more attractive. Try this plan of action, which can be modified according to your circumstances.

Week 1: During this week don't take your dog for a ride in the car. Cover the seat or, in a station wagon, the floor with an old blanket

Below and right: The nausea that dogs experience in a car may be caused by motion sickness. In such cases it can help to secure the dog to a seat belt with a seat harness like this (below). Also, periods spent in a stationary car (right) help a dog lose its anticipatory fear of getting into the vehicle.

for security and warmth. Begin feeding your dog at least two meals a day in the car. At first you may sit alongside the dog and then after a few days, if all is well, close the door with the dog inside for a few minutes. For the first few meals allow your dog to jump in and out when finished. The food, if the dog is hungry, should motivate it to investigate the car. After that, shut your dog in the car for five minutes at each mealtime, making sure you leave the windows ajar for ventilation. When you let him out, make no fuss; behave as if it's no great feat but a part of his routine. If the dog does not drool or show discomfort, you are ready for stage two.

result is achieved. This system works really well as long you don't try to rush the training – patience really is required.

Further Tips

- If practical, buy a seat harness that attaches to a seat belt. You can use this to strap your dog in the rear seat and this sometimes helps to reduce the rocking motion that can cause nausea.
- Avoid journeys in heavy traffic, as endless stopping and starting only serves to exacerbate the problem.
- During the daytime occasionally put your dog in the car for ten minutes or so. Then simply let your dog out of the car without any fuss. In this way your dog won't always anticipate a car journey and this should reduce its anticipatory sickness.
- Don't take your dog on long journeys until it can consistently manage short ones.
- If your dog is extremely frightened of travel, travel sickness pills may help, but in the long-term they will not change the negative feelings that the dog associates with the car. Consult your veterinarian for advice.

Week 2: Continue as with week 1 but now introduce five-minute drives at least twice daily after the dog has finished eating. Five minutes is not long enough for most dogs to start feeling sick. When the dog has reached a stage where it no longer seems uncomfortable or apprehensive about being in the car, we are ready for week 3.

Week 3: Take your dog by car to the park each day, providing the journey isn't more than fifteen minutes from your home. Exercise him and then return home. You can place chews or treats in the car for him on the journey. Give no treats of food at any other time of the day.

By lengthening journey times you can make further progress until the desired

19: Digging Up the Yard

As far as dogs are concerned, digging is a perfectly normal activity. Perhaps they have found an interesting smell, or they want to bury a bone for a rainy day. On hot days they may be trying to find cooler soil to lie on. For some dogs it's an outlet to relieve boredom or anxiety, while for many it's just an enjoyable activity. Although it often appears destructive and pointless to us, it's as natural to a dog as yawning is to its owner.

Prevention Advice

If the digging is a symptom of boredom or anxiety, then the dog is possibly being left alone for too long and the digging is a type of relief mechanism for the dog. Make sure that your dog is receiving adequate exercise and mental stimulation. Possibly giving your dog more attention by playing games with him will be all that's needed to make him content and stop him from digging.

If your dog digs solely in one place or digs up specific shrubs, place a large stone slab in the hole and cover it with a few inches of soil or turf. Alternatively, place slabs on the surface around the base of the shrub. This takes the fun out of digging for all but the keenest excavator.

If you're experiencing digging for the first time with a new puppy or adult dog, the simplest solution may be to fence off the part of the yard you wish to protect. Another possibility is an outdoor kennel and pen. This will keep a puppy out of mischief until he matures and provides a permanent solution for the persistent adult digger.

Mind Games

I teach all puppies to enjoy playing with hollow rubber food toys. These are durable, chewable playthings that can be stuffed with natural sticky foods, which makes the process of excavating the food from the toy hard work for the dog. I let my puppies play in this way every day using a part of their daily food ration as I describe in the section dealing with Separation Anxiety.

The puppies devote great amounts of time and energy to getting the food out and they love it. It also takes their minds off the thought of eating feces.

Another simple solution is to knock a stake into the ground. A 6 ft (2 m) line or chain can then be attached to the dog and secured to the stake, allowing the dog freedom to move around but keeping it from destroying precious plants. Make sure a kennel is nearby if the dog wants to take refuge, and keep periods of restriction to not longer than one hour. Keep an eye on the animal in hot sun and make sure that water is always freely available.

Training Discs

Direct action to stop digging tends to be difficult to enforce, as it is often hard to catch the dog at the moment when it is committing the offense. However, on occasions it can work. Teach your dog indoors to associate the sound of training discs with your commands. When your dog is fully conditioned to respond to the sound that the discs make when shaken in your hand, this reaction can be transposed outdoors. When you see your dog about to dig, rattle the discs. Most dogs stop immediately when they hear the sound,

1

2

1 and 2: *Dogs are no respecters of horticulture – garden flowers, vegetables, even pots and containers can fall victim to a dog that has decided to dig. The simplest solution is either to restrict the dog's movements or to use deterrents.*

3

3: *Spraying a bitter-smelling spray around the base of a plant usually deters a dog from digging it up. Remember to reapply the spray after rain.*

provided the early conditioning has been taught properly.

Another method is to allow your dog into the yard when you are present. Keep the training discs or a large bunch of old keys in your pocket. If you see your dog digging, throw the keys just behind him and command "No" simultaneously. This will distract your dog from digging; when he looks up, call him to you in a kind voice and praise him when he comes. It's important to carry out this method without the dog seeing your action. In this way he may come to associate the command "No" and the clattering noise

with digging, and this will discourage the behavior.

▷ Scent Deterrents

Many dogs that chew newly planted shrubs and plants repeatedly do so because they can smell human scent on them; this stimulates their canine curiosity. One remedy for this sort of behavior is to spray bitter apple, which is quite repugnant to dogs, around the base of the valuable plants. Because rain will wash the spray away, make sure you reapply the spray after rain.

▶ TETHERING – RECAP

▶ • Provide shelter from heat, cold, and rain for any dog tethered outside.

• Don't tether your dog for periods exceeding one hour.

• Do provide distraction items, such as marrow bones, leather chews, and safe toys.

Above: *One tactic to thwart a persistent digger is to restrict his movements to an outdoor pen that is provided with a kennel.*

▶ DETERRENTS – RECAP

▶ • Use the sound of rattled training discs to discourage a dog from digging if it has learned to associate the sound with stopping an action.

• Spray bitter-smelling scent around the base of plants.

• Repeat the application of spray after rain.

Chapter 20: Eating Animal Feces

Dogs seem to have a natural desire to eat the feces of herbivorous animals – cattle, sheep, and horse dung being the favorites. It seems a disgusting habit to us, especially when you know that the same dog will probably jump up at you to give you a big lick as an enthusiastic greeting. Cat litter trays are something else that some dogs seek out for a quick snack. This is a particularly distasteful habit to many people. In this case I purchase a covered litter tray (with a hood on it) and make the entrance just big enough for the cat to pass through.

In reality, eating feces is quite normal. As far as your dog is concerned this is a dietary supplement to meat and it is only following its instincts. This is especially true of puppies and adolescent dogs who are still learning what to eat – they are very curious and eager to explore a new world.

Above: *"I'm pleased to see you, but what were you eating a moment ago?" Dogs that eat feces repel us, even though the habit is quite natural to them.*

Dietary deficiency is often suggested as a reason for this behavior, but this is not borne out by my experience. The dogs I've personally seen are in the prime of health and eat a well-balanced diet. Whatever the cause, the effect produced in you, the owner, is uniformly simple: revulsion! Unfortunately it's not always an easy habit to break. However, you should persist because parasitic infestation from whatever fecal matter your dog consumes can be a problem.

Prevention Advice – Dogs That Eat Their Own Feces

The obvious prevention method in this case is to clean up after your dog has defecated. You can make life easier by feeding the animal healthy food. Some foods on the whole produce more bulky fecal matter, so changing your dog's food to a healthy diet will reduce its output. Feeding once daily will also help to reduce the number of times that your dog defecates.

I believe the most common reason why puppies and young dogs begin to explore their own feces is boredom. Dogs left alone in an unstimulating environment learn to eat feces, especially when the feces are left for long periods in their presence. This early conditioning is very powerful and the answer is clear. Avoid these circumstances and from an early age give your dog a stimulating lifestyle with toy chews to play with and plenty of interaction with you and other animals.

Dogs Eating Feces of Other Animals

Herbivores' feces is very attractive to many dogs who view it as a supplement to their diet. Wolves have no problem with digesting copious amounts of elk, deer, and other animal feces, which complements their nutritional needs. They cannot digest vegetation as thoroughly as herbivorous animals can, so eating part-digested matter is a way of getting the nutrition required. For dogs that eat other dogs' feces, some manufacturers offer preparations that you can mix with their food (they contain sulfur). This apparently has a foul taste in expelled feces, making it less palatable. However, the results are no better than average if you are dealing with a determined feces eater.

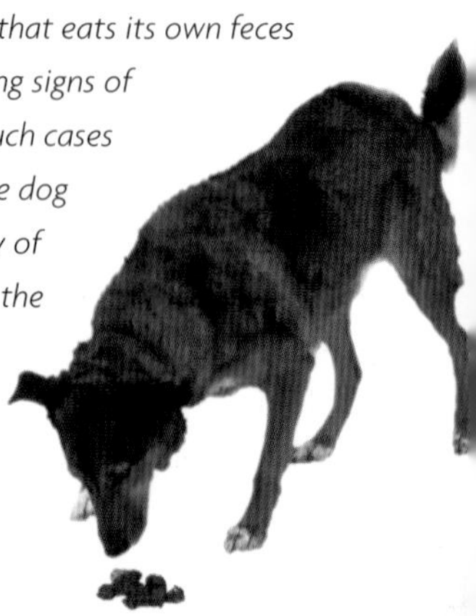

Below: *A dog that eats its own feces may be showing signs of boredom. In such cases ensure that the dog receives plenty of stimulation in the form of toys, play, and the pleasures of human company.*

Left: *Even the kitten looks shocked! Cat litter trays prove tempting fare for some dogs, but the answer is simple – cover the tray with a hood.*

Line Training

If you are out walking in places where the dog is likely to indulge this habit, attach a 30-feet (9-m) nylon line to its collar. While the line is attached, don't let your dog play with other dogs as the line will tangle. When your dog attempts to eat feces, jerk sharply on the line and command "No" at the same time. This can have an effect if the dog is checked consistently in this fashion. Praise him when he returns to you.

Redirect Your Dog's Attention

The success of this method relies on your dog having a favorite ball or toy that it has learned to fetch on command. Now when your dog is about to go near or eat feces, call his name and command "Fetch" as you throw the ball. As the dog returns to you, run backwards and praise him when he reaches you. In this way you can effectively use play as a means to interrupt the undesirable behavior.

Deterrent Methods

Though not always pleasant to the eye, using a cage-type face muzzle is the only sure way of preventing your dog from eating feces, and stopping him from getting the repetitive reward of doing so, which reinforces the habit. I prefer to use this method as a starter for the first month as it is one hundred percent effective in stopping the bad habit. When you stop using the muzzle, some of the other methods can be considered.

The collars that contain a remote-controlled jet spray that are described in the section on training aids provide an excellent way of intercepting your dog as it is about to eat any unpleasant matter. The spray is non-toxic and very effective. The spray collar works by filling the air around your dog's nose with a pungent-smelling vapor which soon makes the target feces less attractive. When properly timed, this deterrent method has a startling and positive effect – but you must be taught how to use it properly by a trainer.

RECAP

• Sometimes this habit can be a sign of boredom. Make sure that your dog has plenty of stimulation from an early age.

• When out walking, keep your dog on a long line and check it when it is about to eat feces.

• Use favorite toys as a method of distraction to divert the dog's attention away from the feces.

• Cage-type face muzzles can be used in persistent cases.

• Remote-controlled sprays are effective deterrent measures.

Above: *Dogs that will not respond to corrective training may have to be fitted with muzzles. It's not a pretty solution but it's certainly effective.*

21: Chasing People and Animals

Chasing animals is one of the strongest natural instincts in dogs. Pursuit and hunting behavior is as natural to a dog as walking is to a human. It is an expression of the desire to chase prey.

Above: *If your dog loves chasing balls and you can get your timing right, it's possible to redirect his attention away from the intended target of his pursuit to a favorite ball thrown as a distraction.*

All dogs may exhibit predatory behavior that involves chasing and biting. Many go through the motions but don't usually attack or bite at the end of the chase, although this can change as such dogs get more practiced at it. If your dog chases other animals or dogs aggressively, refer to the section about dog-on-dog aggression.

The habit normally gets out of control when the dog begins to chase other animals or people persistently. Each successful chase, which is rewarded by the sight of the other animal or jogger trying to escape, encourages the dog to do it again. However, if caught in the early stages, you have a good chance of nipping it in the bud and stopping the habit altogether.

▶ Sizing Up the Problem

Identify the problem as early as possible. High-drive breeds like Border Collies and terriers often become chase dogs because their owners ignorantly allow them as puppies to chase rabbits and squirrels in the local park, not realizing that they may be setting the stage for more serious behavior problems later on. Behavior that it practiced over several months becomes an embedded habit and new targets are found.

Some dogs often become bored when out for a walk with their owner. They start to seek stimulation in other animals and people, usually beginning with anything that is moving quickly away from them. With repetition, this behavior becomes reinforced and the problem becomes harder to correct. Joggers in the local park are easy targets because they always seem to run off when the dog decides to bark and/or give chase. If the jogger were to turn and scare the dog, the dog

would soon find pursuit less attractive. Unfortunately this rarely happens. The end result is that a large number of dogs develop even worse habits, such as biting and serious aggression toward other people.

▶ Obedience Training

Obedience training is the best corrective method to try first. Consult a qualified trainer and train your dog in the environment where the problem arises. The "recall" and the "down, stay" commands given at a distance are particularly useful with this problem and should be taught thoroughly. With time you should begin to attain some leadership over the dog. Also check the section on long line training

Above: *We all expect dogs to chase cats, but the behavior gets problematic when the targets are people, horses, other dogs, or livestock. If the dog goes uncorrected, the habit will get progressively worse.*

in the Recall chapter in this book (see Chapter 4). This enables you to gain control over your dog when it is some distance away from you.

Reverse Chase

(for dogs that only chase people)
Ask a friend whom the dog doesn't know to jog in an area where you habitually walk. Equip your friend with a clean plastic bottle full of water or a water pistol. If your dog pursues this jogger, your friend

The alert eyes and eager nose remind us that dogs are hunters by nature.

should jet water in the dog's face. Alternatively, use a dog-stop alarm (see the section on training aids) or a loud football rattle; these can be activated near the pursuing dog. If the dog has been preconditioned to the sound of training discs, a set of discs can be thrown at the dog's feet to make a clattering sound while it is in pursuit. From the dog's point of view, the pursuit is no longer rewarded by a pleasurable experience and this often is enough to cause the behavior to cease.

Redirecting the Chase

Dogs like chasing things and probably the most popular toy used in chase, catch, and retrieve games is a ball.

Distraction training works with some dogs, especially those that love retrieving. Teach the dog to retrieve to a competent level. Do not play any retrieve games with your dog except when you are out in the areas where the chase is likely to occur. The aim is to transfer your dog's attention from the chase to the retrieve, so timing is vital. You must focus the dog's attention on the retrieve just as it is starting to think of chasing something, not after the chase has begun. Then, at the correct time, throw the ball and reward your dog with verbal and physical praise when he returns.

STOPPING CHASING – RECAP

- Identify the problem early and try to correct it before the behavior becomes ingrained.

- Obedience-train your dog to a high degree.

- Use a jet of water, dog-stop alarm, or training discs to deter a dog when it is in hot pursuit.

- Use a ball to redirect your dog's urge to chase something onto another object.

- Employ the Intelligent Leadership program (see pages 44–47) to assert your authority.

- Check the recall training chapter and practice the recall exercise.

- Consider using a muzzle if your dog tries to bite the target.

Above: *Dogs can get fixated on chasing the most unlikely prey – even ducks in their own element! While this may look comical, the dog could get into difficulties in the water and put itself at risk.*

Index

Index

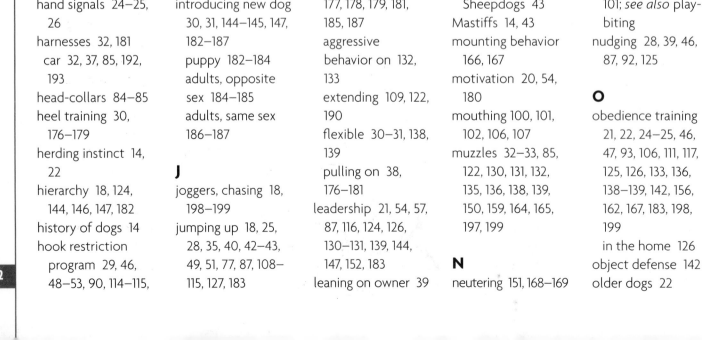

Index

Author's Acknowledgements

I would like to say thank you to all the clients and friends who allowed me to photograph them and their dogs for the purposes of this book. Special thanks also to: Christopher Harvey for studio work; to Gist, Saphie and Lillie, my pets; to John France (canine behaviorist and trainer); to Ross McCarthy (canine behaviorist and trainer); to John Bowe for his technical assistance; to Karl Holt for production and technical advice; and to John Ashford; Stephen, Juliet and Gabriella; Kelly Brown; Charlie Brown; Libby Grey; and Mike Turner, my writing advisor.

A big vote of appreciation to Philip and Malcolm for their tireless support and very adaptable skills in helping me to construct such a complex work on dog behavior.

Picture Credits

Unless otherwise credited below, all the photographs reproduced in this book were taken by **David Ward, Colin Tennant and John Bowe** in a studio established at Colin Tennant's Canine and Feline Behavior Center in Hertfordshire.

Bigstockphoto.com Gvictoria: 157 top right chapter head. **Jane Burton, Warren Photographic:** 135 center right column, 145 bottom right column. **Crestock.com** Marc Dietrich: 97 center right column. godfer: 31 top right chapter head. **Dreamstime.com** John Bell: 15 top right chapter head. Andrew Burov: 109 top right chapter head. Carolina: 95 top right chapter head. Cynoclub: 79 top right chapter head. Lon Dean: 145 top right chapter head. Mitch1921: 155 bottom right column. Tomasz Niewęglowski: 100 top. Ljupco Smokovski: 183 bottom right column. Marzanna Syncerz: 107 center right column. **Fotolia.com** Viacheslav Anyakin: 161 top right chapter head. Callalloo Canis: 189 top right chapter head. Claireliz: 186 bottom left. Cynoclub: 39 top right chapter head. eAlisa: 159 top right chapter head. Jorge Moro: 69 top right chapter head. Martina Reimers: 199 top right chapter head. Alexander Semenov: 153 top right chapter head. **iStockphoto.com** Loretta Hostettler: 87 top right chapter head. Ken Hurst: 55 top right chapter head. Verity Johnson: 195 top right chapter head. Aleksey Krylov: 199 bottom right column. Jim Larson: 74 top right. Gary Martin: 177 top right chapter head. Ivan Mayes: 197 top right chapter head. Pamela Moore: 183 top right chapter head. Pinkpig: 23 top right chapter head. TheBiggles: 171 top right chapter head. **PetSTEP Inc.:** 37 center left. **Shutterstock.com** Willee Cole: 101 top right chapter head. Cynoclub: 167 top right chapter head. Anne Kitzman: 193 top right chapter head. Vilena Makarica: 131 top right column. Miko Pernjakovic: 117 top right chapter head. Martin Valigursky: 133 top right chapter head. Elliott Westacott: 67 center right column. Yuriy Zelenenkyy: 141 bottom right column. **Monty Sloan, Wolf Park:** pages 16 top left (montage, right), 18 top left (montage, right), 19 bottom center (montage, left), 19 top (montage, right). **Neil Sutherland for Interpet:** 23 bottom right, 37 right column, 127 bottom right column, 165 top right column, 177 bottom right column, 179 top right column, 181 top right column.